The Real Pet Detective

The Real Pet Detective

True Tales of Pets Lost and Found

TOM WATKINS

WITH RUTH KELLY

VIKING
an imprint of
PENGUIN BOOKS

VIKING

UK | USA | Canada | Ireland | Australia
India | New Zealand | South Africa

Viking is part of the Penguin Random House group of companies
whose addresses can be found at global.penguinrandomhouse.com

Penguin
Random House
UK

First published 2017
001

Copyright © Tom Watkins and Ruth Kelly, 2017

The moral right of the author has been asserted

Set in 12/14.75 pt Bembo Book MT Std
Typeset by Jouve (UK), Milton Keynes
Printed in Great Britain by Clays Ltd, St Ives plc

A CIP catalogue record for this book is available from the British Library

ISBN: 978–0–241–29227–3

www.greenpenguin.co.uk

Contents

Prologue   1

1. Barking Mad   5
2. Fur Cop   17
3. Grass Roots   24
4. World Headquarters   34
5. Stay Pawsitive   38
6. From Mace to Ace   48
7. The Riddle of Toots   57
8. The Plot Thickens   76
9. The Golden Door, Part 1: Casper the Cat   85
10. The Golden Door, Part 2: Rubens the Rebel   97
11. The Degu   113
12. Mystic Mog   123
13. Psychic Sarita   137
14. Blues and Clues   144
15. No Bone Left Unturned   153
16. Jerry and Jill   161
17. Chairman Miaow   174
18. Sniff! Only I Could Find Him   185
19. Sherlock Bones   192

v

20. Barking Up the Wrong Tree   202

21. Cat-astrophe   209

22. Waggy Tales   217

23. Maggie the Moggie   228

24. Elementary, My Dear Watkins   235

25. Ruby Trap   247

26. Doggelgänger   259

27. Hot Dog   266

   Epilogue   278

PROLOGUE

The mist started to seep through the woods as we searched the undergrowth.

'Any sign of him?' I radioed through on my walkie-talkie.

'Nothing. Over,' crackled the reply.

My heart sank. We'd been searching for hours but still nothing.

We moved forward in an orderly line, one step at a time, sweeping the undergrowth for any sign of life. Bourne Woods in Frensham, Surrey, isn't somewhere you would want to get lost.

I could only imagine how Cody must be feeling. Terrified. Alone. I just prayed he was still alive after a night in the cold and the rain.

The rotting leaves squelched under my boots. The brambles clawed at my trouser legs. I blew into my cupped hands to keep them warm, the hot air rising into the January cold as puffs of steam.

'Torches, everyone! Over.' I gestured to Liam, M and Olivia, who were spaced fifty yards apart from each other.

We switched them on at the same time, their beams cutting through the gloom like lightsabers.

We'd searched three square miles but still had five to comb through before nightfall. The deeper into the forest we ventured, the darker, the more sinister and eerie it became. Luckily everyone was wearing luminous jackets or we would have lost one another.

'Stay in formation. Over.' I reminded everyone to keep the line strong.

Suddenly, the ground dropped away beneath me. I lost my footing and slid uncontrollably into a ditch. I reached out my hand to break my fall, cutting it on the razor sharp brambles. I yelped with pain.

'Tom, are you okay?' Liam cried.

He peered over the ridge and I stared up at him. I was plastered with mud and up to my knees in ditch water. 'All part of the job.' I smeared the grime onto my trousers. I didn't have time to worry about a few grazes.

As I scrambled back onto dry land, my torch caught something next to my boot. I crouched to get a better look, pulling away ferns and branches. My heart leaped.

'I've found something!' I shouted, over the walkie-talkie, to Olivia and M.

'Receiving. We're on our way!'

Five minutes later I had my team surrounding the piece of evidence.

'No doubt about it, it's a print,' M confirmed.

'Looks like he came this way,' I chipped in.

Cody had been through the ditch at some point in the last twelve hours. We searched the immediate area for more signs. We just needed another print to point us in the right direction.

'Anything?' I called hopefully.

'The rain's washed it all away!' Disheartened, Liam prodded the mushy earth with a stick.

He was right: last night's heavy downpour was making our search even more challenging.

I pulled out the Ordnance Survey map and rested it on the trunk of a fallen tree. It must have been hit by lightning, I thought, judging by the burn marks lacerating the trunk. It was a huge old thing, coated with moss and fungi, its roots splayed like the tentacles of an octopus.

Everyone leaned in, alert and ready to plot our next move. Where we searched next would be vital to Cody's survival. We had a lot of area to cover and limited boots on the ground to do it before darkness set in.

'So we know he's heading this way,' I said, drawing my finger along the map.

A splatter of rain hit my forehead and ran down my face. As soon as I wiped it away, another arrived. Pretty soon the drops were ricocheting off the map onto our jackets.

A rainstorm was the last thing we needed. It would wash away any remaining evidence, and if Cody was trapped or injured it would increase the risk of him catching hypothermia.

I shuddered as I zipped up my coat to my neck. 'Quick, let's all get in line again and start working our way towards the clearing,' I instructed, pointing into the distance.

As we fought our way through the rain and the brambles I had an unnerving feeling that something terrible had happened to Cody. Maybe someone had snatched him. He was only young – he wouldn't stand a chance.

The crackle of the radio sliced through my thoughts.

'Tom, I've found something!' It was Olivia's voice and she sounded worried.

I bounded across the woods, weaving through the bracken, ducking and diving over and under fallen branches. My boots were slipping and sliding across the ground.

M and Liam were already there, crowding around. I could tell by their worried faces that it was bad news.

'I found this,' Olivia said, pointing to the red object.

I picked it up and held it between my thumb and forefinger. It was Cody's collar.

Somehow the two-year-old black and white collie cross had lost it. I pointed my torch into the gloom, wondering how we were going to find him.

CHAPTER ONE
BARKING MAD

Hi, my name's Tom Watkins, and I'm a pet detective.

I find missing pets for a living, anything from a cat or a budgerigar to a dog or a tortoise. No animal is too small or too big for me to track down and rescue. I do it because I love animals and because I want to help people.

Pets aren't just animals: to many families, they're like children, and what wouldn't you do to see your child returned home safely?

I wasn't always a pet detective. I used to be a copper. I now apply the skills I learned in the police force to finding missing and stolen animals. I run Europe's largest, and most successful, pet detective agency. I have fifteen staff, a fleet of animal search response vehicles – or pet-mobiles, as I like to call them – a twenty-four-hour missing-pet rescue hotline, up to a hundred lost-pet cases added to my online database each day by owners needing my help. I've reunited thousands of pets with their owners through my detective skills. No fewer than 150,000 have registered a lost or found pet on my website over the years.

I use all sorts of equipment on my searches, anything from thermal-imaging cameras (to spot cats hiding in dark sheds and garages) and walkie-talkies to Dictaphones (to record the sound of the owner's voice). My detective methods are just as colourful and unusual: I've flown a plane with a banner over Surrey to help find a missing terrier and I've filmed a *Crimewatch*-style reconstruction of a dog-napping to prompt witnesses to come forward.

But it didn't start off like that. Far from it. In the beginning I didn't even have a magnifying glass, just a can of dog food and a map of Wolverhampton.

It was April 1999 and I was feeling down in the dumps. I'd left the police force with no clue about what I wanted to do with my life. One night I was sitting on the sofa with a cup of tea and turned on the radio to the local station – Beacon FM. I'd been a regular listener since I'd won one of their phone-in competitions a couple of years back.

After the commercial break, a woman started speaking. She sounded distressed and my ears tuned in. A member of the public, she had called in to say she had spotted an Afghan Hound roaming the streets of Wolverhampton. She described the dog as wet, bedraggled and starving.

From my limited knowledge, I knew an Afghan Hound wasn't the sort of dog to be wandering the streets without its owner. It was large, a pedigree, the kind you were more likely to see at Crufts. Had he slipped his collar? Had he been stolen and escaped his captors? I could take myself out of the police force, but the copper was still inside me.

I carried on slurping my tea. About fifteen minutes later another announcement was made. The dog had been spotted! It wasn't in the Penn Fields area any more, it was now in Perton – it had legged it another few miles.

The reports were coming in thick and fast. I was glued to

the radio. I didn't want to leave the house for fear of missing a detail.

That night I lay in bed gazing up at the ceiling. My mind was working overtime, worrying about where that dog might be now. It was springtime, so it got pretty nippy outside when the sun went down. I hoped the poor thing would find shelter for the night. And I couldn't silence the inquisitive side of me. Why hadn't the owner come forward? As it was a pedigree, it was hard to believe it didn't belong to someone. I thought about the places it had been seen. I turned on the bedside lamp, pulled back the duvet and jumped out of bed.

I opened my wardrobe, which was brimming with my clothes, but beneath the shirt rail was a large cardboard box. I reached in and pulled it out. It was heavier than I remembered.

It had been three years since I'd touched it, since I had left West Midlands Police. I peeled back the sticky tape and started rooting around the various bits and bobs I'd cleared from my desk until my fingers had a grip on what I was after: the *A to Z* – an essential piece of equipment for any bobby walking the beat.

I flicked through until the page opened on the city of Wolverhampton. I felt a spike of adrenalin as my investigative skills were reignited.

'He was seen here,' I mumbled, under my breath, tracing my finger across the page. 'And here . . . and here.' I continued to mark the locations where the dog had been spotted.

I held the map at arm's length and examined the evidence. Were the places randomly scattered across the city or was there a pattern?

'He's moving westwards!' I exclaimed. 'So, he's going to be on this side of the city rather than that side . . .' I jabbed my finger on the spot where he was most likely to be.

When I woke up the next morning I turned on the radio. I couldn't wait for an update. The same thing happened again: people were spotting the Afghan Hound but nobody could catch him. And then came the offers of help. Business owners from Wolverhampton were ringing up to make donations to anyone who could catch the stray dog.

The owner of Luigi's on the high street wanted to give a pasta or pizza meal to the person who could help. Joan, who ran a florist, was the next kind-hearted person to call. She was offering a beautiful bouquet to the person who could rescue the hound.

The donations warmed my heart, but the sightings made for uncomfortable listening. I couldn't bear the thought of that potentially injured dog wandering the streets, alone and frightened. I felt compelled to do something. I wasn't bothered about the meal and the bunch of flowers. I just wanted to rescue that suffering animal. So I picked up the phone, dialled the hotline and spontaneously invented a name for my business.

'My name is Tom Watkins. I'm a former police officer. Now I run Animal Search UK, which is a national pet detective agency based in the Black Country. I'll find this dog.' The Black Country is a term used to describe where I lived in the West Midlands. During the Industrial Revolution, it was a hub of coal mines, iron foundries and steel mills producing a high level of air pollution.

The presenter's voice rose an octave in surprise. 'Animal Search UK? I've never heard of that!'

'It's a relatively new organization, but it's the biggest in the UK.'

Technically that was true – it was the biggest in the UK because nobody else had done anything like it before. I was the UK's first pet detective.

The radio presenter was lapping it up. 'Great one, Tom. Tell us how you plan to find the dog.'

I hadn't got that far! I had to think on my feet. 'I'm going to send out one of our patrol cars.' Patrol cars? I'd shocked myself.

'Lovely! Keep us posted with updates,' the presenter chirped.

As soon as I hung up I felt a tremor of nerves. Thousands of people were now counting on me to save the dog. Not to mention that I'd just become a real-life Ace Ventura pet detective.

All I had was a Fiat Panda and a motorbike, and I couldn't do the search using either of those. How would I transport the dog to safety once I'd found it? I was full of confidence that I *would* be transporting the Afghan Hound to safety. There was no way I was going to let it wander the streets any longer.

As soon as I got off the phone I went to a company who rented vans. But as I was seriously strapped for cash, I had to think on my feet again. I told the man in Reception that I was from a pet-search organization, and negotiated a deal whereby if he lent me a van for the day, I'd give his company a plug on the radio. I couldn't quite believe what I was saying but somehow being media savvy came naturally.

Amazingly he agreed, so I collected the van and went to call on an old friend of mine. Alan worked at a petrol station in Dudley. We'd become friends when I'd been coming in to fill up my tank at two a.m. after late shifts. We used to have a good old chinwag in the early hours.

I pulled into the garage just as Alan was finishing his

night-shift. I wound down my window and shouted, 'Jump in! We're going on a dog search!'

Alan, who hadn't had a clue that I'd be dropping in, shook his head to make sure he wasn't imagining what I'd just said. 'What are you talking about?' he said, rubbing his bleary eyes as he stepped into the daylight.

'Just get in. I'll explain on the way.'

Alan was nineteen, a little chubby, shorter than me, with dark hair and a smiley face. He was a friendly chap and a real good laugh.

Just as we were about to drive off, I remembered some essential dog-search equipment we would need. I dashed back into the petrol station and reappeared balancing a tower of dog food cans in my arms. I had a bottle of water wedged under one arm and a plastic bowl under the other.

Alan's face was even more bemused. I tipped everything into the back of the van and jumped behind the wheel. 'We'll need bait to lure the dog,' I said.

'Will you please tell me what's going on?' Alan begged.

I indicated, turned onto the road and briefed him on Operation Dog Rescue. I explained the story that had unfolded over the past couple of days on the radio. 'This dog is clearly in a bit of a pickle. We need to catch it, so it can be returned to its owner or given veterinary attention. It'll be very thirsty after days on the trot, hence the bottle of water.'

Alan was brimming with questions. How were we going to track the hound down? If we did manage to find it, how would we catch it?

I didn't have all the answers, but I had a hunch my years as a copper would pay off. My experience had taught me it was essential to know what you were up against. In this instance, Wolverhampton and a large dog that could get about quickly. I didn't know the area at all, so we cruised around for a bit, getting our bearings. Our starting point was the street the dog had last been seen in, on a housing estate not far from the city centre.

Within half an hour, we struck gold.

Suddenly, out of nowhere, a large, long-haired dog crossed the road right in front of us. It was going at quite a pace.

'That's him!' I screeched to a halt.

My heart was pounding. By the time we had parked, jumped out and grabbed the dog food, though, the hound had vanished.

'I thought we had him!' Alan said, staring into the distance.

So did I. I couldn't believe our luck that we had stumbled upon him so quickly. But I should have known it wasn't going to be a piece of cake.

'Now, let's try and conduct this search in an orderly—'

'There he is!' Alan yelled. He'd caught sight of the dog in an alleyway between two houses.

'Quick!' I shouted, scampering after him. All order and police formality flew out of the window.

As we closed in on the runaway, I signalled to Alan that he should slow down. I didn't want to scare the animal with our approach. I could see now that it was a he, and he was terrified. The radio reports had been true – he was thin. Bedraggled and frightened, too. His long hair was matted with mud and water. His eyes were wide and he was trembling.

'It's okay, boy, we just want to help you,' I said, as we edged forward.

'Alan, dog food.' I waved to my sidekick to deposit our 'dog trap'.

'Yes, boss,' he said, emptying the contents of the can onto the pavement. He spread it out so it wasn't in an unappetizing lump.

We stood back, hoping the dog would come towards it, so we could gently grab him. We were both poised to pounce.

He was clearly hungry, but when he walked up to the dog food, then sniffed it, he turned up his nose in disgust and carried on. His elegant hair would have swished around his long legs if it hadn't been so matted.

'Quick!' we both shrieked.

Alan got on his hands and knees and scraped the dog food off the pavement and back into the can. A couple walking along the pavement flashed us a surprised look.

'No need to be alarmed, we're trying to catch a dog!' I panted, as we tore off down the street.

The problem was, of course, that we were no match for the Afghan Hound's long legs. He was the hare and we were the tortoises.

Alan must have scraped the dog food off the pavement at least six times over the next two hours. There were just a few chunks left in the tin and we didn't have another in reserve – the rest were back in the van.

'Where is the van?' I looked around, scratching my head. I suddenly realized I had no idea where we were. We'd run miles from where we'd parked, but before I had time to worry, we were off again. This time we took a left along a main road. The cars were whizzing past, and I felt extremely nervous for the dog's safety as he bounded ahead. He appeared unsteady, as if he might step off the pavement at any moment.

'We need to keep our distance,' I yelled, above the noise of the traffic.

I didn't want to frighten him into the path of a passing car. The poor chap was like a drunk driver, weaving across the pavement. Suddenly he put one paw onto the road.

'Noooo!' I yelled. But I was too far off to stop him.

BEEEEEEEP, tooted the approaching car.

Luckily the hound thought better of it and returned to the safety of the pavement. He then sprang into life and legged it down a side-street on the left.

'Here we go again!' Alan spluttered, as we took off in hot pursuit.

I was completely out of breath by the time we turned into a cul-de-sac. I bent over double with a stitch. I wasn't used to so much exercise!

We'd followed the dog to a derelict 1950s red-brick house. The windows were boarded up with sheets of wood. The grass was overgrown and littered with rubbish, such as takeaway cartons and beer cans. The door had been kicked in by what I assumed had been youths or squatters.

Having caught my breath, I approached with caution. 'Stay behind me.' I flagged Alan back.

For a split second I thought I was back on the police force. I instinctively reached for my walkie-talkie, which would have been attached to my belt.

I stuck my nose through the front door and was hit by a strong smell of urine and stale booze. It was hard to see anything because it was dark in there, except for a few shafts of light streaming through the gaps between the window boards. They beamed onto the concrete floor, like spotlights. I wished I'd had a torch on me – something I would have always been armed with as a constable.

I could make out some graffiti on the wall and there appeared to be the charred remains of what looked like a campfire. There was a grubby sofa in the middle of the room. Its cover had been torn to shreds, the springs poking through.

I turned to call to Alan, but he was less than a foot away, hot on my heels. He was keen as mustard to be involved. I was used to situations like this, but it must have been new and exciting for him.

I heard something crunch underfoot, followed by a rustling noise from the back of the room. Was that a shadow moving? If it was our Afghan Hound, I wasn't letting it escape this time.

'Use those boards to block the door,' I told Alan.

I edged my way forward into the darkness.

'Can you see him?' Alan whispered from the doorway.

I heard the dog before I saw him. He was panting heavily, no doubt from dehydration. I placed the bowl on the floor and filled it to the brim with water. Some of it sloshed out, spreading across the concrete.

I took a few steps back and held my breath.

'Come on, boy,' I encouraged him.

Slowly but surely, the weary dog padded towards the bowl of water. He stepped into a shaft of light, his eyes reflecting brightly.

His energy levels had dropped dramatically. He crouched over the bowl, his shoulder blades poking through his fur like spears. His eyes were heavy and sad, as if he was fighting to keep them open.

'That's it, boy!'

My heart lifted as he managed to take a few laps of the water, slurping it up noisily before sloping back to his corner of the room.

'What are we going to do now?' Alan asked.

Good question. We had a bit of a problem on our hands. There was no way we were going to be able to lead such a fragile animal all the way back to the van. Especially as we didn't know where the van was! We couldn't contact the owner because the dog had no collar with an ID tag. I pulled out my mobile and rang the radio station in the hope that the dog owner had come forward at the eleventh hour. No such luck.

'How are you getting on there, Tom?' the presenter enquired. I was live on air!

'The dog is secure, safe and uninjured.' I updated the listeners.

But the buzz I'd had when I was first on the radio had gone. I felt disheartened. What I wanted to say was I couldn't believe that no one had claimed the dog. I'd looked into his big brown eyes – I couldn't believe there wasn't someone out there desperately missing him. He might have been bedraggled but, with a wash, food and a rest, he would look magnificent. The owner might not have been listening to the radio station – that was always a possibility.

I didn't know what to do other than draw on my experience as a copper. In a similar situation I would have called on the dog warden to help trace his owner or rehome him. At least the warden would have the equipment to scan the dog for a chip to see if he had an owner.

It must have been around two p.m. when the van pulled up outside the derelict house. 'All right, mate,' I said, coming out to shake the warden's hand. Alan was watching over the Afghan Hound, blocking his exit.

The sound of the opening of the cage door – the sliding of the metal bolt – sent a shiver down my spine. This wasn't how I wanted it to end. The warden fetched his metal pole, which had a noose at one end to capture the dog. It looked like a medieval contraption, but it wouldn't cause the animal any pain: it was more to protect the warden from being bitten – animals can behave unpredictably when they're frightened.

I led the way into the building and left the warden to get on with his job. The hound was so weak by this point that he didn't put up a fight. He stood motionless, his elegant lion head bowed, as if all the life had been beaten out of him.

I finally got a good look at him as he was led past us into the van. The poor chap was trembling, his tail between his legs. It was heartbreaking to watch.

'What's going to happen to him?' I asked, concerned.

'We'll get him looked over by the vet first, check if he's been chipped, then go from there.'

'Okay, mate, thanks for coming out.' I sighed, sad that I couldn't do more.

The warden gently lifted the dog into the back of the van. He secured the cage and shut the door. I could see little black eyes staring helplessly at me through the window. I wanted to do something, but my hands were tied.

It was at that moment I knew what I wanted to do with my life. I wanted to reunite owners with their missing pets. I wanted to make a career that combined my love of animals with my investigative skills. I was going to become a pet detective and be the best in the world at it.

But I still had a lot to learn . . .

CHAPTER TWO
FUR COP

Watching the helpless Afghan Hound being led away by the dog warden had reminded me of my days as a copper. It took me back to those emotional moments at the police kennels when I'd had to say goodbye to the dogs I'd made friends with.

My station in Halesowen, near Dudley, had a few kennels, which were used to house strays that members of the public had handed in. The police saw it as a burden to receive those dogs, so no one paid them any attention. The door was shut behind them. They had a bowl of water and a bowl of food and that was it. It was like a mini prison for sometimes up to twenty-four hours, until the dog warden picked them up at four the next afternoon.

I felt sorry for them being locked up in concrete cages. On my break I made a point of going to see them, to give them a stroke and a cuddle and sometimes take them for a little walk. One day I took two for a leg stretch and they both slipped their collars. I was running around the car park trying to catch the rascals. I've only got ten minutes left of my break! I'd better get these dogs back in their cages before someone notices, I thought, as I panted around the yard. It was a nightmare, but in the end I recaptured them. Luckily no one saw or I would have been under questioning.

My colleagues used to take the mick out of me for being so soft, but I've always been an animal lover. Ever since my mum brought home a puppy when I was fourteen. We named her Maggie.

Maggie was a mix between a sheepdog and a spaniel – a mongrel, if you like. She was adorable, with her little wavy ears, her glossy black and white coat, and her four white socks. Mum would never admit it, but she'd bought Maggie as a 'softener' after the blow of her divorce from my dad. I shared her with my three sisters, Naomi, Charlotte and Hannah, but it's fair to say she was my dog. I took her for walks. I fed her. Maggie slept on my bed every night. She liked to curl up in a tight ball at my feet, with her nose tucked into her flank. Her deep sighs of contentment and gentle snoring would send me to sleep.

She meant the world to me. She was intelligent, loving – Maggie was my rock. Since Mum had left Dad, I'd felt a bit lost and I'd cuddle Maggie for comfort. She'd lie on the floor with her head on her left paw, panting, and I'd stroke her tummy while we watched the telly. I used to talk to Maggie, run through my quandaries and problems with her. I'd cuddle her and say, 'What would you do about this, then, Maggie?' Of course she couldn't answer me as a person would, but she showed me she cared by licking my nose, jumping up or pawing my leg. She'd show her support by gazing up at me and wagging her tail.

I loved playing tennis with her. My mum's house had a big

wall outside and I used to whack the ball against it. Maggie would retrieve it within seconds. She'd drop it at my feet, poised for me to serve again.

One of my biggest worries was losing her. I was always terrified of letting her off the lead when we went for walks in case I never saw her again. When I did let her go, I watched her like a hawk.

Maggie was there for me when I was sixteen and joined West Midlands Police. She supported me through my two years of training as a cadet and then as a constable – or bobby, as we were called back then.

At seven a.m., on my way home after a long night-shift, I'd stop at the corner shop to pick up some milk and Midget Gems to share with Maggie while I wound down watching breakfast TV. She would greet me after a tough shift with an enthusiastic tail and a lick to my face. I couldn't communicate with people as I could with Maggie. There was something about animals – their unconditional love and loyalty – that I hadn't found in any person.

Not surprisingly, my love of dogs spilled over into my job as a copper, which explains why I was down at the kennels, looking after the stray dogs whenever I had a spare moment.

But canine company wasn't the only thing I gained from the force. I wouldn't be where I am today if I hadn't spent all those years as a bobby. The police force was like a degree in life. I learned about human interaction, about investigation, about being organized, professionalism, infrastructure, logistics and communication.

The headquarters were in Birmingham, but I worked as a PC in Halesowen and Stourbridge, next door to each other. Mostly I walked the beat through the town centre in Stourbridge and drove around in my marked car. I dealt with everything from stolen bikes and serious assaults to burglaries, road accidents and pub fights.

Although I'm a big guy at six foot one, and quite sturdy on my feet, I was always a bit of a wimp in my dislike of violence. My strength was my ability to talk through situations rather than going in aggressively, as some coppers would. I took control in a diplomatic way.

Sadly, as time went on, I started to become disillusioned by the justice system. I felt frustrated that we spent all our time catching the bad guys only for the courts to let them off. Even though the police force was incredibly organized, there was much that I found difficult to cope with – primarily there weren't enough bobbies on the beat so our lives were thrown into jeopardy while we were arresting criminals. The final straw came when one of the defendants, Jimmy, at a criminal trial I was involved with threatened to slit my throat right under the judge's nose for grassing him up.

I didn't sign up for this, I thought, as I raced on my motorbike from the court to my mum's house in Dudley. I was sick with worry. What was Jimmy going to do? I feared he would track me down.

As soon as I screeched to a halt on Mum's driveway I rang the inspector at Dudley police station. I explained I'd been in court and what had happened. He agreed it was a concern and reassured me that his boys would pay 'passing attention' to my mum's house. It's called 'passing attention' when a police officer takes a regular drive-by to keep an eye on a place.

'What's happened, love?' Mum came into the living room, clearly anxious. She'd overheard my conversation with the inspector.

'It's nothing to worry about, Mum,' I lied. 'I've had a bit of trouble at the courthouse so I've asked the station if they'll keep an eye out for us.'

Mum's eyes widened like saucers.

'Honestly, Mum, it's nothing to worry about,' I insisted, placing my hand on her arm reassuringly.

'Okay, love,' she said hesitantly. 'Tea will be ready in a minute.'

I found it a challenge to mask my fears as we all sat around the table for supper. I was on tenterhooks, listening for any noise that might indicate trouble. I watched the telly from a chair by the front window. Every twenty minutes or so I would pull back the curtain and survey what was going on outside.

I struggled with terrible thoughts about what that bloke might do to my family in revenge. He was a nasty piece of work. I turned to Maggie for support. 'So what should I do about this?' I asked my best friend.

She was stretched out in front of me, resting her head on her paws. She let out a little whimper, then pulled herself to her feet and came to my side.

'I'm going to need your help, mate,' I said, stroking her head and scratching behind her ears.

She 'woofed', as if to say, 'No worries, I'm here if you need me.'

As I made my way up the stairs to bed, Maggie was hot on my heels. 'Stay!' I said, pointing to the hallway by the front door.

She tilted her head and let out a snuffled whine. Maggie had spent every night on my bed since we'd got her eight years earlier.

'I need you to stay on guard for us tonight,' I explained.

She didn't know why I was asking her to sleep in front of the door, but she realized, because I'd asked her to do so, that it must be important.

'Thanks, mate.' I gave her another stroke, then climbed the creaky stairs.

That night, not surprisingly, I hardly slept a wink. Any slight noise jolted me awake.

It was 2.32 a.m. when I woke to the hum of a car engine outside our house. My window was juddering. The beam from the headlights had crept through my curtain and was projecting a light across the ceiling. My heart was in my mouth. I could hear Maggie's paws scratching on the floorboards downstairs, which meant she was wide awake and also wondering who was outside. I crept downstairs on tiptoe, doing my best to reduce the noise of the squeaky stairs. I didn't want to alarm my mum and sister unnecessarily.

Maggie was waiting for me, ears pricked. She appeared agitated. She followed me through to the living room, where I peeled back the curtain onto the street outside.

From the dull glow of the streetlights, I could make out a man behind the steering wheel of a red Vauxhall Vectra. A woman wearing a black coat, skirt and heels got out of the passenger door.

'No need to worry, mate.' I turned to Maggie. It was just a neighbour being dropped off after a night out.

Maggie slept downstairs for a week until the dust settled.

But the scare had left a bitter taste in my mouth. This guy was my breaking point – the last in a long line of arrests that had ended up with the criminals getting off. We were continually undermanned, under-resourced and under-protected.

The next morning while I was on my rounds I made a snap decision. I didn't want to spend another moment of my life doing something I didn't believe in. I was going to quit the police force and use the valuable set of skills I had acquired for a greater good.

At that moment I had a flashback to my interview for the cadets all those years ago.

'So, Tom, why do you want to join the police?' the chief inspector had asked.

I'd answered with five simple words: 'I want to help people.'

That was my goal then, and it was still my goal.

One way or another, I was going to help people.

CHAPTER THREE
GRASS ROOTS

'When did Bertie go missing?'

'Wednesday night.' The woman at the other end of the phone line sniffled.

'What time in the evening?'

Why was I asking that? Well, the search for the missing Afghan Hound had been a steep learning curve for me, and in the past six months I'd honed my pet detective skills. I needed to determine whether it was light or dark outside when the black and white moggie had disappeared three days ago: if it had been dark, then the chance increased, unfortunately, of Bertie having been hit by a car.

'I can't say for sure, but I think it was near eight o'clock. I was just settling down to watch *Midsomer Murders*, you see. That's why I remember the time.'

I scribbled *eight p.m.* in my notebook. 'Does he normally go out at night, Mrs Perry?'

'Yes, he does, right after I feed him.'

Likes to go out at night. Likes to roam? I jotted down on my pad. 'And how long does he normally go out for?' I asked.

Why was I asking Mrs Perry this? Because if Bertie normally ducked out for ten minutes to go to the toilet, there was a higher chance something had happened to him. If he was a regular 'all-nighter' – exploring, travelling and investigating his neighbourhood – he was more likely to have got lost.

'I – I don't know . . .' Mrs Perry stumbled. Her voice quivered. I could tell she was deeply upset by the disappearance of her beloved cat.

'I know this is hard for you, Mrs Perry, but please don't give up hope. If we can establish his movements, there's a very high chance we'll find him,' I reassured her.

How did I know what questions to ask? Having lived on housing estates most of my life, I knew that cats didn't generally wander too far from their home. I'd observed that the local cats were creatures of habit – they frequented the same haunts, at the same times; they ran like clockwork.

I also drew on my experience as a copper. The questions I was asking Mrs Perry were exactly the same as I would have put to a parent to assess whether their missing child had been abducted, was playing truant, had got lost or simply forgotten the time. Just as the police build up a personality profile of a missing person, I was building up a character profile of a cat.

I continued with my line of questioning. 'Do you know how far Bertie normally goes?' I wanted to establish his territory in order to work out whether the search needed to be extended beyond Mrs Perry's backyard and next door's garden. If a cat doesn't typically leave the owner's property, it'll most likely have been accidentally locked in an outbuilding nearby or had an accident close to home with a car or been adopted by someone. There was a pause, as Mrs Perry searched her memory. 'Oh,

25

I don't know, really. I've seen Bertie sitting on next door's wall. They have a bird feeder and he likes to watch them fly in and out.'

'You're doing really well, Mrs Perry. Just a few more questions,' I said. 'Has anyone on your street gone on holiday?'

This was a crucial question because Bertie might have been inadvertently locked in their house or gone through their cat flap and was now trapped inside.

There was another long pause.

'I don't think so . . . Hang fire a minute. I think the Barretts over the road might be away. I haven't seen their car in the drive for a week now!' Mrs Perry exclaimed.

The Barretts might be a first port of call to find missing Bertie.

'And the last few questions, if you don't mind, Mrs Perry. Is he on any medication? Does he have any health problems that may have caused his disappearance?'

'Oh, no, not my Bertie! He's fit as a fiddle.' Mrs Perry gasped at the idea of her cat being ill.

'I'm sorry, it's just necessary to ask.' I jotted down the last bits of information on my notepad and then drew a circle around the Barretts' name. *This is where the search for Bertie begins.*

It was Christmas 2002, and I'd launched Animal Search UK as an official pet detective agency.

'Your tea's getting cold,' my partner Jenni reminded me, tapping her watch. We had a baby on the way.

'Five more minutes,' I mouthed, holding the receiver into my chest. I'd been on the phone for at least half an hour, giving advice to Mrs Perry. But I wasn't about to leave her while she was sounding so distraught.

Since I'd set up the twenty-four-hour free helpline, I'd spent most evenings holding a phone to my ear. The majority of calls had been from cat-owners, although I'd quickly realized, from hearing the distress in their voices, that it wasn't just 'the cat'. It was 'Tigger' or 'Felix' or, in this instance, 'Bertie'. All of the cats had names and personalities. They were like family members and I had to be very sensitive to that.

Pet-owners would often start the conversation strong and determined, but gradually, as they described what had happened and were reminded of the fateful day when their pet had gone missing, their tough exterior would crumble and they would often cry. My police experience had taught me they were in shock. It wasn't uncommon to find an owner who hadn't slept since their beloved animal had disappeared. They were often knackered and worried sick.

On many occasions as a policeman I had encountered people who were distressed by what they had seen or by something that had happened. I'd dealt with the situation by taking control and calming them down. Bertie's predicament wasn't any different. It was my job to reassure Mrs Perry. How did I do this? By being professional and methodical, and by giving constructive advice.

Like many cat-owners, Mrs Perry's first instinct was to run out of the house and have a look. 'Before you do, take with you a torch, a cat basket and some food. That way you're mentally prepared for the search and ready for Bertie if you do spot him. I'd also advise taking a friend for support,' I suggested.

I told Mrs Perry to make door-to-door enquiries, hand out posters featuring pictures of Bertie to local schools, hairdressing salons, libraries, pubs, corner shops, local buses, taxis and postal delivery offices. 'You need to get your posters seen by people whose jobs take them all around your neighbourhood,' I explained. She should also walk around the community, rattling cat biscuits and calling Bertie's name. 'Don't forget to try the Barretts' house.' Cats can be responsive to familiar voices, so calling to Bertie in the streets around which she lived could prove fruitful. I said she should venture out early in the morning: if Bertie was roaming, she might catch him. One of my top tips was to check if there was any building work going on. If there was, Mrs Perry needed to ask the workmen to check the scaffolding, as Bertie might have got stuck up there. Builders often remove the ladder at the end of the day so kids don't climb up, not realizing that a cat is stuck at the top.

'If you hear of any sightings of Bertie, make a record of them and mark them on a map. From the crosses, you'll be able to see what area he's most likely to be in and if he's moving in any particular direction,' I said, drawing on my Afghan Hound experience.

'Tom, tea!' Jenni said, more impatiently this time.

'Okay, okay!'

She walked off, rolling her eyes.

Mrs Perry was still on the line, stifling her sobs.

'Never give up hope, Mrs Perry. And I'm here on our helpline if you need any more advice.'

'Thank you, Mr Watkins. I hope it will help me find my poor boy.'

As I hung up, I felt uneasy. I wished I could travel to Kent to help Mrs Perry find Bertie. Sadly, there weren't enough hours in the day. Any spare second I had, I dedicated to Animal Search UK. I would answer the hotline until eleven p.m. some nights. I didn't go to bed much before one o'clock as I was beavering away on strategies to turn my dream into a successful business.

I was living in a two-up, two-down semi-detached house in Bobblestock in Hereford. Every street in Bobblestock was named after a racecourse because Hereford racecourse was around the corner. I'd moved away from Birmingham to be closer to my dad, a vicar in a village near Ledbury.

I'd set up Animal Search UK from my kitchen table. I'd bought an old PC and I'd read a book *HTML for Dummies*, which enabled me to grasp the basics of building a website. I ended up with a very simple home page, which featured a few dozen pictures of missing pets from all over the UK, and a little info about where they had disappeared. I charged owners a bit for putting it on the website – but not for my advice. I also offered a missing-pet poster service to help publicize the disappearance.

I'd design and print one poster, then hop on the bus into town and photocopy it a hundred times at a stationery store. When I first started the website, I would send the posters to a hundred different addresses in the area where the animal had been reported missing – everywhere from the school to the post office to the butcher. This involved a bit of research and detective work. I often turned to Yell.com to look for shops and amenities in the appropriate postcode. (I charged fifty pounds to do all that and only made about a tenner but I didn't care: I was helping someone, which was a brilliant feeling.) Sending out the posters was time-consuming, though, and hit and miss: I never knew whether the recipients would display them. I quickly realized it would be better to send them all to the pet-owner and give them guidance on where to distribute them. That meant targeted results: the owner of the missing pet would be putting them through doors at the heart of the search area.

That was what I was doing with Mrs Perry.

When I finally made it to the dinner table, I had a cold plate of meat and veg and a disgruntled Jenni waiting for me.

'Tom, the business is taking over our lives and our home,' she said, stroking her growing bump.

'I know, Jen, but I love doing it. And I've got to keep the momentum up. One day, when we're as big as the RSPCA, and the Cats Protection League is recommending us, all the long hours and hard work will be worth it!' I pleaded.

'I'd just like the kitchen to be a kitchen again.' She sighed, glaring at the computer and the mountain of books and paperwork engulfing the table and shelves.

Even when Jenni was cross she still looked pretty. As gorgeous as the day I'd met her at a New Year's Eve party in town. I remember her being dolled up in a purple dress with her curly hair pinned back in a fancy do. She had lost her purse and was frantically checking the floor by the bar to see if it had fallen out of her bag. She was a damsel in distress and the copper in me immediately came to her rescue.

'I'll help you find it,' I'd said, confidently offering my assistance.

'Thank you!' she'd replied, shyly tucking a ringlet behind her ear. She was a reserved young lady, which made her even more adorable.

We chatted as I searched the cloakroom and under tables and chairs. Sadly I didn't find her purse, but I did end up walking her home. To be honest, I wasn't really that interested in finding it – I wanted her phone number!

Amazingly, Jenni rang me the next day. I'll never forget the first time she came to my house and made me dinner. No girl-friend had ever cooked a meal for me before. It wasn't a big deal, but it meant a lot to have someone show they wanted to look after me. When I found out what she did for a living – she worked with Riding for the Disabled – I fell even more in love with her because she was clearly an animal lover too.

Now, just as she had once won me over with a meal, I tried to get back into her good books with her favourite dish. 'Why don't I get us a nice pizza tomorrow night?' I suggested.

Jenni loved pizza, and a large ham and pineapple normally helped to cheer her up. 'Go on then.' She softened.

As Animal Search UK got busier, gradually the 'office' – which was an Ikea computer desk with a slide-out platform for the keyboard and a little foldaway camping table in the corner of the kitchen – grew. I bought a second-hand filing cabinet and fitted shelves to store my mountain of ring binders. I was fanatical about labelling things – there was a binder for the bank, and others for suppliers, To Be Done (TBD) and, my favourite, Ideas.

Even though Jenni moaned about the increasing amount of office equipment, she was as good as gold and would check the emails that came in from pet-owners while I was out during the day. Secretly she wanted the organization to grow as much as I did. She knew it was my dream to make my pet detective agency the best in the UK.

The next day, when I arrived home, she was waiting at the front door to greet me. She had a big grin on her face, as I pushed my bike up the drive.

'You'll be happy!' she said.

'Go on.'

'We've had two cats return home today from your advice.'

'Get in there!' I cheered. I pulled her in for a one-armed bear hug while balancing the bike in my other hand.

'Yep. One was found in the neighbour's shed and your hoover bag idea worked for the other.'

The hoover bag trick was something I had researched on the internet. I'd heard if you empty your vacuum cleaner in your garden, lost cats will be able to detect the familiar smells of your home. They will find their way back following the scents.

I was constantly researching new ways to find missing pets. I was waiting for the break that would allow me time to go out on searches myself.

My plans had to be put on hold for a little longer, though, as in September, Polly was born. Along with our beautiful baby daughter came a pram, a play pen, a changing mat, a car seat and cradle, and about a million teddy bears. Space was now at even more of a premium at Animal Search HQ.

Life became more cramped with every month that passed. Polly was getting bigger and toys were filling every remaining nook and cranny.

'We need to move house, Tom,' Jenni said.

'I know, Jen.' Things were getting tough. Luckily I'd done my research.

'A bigger house would be doable if we can get on the shared-ownership scheme.' It was an initiative run by our local housing association whereby they would buy part of your property and rent it back to you.

'I could get a Welsh dresser like my nan had.' Jenni was dreaming of our new place already.

I could get another two desks and a second filing cabinet, I thought, but kept it to myself.

The application was successful and Polly was reaching her third birthday when we finally got the keys to our new home.

The three-bed semi-detached house in the village of Credenhill was three miles out of Hereford. It was originally built in the 1960s as accommodation for the RAF pilots who were based nearby. The rooms were big and we settled in quickly. Jenni was over the moon, although the dining room wasn't furnished with a Welsh dresser: I immediately turned it into an office – which meant dinner on our laps in front of the TV.

I celebrated our move by buying a laser colour printer. It was a big investment – but worth it because it meant no more hopping on the bus into town to get photocopies done. The high-tech piece of equipment could print twenty pages in a minute, enabling me to produce a missing-pet campaign of five hundred leaflets and thirty posters really quickly. I also splurged on three A4 laminating machines to create posters that would be protected from the rain. Pretty soon I had a mini production line going: while the posters were creeping through the heat-sealers and coming out the other side encased in plastic, I would guillotine the rest of the leaflets from A4 down to A5.

I could chop four leaflets at a time, but the new equipment transformed the business. Pretty soon I had a regular trickle of campaigns being ordered each week.

The website was also going strong – the number of people registering a picture of their missing pet had jumped from thirty in total at my last house to ten a day. Our poster campaigns were proving a massive hit, with more and more owners finding their pets because of them.

It was time to update the Animal Search UK website so that it looked more professional. I paid a bloke called Pete to come up with something that looked more 'pet detective', with a picture of a magnifying glass and some paw prints. He designed a program whereby owners could upload their own photo. It was a huge leap forward.

But the more successful Animal Search UK became, the more frustrated I felt. I just wanted to be out on the ground, investigating and responding to enquiries. I wanted to have a patrol car and a uniform, to be like a copper again, only looking for animals. My prayers were finally answered just after the birth of my son, Sam, in 2006, when I landed a job working as a traffic officer for the Highways Agency to make ends meet. My new role gave me a good income but, most importantly, flexible working hours – six days on, three days off – so I had a chunk of time in the week to focus on Animal Search UK.

It was the breakthrough I'd been waiting for.

CHAPTER FOUR
WORLD HEADQUARTERS

Jenni finally put her foot down. She'd had enough of me taking over the dining room and said I had to find an office for Animal Search UK. We weren't doing well enough to afford to hire premises, so I had to come up with another idea. As I sat having a cool beer on the patio one evening, staring at the knackered old garden shed, I had a eureka moment. What if that was knocked down? I could build a much bigger shed and turn it into my ASUK headquarters. I was already dreaming big.

The next weekend I got to work dismantling the old shed. Jenni, of course, couldn't have been more delighted to get her hands dirty if it meant seeing me out of the dining room. Once we'd removed all that was left of the roof we kicked the remaining rotting panels down from the inside and it fell to the ground.

Once the debris was cleared I was left with a nice flat patio and a space the size of a double garage.

That'll make a great base, I thought, surveying the new terrain. I pulled Jenni in for a celebratory hug. 'The new one will sit in the garden nicely. It'll be like our own little empire.' I beamed.

'What are you like?' She laughed.

Polly came out and helped me sweep up the mess while Sam, who was now a year old, looked on from his buggy, giggling merrily. We loaded the car with all of the junk to take to the tip. Sam would have liked to travel in the trailer with the wood but I decided that would be unwise, so he had to settle for his car seat.

Four tip trips later we were back in the garden, measuring up. Polly and Sam helped hold down the tape measure and Jenni wrote down the figures. Twenty-one foot by eight: I couldn't believe how big it was going to be.

I spent the evening trawling the internet for companies that could build a shed for me. Sheds R Us – that'll do nicely. Finances were tight but I was making a little bit of income from the poster printing, and Jenni was fully supportive of the move. 'At least we can have our home back! And it'll help you expand the business, so it will be an investment,' she said.

We decided to take the plunge.

I thought it would be a good idea to speed things along by laying the foundations for the shed before it arrived. At the time, only half of the area had a patio covering it. I spent the next week digging up soil in the evenings, then laying down sand and patio slabs . . . only to be told by my mate, Jason, who lived across the road, that the two patio levels weren't even. There was about an inch difference. 'Unless you want your shed on a slant, we'll have to do it again.' He sniggered.

I was gutted, and so were the kids – Polly had been so proud of her slab-laying. I had to start from scratch.

Jason painstakingly helped me lift all the patio slabs and re-lay them half an inch lower. 'At least you can start with a level playing-field,' he quipped, patting me on the back.

'Very funny!' I replied.

The following weekend Sheds R Us arrived with my new office. It came in bits, which the team assembled there and then. I was asleep when they arrived because I'd just done a night shift on my Highways job. I'll never forget the moment I stepped out of the patio doors into the bright afternoon sunshine. I blinked a few times to adjust my eyes to the light, and there in front of me was a brand new office in all its glory.

It was magnificent.

I'd waited so long for that moment. Although Animal Search UK was off the ground, its new headquarters would be a game-changer. I imagined a bustling control room, just like a police station, from where I'd be taking calls and planning my missing-pet search investigations. But, more than anything, I was buzzing with the prospect of reuniting owners with their beloved pets.

The shed people were just putting the finishing touches to it – laying the felt on the roof so it would be protected from the rain and treating the wooden walls with preserver. I was keen to look after my new office from the word go.

Over the next couple of weeks I spent any spare time I had doing up the shed and turning it into a missing-pets operations room. I insulated, plastered and painted the walls. I installed electrics. I bought a carpet from an online warehouse. I furnished the place with bits and pieces I found at bric-à-brac shops, and at my neighbour's garage sale I acquired a couple of desks for twenty pounds and the chairs to go with them. It looked a hotchpotch of different furnishing styles and colours, but I didn't mind: I was as pleased as Punch with the end result. I was on track to fulfilling my dream of becoming a fully fledged Ace Ventura pet detective.

The final touch was a map of the UK, which I had framed and mounted on the wall above my desk. I was going to use it to help with my investigations. Any animals needing to be found would have their photo pinned next to the location where they were last seen. That way I would have a constant reminder of them. I would only have to raise my eyes to see their faces, which would spur me on to find them.

'There's one more thing you need,' Jenni said, hiding something behind her back.

'What's that?' I asked, curious.

She revealed a name plaque for the shed door made of granite. It was a gift from her mum and dad.

I held it at arm's length, admiring the engraving: *Animal Search UK HQ*. 'It's lovely.' I gave her a big kiss.

But that wasn't all. Jenni disappeared, only to return a few moments later with a cake she'd made in the shape of a garden shed. She wanted to make the grand opening official. We all sat around the desk, eating chocolate cake and drinking tea.

I swung my feet up onto the desk and leaned back in the creaky second-hand swivel chair. I was already feeling at home.

CHAPTER FIVE
STAY PAWSITIVE

Did I mention I was allergic to cats? It's a slight disadvantage when you're a pet detective, but it didn't stop me throwing myself into my first cat search.

It was a chilly December evening in 2008 when I was driving back through the village of Tarrington in Herefordshire on my way home after a long shift in the Highways job. The car heater was on full, blasting hot air into my face. It was freezing and a slippery layer of frost was settling on the roads. I knew Tarrington well because it was where my dad lived. It had also been my home for a year before I had moved to my own place in Bobblestock.

Out of the corner of my eye I spotted something flapping from a lamppost. I pulled over and parked, then ran across the road to the sign to see what it said. It was handwritten and there was no picture: *Rufus. Cat missing since 5 December.*

That was two weeks ago. How awful to have your cat go missing just before Christmas, I thought. This is an opportunity to help a local family.

I pulled out a pen, which I always kept handy in my pocket, a throwback from my copper years, and jotted down the owner's details on the back of my hand. She was called Emma Webster. I didn't recognize the name, although I knew most of the community, thanks to my dad.

As soon as I got home, I told Jenni, 'A cat's gone missing in Dad's village . . . I wonder if he knows the owner.'

'Maybe! Are you going to ring her?'

'I think I will,' I said, already dialling her number.

Emma picked up immediately. She sounded as if she had been waiting by the phone for any news of her beloved Rufus.

'I haven't seen your cat, but I may be able to help find him. My name is Tom Watkins and I produce professional posters and leaflets for people who have lost their pets.'

After the initial surprise of me ringing out of the blue, she sounded relieved and comforted at the prospect of receiving some support and professional help. It was then that she revealed a very important piece of information about her moggie. Rufus, a year-old ginger and white cat, had a habit of hitching a ride with strangers. 'A number of neighbours have been down to the village hall to drop off recycling at the bins and Rufus has jumped into their car,' Emma said.

Her information helped me build a character profile of her cat. Clearly Rufus was an adventurer and Emma confirmed he liked to wander long distances from home.

'We should definitely spread the net wider and put up posters in nearby villages,' I suggested.

She jumped at the idea and asked if I would print off a batch.

After we had agreed on a plan of action, Emma confided in me some more. She told me that all her kids had grown up and flown the nest, so Rufus was like a child to her. 'He's a really loving cat who likes to follow me everywhere I go. He'll keep me company when I'm doing the ironing or the washing. He'll sit on the arm of the chair purring.'

She was brave and didn't cry, but her voice started to tremble when I told her not to worry, that I would help her spread the word. Just before I rang off I told Emma to email me some pictures of Rufus, which I could use for my poster designs. I opened the file to see a cheeky ginger cat staring back at me. Suddenly I got a much better sense of what we were up against. I could tell by the way he was sitting and looking out from the corner of his eye that he was a bold and brazen cheeky chappie. I suspected he had wandered further than he should have and got lost on the way back. Either that or he had hitched a ride with some unsuspecting member of the public and now didn't know where on earth he was.

I stayed up late that night with a cup of hot chocolate, printing off three hundred leaflets and making twenty-five laminated posters.

'Get some rest!' Jenni massaged my shoulders and kissed me goodnight.

But I wouldn't slow down until the printing was done. I had to be up early for the Highways job but I'd made a promise to Emma, to Rufus.

I'd had only a few hours' shut-eye by the time my alarm sounded at four the next morning. I peeled myself out from the warmth of the duvet, showered, shaved and threw on my uniform. I had to be out of the door quickly because I had a detour to make on the way.

I wanted Emma to have the posters first thing, so I thought I'd drop them off at her house on the way to Worcester, where I was stationed that day. She lived in a big cottage near the centre of Tarrington. It had its own private lane, with a gate and an old-fashioned letterbox on a post next to the five-bar gate. It was still pitch black as I pulled up outside. I kept the car engine running, the hot exhaust fumes rising through the frosty air in clouds.

I pushed the wodge of posters into the letterbox and they landed with a thud on the bottom. I hope this works, I thought, because a success story for a local family from the same village where I had once lived would be wonderful.

Emma texted me at eight a.m. to say she had received the posters. I carried on with my Highways duties, but as the hours crept past I felt a gnawing inside me.

Suddenly I realized what it was about. I'd had enough of taking a back seat. I wanted to be out on the street doing what I did best – investigative work. Rufus would be my first case as a pet detective.

I was nervous with excitement when I texted Emma back to say I'd come to the village later that day to assist with some door-to-door enquiries and putting up the posters. Often a pet-owner delivering posters singlehanded can find it emotionally draining, so I wanted to lend a helping hand and bring Rufus back in time for Christmas. Wouldn't that make the best gift ever? Plus, I knew the area back to front. Combined with my police skill set, I was confident I could crack the case.

I managed to clock off a little earlier than expected and decided to make a start on the door-to-door enquiries. I was changing my clothes in the front seat of my Volvo when it dawned on me that a pet detective needs an official uniform. Something that stood out, that looked official, that showed people I took my job very seriously.

But that would have to be put on the back burner for now . . .

Instead I improvised, wearing a luminous work vest over my white T-shirt. It was cold, so I threw on my warm parka jacket, but the fluorescent colour was still peeping through, enough to give people the idea I was on official work.

It had been some time since I'd knocked on doors to gather information. When police are establishing what happened in a case, they use Witness Recall where they go over things step by step to find out what really occurred, with times, dates and places. Then they plot a chart of information. I would ask what I called the six WH questions – Why, What, Who, Where, When and How – adapting them for my pet detective work. Have you ever seen a cat like Rufus? When did you see him? Where did you see him? If you see him again, or a cat like him, could you take a photo of the moggie on your mobile phone and ring us? And, by the way, please may I search your garden, in case he's hiding there?

I took a deep breath and plunged in.

'Oh, hi, Tom, how are you?' Mrs Evans greeted me on her doorstep with a welcoming smile. She knew who I was, of course, via my dad, but was surprised to hear I was now a pet detective.

She invited me in for a chat, but I had to decline. I told her daylight hours were running out and I needed to press on. She seemed genuinely intrigued by my new part-time job, as did many of the people whose doors I knocked on that afternoon. Sadly, no one had seen Rufus.

As I worked my way through the village and spoke to numerous people, I also stopped dog-walkers. They're wonderful people to hand a leaflet to because they're out and about each day in the area and can keep an eye open for a missing cat.

As I got closer to my dad's vicarage, I thought I'd drop in and show him what I'd been up to. He was the eyes and ears of the community. He might be able to shed some light on the case.

I hadn't told him much about Animal Search UK because he'd never been keen on the idea of me being self-employed. Dad had always stressed the financial benefits and security of working for someone else. He was just being a protective father. I was looking forward to telling him about a job I'd got in the village to prove to him that my business model was working, slowly and steadily.

I knocked on Dad's door with my armful of posters and leaflets.

'Hello, love, come on in.' Dad called everyone 'love'. 'Cup of tea?'

'Yes, but make sure it's in the pot, Dad.'

By 'the pot', I meant the stainless-steel teapot Dad had won at my school's summer fair when I was eight years old. It had become a bit of a tradition for him to make tea in it ever since. We'd had many a cuppa from that pot to discuss jobs, work and the meaning of life.

I sat down in his kitchen on the country pine chair.

'So, Thomas . . .' Dad said. He liked to call me by my full name. He had a calming manner that made you relax immediately.

I filled him in on my case file. 'Do you know Emma Webster?' I asked.

Dad said her husband Bernie used to do bell ringing on Thursday evenings.

'Well, she's lost her cat!'

'I didn't know. I saw her walking through the village today. I was in my car so I didn't get a chance to stop and chat.' He looked perturbed by the information.

'I hoped by spreading the leaflets further afield we'd get some good news. I'm going to do all I can to try to bring him home. Emma and I are working on it together,' I said triumphantly.

A big smile spread across my dad's face. His eyes lit up. I could tell he was proud I was helping someone. 'Marvellous. Well, best of luck with it.'

It meant a lot to have my dad's approval. Before I left I handed him some leaflets and told him to spread the word.

Just as I was setting foot out of the vicarage, Emma was calling me on my mobile. The timing was perfect. She said she was ready to travel further to hand out leaflets: would I come with her?

I hadn't met Emma yet, so I was keen to put the name to a face. I drove to her house, where she was waiting outside her gate, dressed appropriately for the weather in a warm black coat and gloves. 'You must be Emma,' I said, winding down the window.

She had rosy cheeks and short brown hair, and I instantly warmed to her friendly personality. I was good at reading people and I could tell Emma was a kind, caring woman. She felt more like a family friend than a client because of her husband's connection with the church. She jumped into the car and I gave her a little hug. 'I've got a torch with me,' she said, pulling it out of her pocket.

'Good thinking!' It was now four thirty p.m. and dark.

Emma was putting on a brave face, but she appeared very tired because she hadn't slept well for several days. She was also a little frantic, wanting to do as much as she could. She kept her hands busy, restlessly curling the posters into a funnel.

Doing my best to calm her down, I explained we needed to approach the search methodically and steadily. We were going to visit each village in turn, first Stoke Edith, then Alders End, Durlow and finally Checkley. No stone would be left unturned in our search for Rufus.

'He's either wandered cross-country or he's hitched a lift with someone.' I shared my theory, from my character profile of Rufus.

Emma seemed to calm down when I told her we had a plan. Which was just as well, as it was turning into a grim night: not only was it cold, but it had started to drizzle. I was glad I was accompanying her around the villages – it wasn't a nice thing to have to do on your own in those conditions, both weather-wise and emotionally.

I cheered her up with a few of the Animal Search success stories, thanks to our poster campaigns. I could tell she was glad that she wasn't on her own looking for Rufus. It had always been my aim to offer the personal touch, to feel connected to the owners in a supportive way rather than just sending out posters.

It took a few hours, but we worked tirelessly, successfully managing to put laminated waterproof posters up in all the villages. Emma invited me for dinner, but I said I had to get back to the kids, though I promised to stop by soon for a cuppa. I felt pleased that we had covered a wide area and that I was leaving Emma feeling calmer and more positive. I couldn't explain why, but I had a good feeling that we were going to find Rufus.

Over the next couple of days I couldn't get the ginger cat out of my head. As I cruised up and down the motorways, looking out for stranded motorists on the hard shoulder, I thought about Rufus. I hoped he was sheltering from the cold somewhere.

On the third day, Emma called. I knew what she was going to say from the tone of her voice. 'Tom,' she said.

My heart started to gallop.

'We've got him! One of your posters worked!'

My feet could have lifted off the ground, I was so happy.

'Where was he?'

Emma explained that the gardener at a big house in the

village of Checkley had seen the poster shortly before spotting a cat that looked very much like Rufus sleeping in a barn on the property he was managing. He'd double-checked and got on the blower immediately. As soon as Emma heard, she had jumped into a car and rushed around to see if the ginger and white moggie was indeed Rufus.

Just as we'd thought, he'd wandered too far. Emma said there was a cross-country route through fields to the village from her house, which Rufus had probably taken.

'He was thin and frightened, but it was my boy all right,' Emma said, close to tears. 'He's in my arms now, purring away.'

There was only one thing for it: I was going to have to pop around to hers tomorrow and meet the cross-country adventurer.

The next afternoon, after work, I made a detour through Tarrington. The warm glow of the Christmas lights twinkling through the windows was much more welcoming this time around, as I imagined the happy Christmas Emma's family would have now Rufus was returned home safe and sound.

As soon as I had driven my car through Emma's gates and stepped out to close them behind me, I heard dogs barking. Spinning around on my heels, I saw a Dalmatian and a Boxer racing up the driveway towards me. I froze on the spot. I knew from my police training it was better to stand completely still than to leg it. That way they wouldn't think I was a trespasser.

I was a bit afraid, but Emma appeared from out of her front door with Rufus in her arms. 'Don't worry, they won't hurt you,' she said.

So I stayed calm and they stopped barking, then started wagging their tails. Rufus didn't seem in the least bit fazed by the dogs. I got the distinct impression that the cat ruled the roost.

'Here he is, the little tinker.' She nuzzled her face into his fur.

Although I'm allergic to cats – their fur makes me sneeze and my eyes water – I'm okay if I wash my hands afterwards. And I couldn't resist giving Rufus a little tickle under his chin. He lifted it up in the air and purred enthusiastically, calm and collected as anything. He looked at me, blinked, and looked away.

'You know exactly what trouble I went to for you, don't you, matey?' I said to him.

Rufus turned restless and wriggled in Emma's arms, indicating he wanted to roam free. She set him on the ground and, in the blink of an eye, he had sprung off the gravel drive and onto the bonnet of my car.

He sat there majestically, as if he owned it, licking his paws, keeping a close eye on what was going on around him. He was nonchalant, a very cool cat indeed.

'He likes your car! You'd better watch out he doesn't climb inside,' Emma teased.

I won't be at all surprised if that happens some day, I thought.

CHAPTER SIX
FROM MACE TO ACE

I had made the papers. The *Hereford Times* had got wind of my Rufus rescue and wanted to print a story. The publicity snowballed and, next thing I knew, *Midlands Today* – my local BBC news programme – wanted to film my 'search team' in action.

Cripes! Search team? It was just me, a yellow vest and the family car. I needed to revamp my image – and fast. If I wanted the world to take me seriously as a pet detective, I needed a uniform and a car to match. The problem was I had only forty-eight hours to sort it out before the TV crew would arrive at my door. What was I going to do?

I knew of a local company that specialized in uniforms and embroidery work. Margaret, the owner, was a bit of a legend in the area and I hoped she'd be able to turn something around for me in time.

'Do you think you can have it ready by tomorrow?' I asked tentatively, as I stood in front of Margaret's desk.

The whirring of embroidery machines and feverish activity on the workbenches outside her little office told me they were busy. Samples of clothing from different local companies were hanging and draped everywhere. Inside Margaret's office mountains of paperwork were piled high. Sunshine streamed through the small window of her industrial unit, lighting up the sewing machine on her desk.

Margaret, who must have been in her late sixties, wore jeans and a shirt, the sleeves rolled up to her elbows. Her thick-rimmed glasses were nestled in her grey curly hair. She pulled them down and used her middle finger to push them up her nose.

'I need it to look official,' I explained.

'What sort of job is it for?' she asked.

'Pet detective work.'

A bemused silence followed.

'Sorry? Do you mean like Ace Ventura?' She smiled.

'Sort of, but a lot more professional!' I cringed at the thought of Jim Carrey's loud tropical-print shirts.

She cast a smirk my way, then beckoned me to follow her into the next room. She flicked through a rail of brightly coloured uniforms, coats, high visibility jackets . . . As she searched for a uniform that would work, I kept firing questions at her. Would the Animal Search UK logo be printed or embroidered onto the jacket?

'Embroidery takes a week.' Margaret cut me dead.

A week?

I panicked. 'Can you print it on the back more quickly?'

'Twenty-four hours for printing,' she said, as she pulled out an orange jacket with reflective stripes across front and back. She held it up to my chest on the hanger. It was bright but not silly. With an ID badge, an ironed white shirt and a clip-on tie, it'd be just right, I thought. My imagination started to race away from me. When I had a team behind me, I'd need . . .

'I'll take four, Margaret.' A small, a medium, a large and an extra large should cover all bases.

I'd come prepared with my logo on a memory stick, so Margaret could see what she was dealing with. It read 'AnimalSearchuk. co.uk', with a magnifying glass over the 'A' and a couple of cat paw prints above the letters.

Within a few clicks of the mouse, Margaret had put together a mock-up of the back of the jackets on the computer screen. It looked impressive.

'I just need the words "MISSING PET SEARCH TEAM" in block capitals, too, please,' I said, drawing my finger across the screen.

Margaret stared at me. 'I thought you were joking about the missing-pet search!'

'No, it's my business,' I said proudly. I'd better get used to this, I thought. To me, it sounded normal, but to your average Joe I guess a pet detective is not run-of-the-mill. 'Most people haven't come across Animal Search because they don't ordinarily need us. If you google "lost cat", you'll find me, though.'

'When did you want these again?' Margaret asked.

'Tomorrow,' I said, crossing my fingers behind me.

Margaret pulled out her diary from underneath her papers. She thumbed through it and ran her index finger down a page. There was only a little gap on the visibly full schedule. Please let that be enough for me, I prayed.

She peered up at me through her glasses. 'I can get them done for end of play tomorrow and delivered next day, if you like.'

'Deal,' I said, with an outstretched hand. We shook on it. Then I realized I hadn't even asked how much they would cost but, to be honest, I didn't care. I needed them pronto and Margaret was saving the day.

That was one problem solved. Now for the next. I needed a pet-search vehicle. Something that people would stop and stare at. Something that would be recognized up and down the country and would draw awareness to the missing pets we were searching for. The vehicle would be our secret weapon. The ace up the sleeve of an Ace Ventura. I stared at my Volvo S40 saloon car. I was going to need some sort of miracle to turn this hunk of metal into a glamorous pet-mobile. It wasn't ideal, but it was all I had, so I was just going to have to work with it. I jumped behind the wheel and headed to the other side of town.

Roger was a sign writer and had come highly recommended by a mate. He ran his own sign and engraving business with his wife, Nora. Just like Margaret's, his diary was filled with job requests.

'A pet detective search car?' he exclaimed.

That day I was getting a lot of strong reactions.

'I need this Volvo to look like a cross between an RSPCA van and a fast-response police car.' I imagined myself racing down the motorway as I responded to a missing-pet call-out.

Roger crouched and ran his hand along the paintwork of my old family car with a bemused grin on his face. Before he had time to make any wisecrack comments, I waved the memory stick with my logo under his nose. 'Would you be able to show me some designs?' I checked my watch. Time was racing past.

'Sure. Come on in.' He sensed I was under pressure.

As we entered his office we walked past a load of trophies in a cabinet. There were stencil cutouts and rolls of sticky coloured vinyl on the tables next to a large printer and cutting machine.

'Don't step on the duck,' he said, as we sat down on well-worn swivel chairs.

'Duck?' I exclaimed. I peered under the desk and couldn't believe what I was seeing – a real live duck nestled on a blanket. It looked at me with its beady black eyes and let out a little quack.

'We rescued her. She comes to work with me every day and sits under my desk,' Roger explained.

'Hello, mate,' I greeted her. She looked very comfortable on her bed.

'Quack!'

'She likes you.' Roger grinned.

At that moment I knew Roger would do a sterling job of transforming my car because he was a pet person. That was the only credential I needed.

After choosing and designing the stickers for the car, I caught the bus home. I was on to my next problem – Jenni.

How was I going to break the news to her that our family car was about to undergo a radical transformation?

I approached the kitchen with caution. 'Hi, love,' I said, giving my wife a peck on the cheek as she was cooking the tea.

Jenni is an intuitive woman. 'What have you done?' she quizzed me.

I skirted around the subject. 'The BBC would like to come and see our set-up – the shed that's been turned into Headquarters, our search team response vehicle –'

'But we don't have a search team response vehicle!' She swung around with a wooden spoon in her hand.

I took a big gulp. 'About that . . .' I then confessed to having left the Volvo at Roger's for a makeover.

She was staring at me, dumbfounded. 'What – the Volvo?'

'Yeah. We're putting stickers on it to transform it into the UK's only missing-pet search vehicle.'

'Who're you kidding?' She shook her head. '*My* family car that I go shopping in and drive around in is going to look like the *Ghostbuster*-mobile?'

I told her to have a bit of faith – she might even think it was an improvement.

I got the cold shoulder for the rest of the evening. But by bedtime Jenni had softened and agreed that if I was going to be a TV star I needed to look the part.

That night I couldn't sleep. My brain and body were whizzing with adrenalin: in less than twelve hours' time I would be back in uniform, driving around in a marked car. I would be like a bobby on the beat, only this time doing what I loved – helping people find their missing pets.

Roger had left a message on my answerphone saying the Volvo would be ready for collection at five p.m. Jenni said she would wait at home with the kids for the big unveiling.

I hopped back on the bus into town. I was filled with anticipation as I turned the corner into Roger and Nora's yard. Would it look professional? Would it look over the top?

There she was. The dark blue bodywork had been transformed with the fluorescent orange stripes that now ran down the sides and over the roof and boot. The logo was bold and unmistakable. All that was missing was flashing lights and a siren. I was as proud as a father over a newborn baby.

Roger appeared from the other side of the car, dusting off his knees. 'Just finishing the last logo,' he said, with a smile.

'She's looking a dream, mate. Thank you so much for fitting us in.'

'Pleasure,' said Roger. 'It's a very good cause.'

As I drove the Volvo home, I noticed interested glances from lots of people. 'Missing-pet search team,' passers-by were mouthing as they pointed at the car.

A big grin spread across my face. 'That's right! I'm a pet detective!' I said out loud.

I stood out from the crowd and that was just what I wanted.

I hoped Jenni would be as pleased with the transformation as I was. I reversed into the drive, and as I got out I looked through the kitchen window and saw her face. She was shaking her head and smiling as she did the washing-up. I gave her a thumbs-up and she gave me a soapy one back with a wink.

I think she was secretly proud of me.

And I was proud of myself because somehow I had managed to pull it off. Well, almost . . . I was still waiting on the uniforms to arrive. Margaret said the delivery would be between nine and ten the next morning. The TV crew was turning up between ten and eleven. I took a deep breath and swallowed my nerves.

We're cutting it fine, but I'm sure it'll be okay, I persuaded myself.

Of course I couldn't sleep. I was worrying about the delivery, how I would come across on TV. So much was resting on my performance. *Midlands Today* was a chance to catapult the missing-pet agency into another league.

'Go to sleep!' Jenni hit me playfully with the pillow, as I wriggled next to her. She was a star when it came to looking after me.

I woke at six to the smell of well-cooked bacon and pork sausages from the local farm shop drifting up the stairs. Jenni sorted the logistics of life while I sorted the logistics of the business, and we both recognized how much we needed each other.

I was as nervous as anything as I buttoned up my freshly ironed white shirt and laced my army-style black leather boots. Most of all I wanted to create an impression of professionalism. It had been my aim since deciding to leave the police and follow my own path. Everything was now riding on those uniforms turning up.

The time ticked by . . . Ten a.m. came and went, but no postman. Ten past ten . . . nothing. I was shifting nervously from one foot to the other. A veil of sweat had formed on my brow. At ten twenty-five I heard the distinctive sound of a diesel engine pulling up outside.

'Please let it be the postman,' I muttered. I stepped into the kitchen to peer out of the front window. The bright red van brought with it a massive sense of relief. I opened the front door to be greeted with a box so big all I could see of the postman was a pair of legs walking up the pathway.

'Morning,' I greeted him.

'Morning. Delivery for Animal Search UK?'

'That's us!' I replied, passing the box back into the hall to Jenni.

'Open that, love! Pronto!' I called, as I signed the man's clipboard.

'Cheers,' shouted the postman, giving us a wave as he climbed back into his van.

Jenni was into the box and pulling out fluorescent items, like fish from a lake; they were wrapped in plastic bags and had several tags attached to the zips. The hallway looked like a scene from a toddler's first Christmas: cardboard, tissue, plastic bags and tags.

I checked my watch. 'Quick, where's mine?' I panicked. I needed the extra large size as I did enjoy a fry-up, contrary to doctor's orders. Jenni passed me a very soft and very bright orange jacket. I held it up like a footballer who's just been signed and is standing in front of the press with his team's shirt. The white logo panels on the back looked great and I was incredibly proud to see the 'corporate image' for the first time.

I slipped it on as Jenni bundled the boxes and debris out of sight into the under-stairs cupboard. The door knocker went as I was zipping up the front. I glanced behind me. 'Here we go, love,' I chirped.

'Andy? Good morning,' I said confidently, as I opened the door to the slick-looking presenter. We shook hands.

'So this is Animal Search UK, I gather?' said Andy, wiping his feet on the doormat before coming in.

I heard a peeling sound, like Sellotape being torn off fabric, from behind me. Jenni was scrunching up a sticky XL label that she had pulled off my back.

'It is . . . The world HQ.' I chuckled. 'Where shall we begin? How about a guided tour?'

As I led the way I gave a deep sigh of relief. I'd pulled it off.

CHAPTER SEVEN
THE RIDDLE OF TOOTS

Business was booming. I was getting twice as many call-outs on searches and three times the number of hits on our website, thanks to my TV appearance. I was so inundated with work that I needed an extra pair of hands. I decided to post an advert in the local job centre: 'Missing Pet Search Coordinator'.

I had a bit of interest, seven applications, but only one caught my eye.

Zoë was an animal lover. That was evident from her home situation: she had more than twenty different pets living at the home she shared with her mum. She had ten rabbits, two cats, two dogs, one bird, guinea pigs and a goldfish. She had the lot.

One of the first things I asked her in the interview was where she kept them all. The nineteen-year-old explained that half of them lived in the house, but the bird and the rabbits had a big coop in the garden to roam and fly around in.

'My mum puts up with them because she knows how happy they make me.' Zoë giggled nervously.

Zoë, who had dark hair and piercings through her nose and lip, appeared shy and a little nervous. It was obvious she had an affinity with animals: not only did she have dark blue paw prints tattooed across her wrist, but she explained her pets were companions.

It struck a chord in me, as I remembered my best mate, Maggie. 'They're my hobby, I love them all,' she said. 'They all have names and they're all very much part of the family.'

Her words warmed my heart. 'That's lovely.' I smiled, knowing full well how comforting it can be to have an animal friend. She had demonstrated that she really cared about animals, which was a prerequisite for the job. But, however much I liked Zoë, she still had to go through the official application process: I needed to find out whether or not she had the skills to become a trainee pet detective.

I handed her a little test, which I had designed to work out how much empathy she had. It was an email from a bereaved pet-owner asking if someone could take the picture of their cat off the Animal Search UK website because it had been found, sadly deceased. 'How would you reply to this?' I asked. I passed her a piece of paper and a pen.

Zoë looked thoughtful as she wrote her answer. She slid the paper back across the table and waited anxiously for my feedback.

She had put together the perfect reply, saying how sorry she was to hear the news and how she would remove the photo immediately. Zoë delivered under pressure, which was just the skill I was looking for. I could also tell from her manner that she would be dependable and committed. 'You've got the job,' I told her there and then.

Zoë let out a little shriek of excitement. 'Really? I'm so happy!' She was over the moon because she had been washing up at a children's play zone in town and, as much as she loved kids, animals were her true passion.

I explained that the job predominantly entailed answering the hotline, telephoning owners who had registered their pets as missing to offer them tips and advice, and to explain how ASUK could help them, and assisting with the printing and postage of the poster campaigns. She would man Animal Search HQ while I was out on traffic-officer duties.

It wasn't long before her duties increased. Five weeks after Zoë had joined the team we received our first celebrity enquiry.

Zoë had knocked off for the day and I was alone in the shed – or, rather, in the Animal Search UK headquarters, as I preferred to call it. It was a very cold January night and condensation had clouded the little sash windows that looked out onto my back garden. The phone rang.

'Animal Search UK, how can I help?' I answered.

The woman at the other end of the line had a thick Scottish accent. She was also the mother of a pop star who had recently had a number one in the charts. 'I'm sure you've heard of Sandi Thom!' The mum went on to divulge more details about her daughter. Not being particularly clued up on pop culture, I didn't have the foggiest who Sandi was.

'We'll help anyone,' I assured her.

'Well, I need your help to find her cat,' the mum, who was also her daughter's manager, blurted out.

This was something I knew lots about. I pulled out my pad of paper and a pen and started taking notes.

Sandi Thom's mum described how she had been looking after Toots at her house in Scotland while Sandi was touring the world. The black and white cat had been missing for three days now and she was worried sick for its safety. 'I understand you have a search team,' she said. She'd clearly seen my new website, which boasted my 'professional missing-pet search team service'.

'Yes,' I confirmed.

'I'd like to hire you,' she replied immediately.

'Great! We're here to help.'

'A team of three,' she went on.

Ah, that was a problem, mainly because there was only me. In my enthusiasm to grow the business, I might have embellished the team on the website . . . I knew I'd find a solution, though. 'We'll leave first thing in the morning,' I said, and promised Sandi's mum we would do everything in our power to find Toots.

As soon as I put down the phone, I googled the location. It was 450 miles away – Edzell, Angus, a small town in the remote Scottish countryside.

Never mind: no distance was too great to travel if a missing pet needed my help. All *I* needed was a 'team'. I picked up the phone and dialled my first recruit. 'How would you fancy coming with me to Scotland tomorrow?' I asked.

Zoë was very new to the job: I was throwing her in at the deep end. 'Umm, how far is it?' she asked tentatively.

'Four hundred and fifty miles.'

There was a long silence.

'And can you think of anyone else who might want to help out?' It was another big ask.

There was an even longer silence.

'Someone sensible, mature, who can carry out a search,' I elaborated. 'How about your mum?'

I knew Zoë's mum must be as big an animal-lover as her daughter because she'd let their home be turned into a zoo. I had chatted to her a few times on the phone and she seemed level-headed and caring. As long as Zoë's mum was confident enough to stop people and question them about the possible whereabouts of Toots, we were in business. Zoë said she'd talk to her and ring me back.

Five minutes later, I picked up the phone and heard Zoë's voice. 'Go on then. Mum's up for it!'

'Yes!' I cheered to myself in the shed.

I spent the rest of that evening researching the terrain. I looked on Google Earth to see how urbanized or rural Edzell was. Despite being in the countryside the area surrounding Mrs Thom's house was built up, which meant we'd be knocking on doors rather than searching the undergrowth.

My alarm went off at the crack of dawn. I tiptoed around the bedroom, doing my best not to disturb Jenni. I had a shower and a shave and got dressed in my new uniform. Jenni had sweetly ironed my dark trousers and white shirt the night before, so I'd look smart for our first celebrity client. I kissed the kids, then made my way out to the drive, where my pet-mobile was waiting for me.

Work had been going so well that I'd transformed our second family car – a silver Vauxhall Vectra Estate. It had luminous orange chevrons, matching the Volvo, along the side and across the boot and a 'MISSING PET SEARCH' sticker on the back.

The boot was loaded with our equipment: there was a spring-loaded trap, which could be used to catch the cat safely and humanely and, of course, cat biscuits for bait. I also packed extra orange fleeces for the cold weather.

As I turned the key in the ignition and the engine roared into life, I was overwhelmed with pride. Twelve years after leaving the police force I had everything I had dreamed of: my own pet detective force.

Zoë and her mum were already waiting outside when I turned up at their house. I was pleased to see them both suited up in the new Animal Search UK uniform – bright orange fleeces, with our logo stitched across the front.

'Ready?' I grinned.

'Let's do this,' Zoë and her mum replied enthusiastically.

They threw their overnight bags into the boot and jumped into the back seat. As we headed for the motorway I briefed them on the situation. I told them Sandi Thom was so distressed by the disappearance of her beloved Toots that she had cut short her tour and was going to meet us at the other end. She had offered to put us up in a hotel for the two days we would be searching.

'Is she the singer who did "I Wish I Was A Punk Rocker"?' Zoë's mum piped up.

'Mum, I didn't know you listened to the charts!' Zoë was shocked.

'There's a lot about me you don't know, my dear.' Her mum patted her daughter's leg.

Listening to the mother–daughter chat, I knew I'd selected the right team for the job. They were both clever and level-headed and would catch on quickly to what I was after. They were also sensitive souls, which would help enormously when it came to meeting Sandi Thom. It was hard to gauge how the pop star would be feeling, but I anticipated finding her in a state of distress, as she was travelling thousands of miles to help with our search. Our pets are close to our hearts whoever we are.

As we travelled the length of the country, Zoë and her mum

spent the next eight hours listening, as I gave them a crash course in pet detecting.

Most importantly, I had to teach them techniques for questioning people when they knocked on a door. 'For example, if you were to ask a question like, "Have you seen anything?" it invites a yes or no answer,' I explained. 'But if you were to make the question more open-ended, such as "What do you know about Sandi Thom's cat going missing?" it will invite a bigger response.'

I broke down the search into the smallest of details, such as showing them how to fold a missing-pet leaflet so that Toots's picture was on the outside when it landed on the doormat. Otherwise home-owners might mistake it for unwanted advertising and dispose of it without reading it, which was the last thing we needed. We had printed a thousand Missing Toots flyers to saturate the area. We were going to be a long way from base and I didn't want to risk running out.

The most crucial thing of all was not to let anyone slip past unnoticed. 'Speak to everyone you see. Don't let anyone pass without talking to them. Make sure you take your notepads with you so you can record everything you see and hear.'

'Got it,' Zoë and her mum said.

After we were done with doorstep techniques, I ran through the walkie-talkies. We couldn't resist having a bit of fun practising. They were in the back with a radio and I was in the front. It didn't take them long to catch on to my police jargon.

'Can you see the sign on the left? Over.'

'Affirmative. Over.'

We tried it the other way around, too.

'What time are we arriving? Over?' Zoë asked.

'Our ETA is seventeen hundred hours. All received?' I responded.

'Yes, received. Over.'

We even had a conversation about stopping at the services.

'Front to back . . .' I started.

'Yes, back receiving. Over.'

'Do you need a coffee?'

'Affirmative. Over and out.'

I'd learned from the police force that it's essential to have camaraderie among your team. A positive attitude leads to positive results! As we drove the last hundred miles across the border I felt we had a very strong unit, dedicated to finding out where poor Toots had gone.

We arrived at Edzell as the sun was setting, an hour ahead of schedule at four o'clock. I took the right fork at the junction, which led me down a long road. The houses petered out and there was nothing in front of us except an open road and woodland. Hereford was beautiful but the highlands were something else. I could see for miles, the air was so clean and crisp.

The pet-mobile juddered as we crossed an old stone bridge over the river that separated where Mrs Thom lived from the main town. In front of us we could see a series of bungalows and outbuildings. I concluded it must once have been a farm or an estate before it was turned into residential housing.

'What number?' I asked my back-seat navigators.

'It's a house name, not a number. Geranium Villa.'

It was easy enough to find as it stood out from the rest with its manicured front garden and the bright flowerpots that lined the driveway. As a copper, I'd found you could tell a lot about someone from the way they kept their house and garden.

After such a long journey it was a relief to get out of the car and stretch our legs. I took a deep breath, inhaling the Highland air into my lungs. The sound of the river running past reminded me of childhood camping holidays in Scotland. It was a nice place to be, but we knew there was a serious job to do.

As I was opening the boot, a woman appeared around the corner of the bungalow and waved at us. She had to be Sandi Thom's mum, I thought.

She was tall and slim, with highlighted grey hair. She looked like a woman who took pride in her appearance. She held out her hand, which we shook in turn. We all were a little nervous to be meeting a pop star's mum, although we couldn't show it because that wouldn't have looked professional.

Mrs Thom invited us in and we sat down on the sofas in her living room. Sandi was out looking for Toots while there was still daylight, and she'd be joining us for dinner later.

Mrs Thom looked strained as she sat on the chair opposite us. Her hands were folded in her lap but her tightly crossed legs gave away how stressed she was. I'd got pretty good at reading body language when I was in the force.

I dived straight in. 'Let's start from the beginning, Mrs Thom. Why don't you tell us a bit about Toots and when you noticed she was missing.' I wasn't one for beating around the bush. It was important to get the facts.

Mrs Thom explained that she had been looking after 'wee Tooty' while Sandi had been touring America. 'She's a homely cat who never ventured far away from the house. But three days ago she didn't come home,' Mrs Thom said, her voice wobbling.

Toots was a distinctive cat with unusual black and white markings. She had a white nose with a single black spot on the end and a black splodge under her chin, like a bib. I pulled out the missing-cat posters we had printed and placed them on the coffee-table. Toots looked up at us from the page, her bright eyes willing us to bring her home. The photo brought silence to the room, as we all took a moment to wish for her safe return.

Mrs Thom continued. She told us that Toots normally lived with Sandi in London and had been with herself for three weeks.

So Toots was familiar with the lie of the land here by now, I thought. I noted it down in my pad, along with the fact that Toots was a city cat and used to urban environments.

Mrs Thom was particularly upset because she felt responsible for what had happened – Toots had gone missing on her watch, so to speak. She was so agitated and distressed that she couldn't sit still. She kept jumping up from her chair and pacing the room. She tried to distract herself by offering to make us a hot drink.

'That would be lovely,' we chorused.

As the kettle shrilled in the background, Mrs Thom went over her story again and again. She was clearly haunted by what had happened.

I tried to keep her calm by telling her that I would do everything in my power to find her daughter's beloved Toots. 'No stone will be left unturned,' I promised.

I didn't have much to go on, but even the tiniest bit of information could help point me in the right direction. Thanks to a final question-and-answer session, I established that one of the local residents wasn't very friendly and might not cooperate with us. Mrs Thom frowned as she described Mr Jones. It wasn't uncommon for people not to get on with others in their neighbourhood but I made a mental note of it.

We had been in the living room twenty minutes when Sandi arrived.

She was small and pretty, with long, dark shiny hair. She looked just like the photos I'd seen of her on the internet but today she was evidently knackered. She'd travelled up from

London the night before and had spent the day conducting her own search.

'Any joy?' I asked tentatively.

'No.' She shook her head. She was doing a good job of putting on a brave face, which I admired. It couldn't have been easy for her.

That was my cue to tell Sandi how we would find Toots. Sandi was keen to establish what we were going to do, how long it would take and where we would be looking.

I explained that we would start with door-to-door enquiries, then approach the press to get some publicity for her. I was keen to reassure her we would do everything we could – that our presence in the town would attract more publicity than she could achieve on her own.

Sandi told us she had contacted the police but they hadn't been very helpful.

'They wouldn't be because they don't deal with missing cats,' I explained.

She looked disheartened.

Zoë, who had been quiet so far, stepped in. 'Don't worry, Sandi. We'll do everything we can to find her,' she squeaked. Zoë was sweet: she really felt people's pain and wanted to do her best.

Sandi dropped her eyes to the floor. She didn't reveal any details about her connection to Toots, but it was clear her cat meant the world to her.

We were all tired after such a long day, so we agreed that our next move would be to check in at the hotel. We'd have a meal later with Sandi and talk more about how we were going to find Toots.

The hotel wasn't far away – back over the bridge and into town. As we parked the car, some chefs were having a cigarette at the back of the hotel. They started nudging one another, mouthing 'missing-pet search' as they read our window banner. I guess it was like the Ghostbusters arriving in a sleepy town in Scotland. They gave us a cheeky chuckle as we walked past and one muttered, 'All right, Ace.'

I nodded and grinned. Something told me that that wouldn't be the last time I'd hear that joke.

The hotel was small with about thirty rooms, a bar and a restaurant. It wasn't the Ritz, but it was clean and comfortable so I'd be happy.

'We're here to find Sandi Thom's cat,' I said, as I introduced myself at Reception.

Word of our arrival had got around, as the receptionist knew who we were when we checked in. It was a small community so the chance of speaking to someone who was a friend of Sandi was high. I was on my guard, making sure I never acted unprofessionally or commented on anything that wasn't our business.

We checked into our rooms. In mine, I dumped my bags on the floor and collapsed onto the bed. My muscles ached and pulsed from all the driving as I lay back, took a deep breath and prepared myself for the next stage of the search.

After five minutes' rest, I peeled myself off the comfy mattress, jumped into the shower and got ready for the meal with Sandi.

Normally, I'd want to take my downtime away from pet-owners otherwise I'd never be off duty, which could affect my performance. For that reason I didn't really want to have a long evening with Sandi and the team, but I knew the singer was distressed and needed my reassurance.

I threw on a clean shirt and finished off the look with my orange fleece. I was making a point of wearing my uniform everywhere I went so I was recognizable – whether I was at work, off work, even going to pick up groceries in the supermarket.

When I got downstairs, I found Zoë and her mum already in the hotel restaurant-bar having a natter, and Sandi walked in shortly after me. The room fell silent, as everyone stopped talking and stared at the local celebrity. I could hear whispering, followed by a clatter of cutlery as everyone got back to eating once they had stopped gawping.

In the restaurant we sat in a booth. Even though it was dimly lit, I could see that people were trying to listen in to our conversation. Nevertheless, we chatted for hours, masterminding our plan to track down Toots. 'I'll carry out methodical door-to-door enquiries, starting with your next-door neighbour. We'll expand into the town, going as wide as we can. I estimate we can cover two or three hundred properties tomorrow,' I said, between mouthfuls of my dinner.

I explained to Sandi the most likely causes of cat disappearances.

'Four things can happen to them. They can get locked into a shed – we'll cover that possibility by searching locally, focusing on the houses surrounding your mum's. They can be adopted by people. Often when we knock on doors, I've found the home-owner either declares it, or lets the cat out later once we've left.'

There was no easy way to say the next bit.

'Sadly, another reality is that the cat may have been knocked down by a car.'

Sandi's face dropped.

'Often there's a witness. If Toots had been killed on the other side of the river, there's a good chance someone in town would have heard about it.' I tried to explain to Sandi that if that had happened to Toots, it was better to know than to be left wondering if she was out there somewhere suffering. Sandi was pragmatic and could see where I was coming from.

'The other option is that Toots has got lost. And if she has, we'll do everything we can to find her!' I ended on a cheerier note.

An idea suddenly popped into my head. 'If you really want to raise Toots's profile, you could hire a plane and fly it over Edzell with a banner saying: "Where is Toots?"'

'To find a cat? That's ridiculous!' Sandi scoffed. Zoë and her mum also found the idea hilarious. At least it lifted the mood.

I still thought it was a good idea, though. And one day I was certain I'd prove it.

I went to bed exhausted. My body was tired, but my brain was swirling with unanswered questions. What did I think had happened to Toots? I had a few theories, but her disappearance was a mystery. I sensed it wouldn't be an open-and-shut case.

I was pretty certain we wouldn't find Toots in a garden in Edzell. Why? Because I'd observed a quarter of a mile of open countryside between the small cluster of bungalows where Sandi's mum lived and the rest of the town. It wasn't likely that Toots would wander a quarter of a mile to town, then get lost in a garden.

I did wonder whether she had been stolen because she was Sandi's cat. And whether a ransom demand would arrive soon.

But, as with every case, I was going into it with an open mind.

I woke up early the next morning, refreshed, and tucked into a fried breakfast with Zoë and her mum, wearing our new Animal Search UK T-shirts. We were going to start our enquiries by knocking on doors and looking into sheds in the immediate area surrounding Sandi's mum's bungalow.

But the first stop was at Sandi's mum's. It was nine fifteen a.m. and we didn't have a moment for a cuppa: we had too much ground to cover. Sandi and her mum told us they had made lots of enquiries locally and were keen for us not to repeat them – perhaps assuming it would take time away from finding Toots elsewhere. However, it was very important that we repeated all the questioning. If a neighbour had any sensitive information, they might not have told the owners, whereas they might tell us.

At nine thirty-five, we started our 'door-to-door enquiries'. 'You two go together in that direction, and I'll start on these houses,' I told Zoë and her mum.

Zoë looked a bit nervous at the prospect of approaching people on their doorstep, but I knew she'd be fine because she had developed a strong and confident manner chatting to strangers on the Animal Search hotline. She also had her mum as back-up.

'Do you remember the questions I told you to ask?' I double-checked.

'Yes.' They nodded cheerily.

'Okay, let's find Toots!'

I had about a dozen properties to search – 'search' being the operative word, as obviously I couldn't check anyone's garden or shed without prior consent. It was my job to be assertive and talk them around.

A young man answered the first door I came to. He was aged around twenty, wearing a T-shirt and tracksuit bottoms.

'Hello, I'm looking for a missing cat. Can I leave this with you, please?' I said, thrusting a leaflet in his direction.

He studied the picture of Toots and thought long and hard. 'You'll be lucky to find her around here,' he said at last. 'She could have been shot by a gamekeeper.'

I didn't like the sound of that. 'Where can I find these game-keepers?' I revved up my enquiry.

'I know them. I'll ask them for you.' He clearly wasn't going to give me any names.

If a gamekeeper had shot Toots accidentally, they might be feeling bad and not want to come forward, I thought.

I told the young man that our phone line was open twenty-four hours a day and was confidential. I wanted him to know that if he needed to ring anonymously he could.

I radioed to fill the team in on my movements. 'I'm going to see the "grumpy" guy now. I'll be with you at ten hundred hours back at the car. Over.' I was referring to Mr Jones, the man Mrs Thom had described as not very helpful.

I heard a few crackles, then Zoë's voice: 'All received, over.'

I felt pleased my walkie-talkie lessons in the car had paid off.

Even though Mrs Thom had described Mr Jones as unfriendly and not very cooperative, it was my job to give him the benefit of the doubt. I approached him, being very diplomatic, professional and polite.

'Good morning, I don't know if you're aware . . .' I started the proceedings, knowing he was fully aware '. . . but Mrs Thom, who lives nearby, has lost her cat, Toots.'

Mr Jones, who was in his mid-thirties, was leaning on a shovel. The neck of his shirt was wide open. He was wearing jeans. He looked like he'd been gardening from the grass stains and mud smeared across his knees. 'I know.' He shrugged, his eyes avoiding my gaze.

'Do you mind if I give you a poster?' I asked, holding it out for him to take. I always try to get a leaflet into their hands, as you never know where it can lead.

'I don't need one,' he said, as he fanned it away. 'I haven't seen anything.' He crossed his arms defensively.

At this point I was starting to think he was either thoroughly unpleasant or he knew something. 'Okay. Well, if you do hear anything, you can ring us anonymously.' I kept things civil.

I laid it on thick about our search team to drum into him that we would not stop until Toots was found. 'There are two teams here today and we're going to be searching for a few days until we find Toots.'

That'll help to flush him out, I thought. I wasn't sure what had happened, but I suspected he might have Toots in his house or in his shed.

'Would you mind if I take a look in your garage to see if Toots might have got trapped in there?' I made one last attempt to unearth what was going on.

He point-blank refused.

That was a blow, although sometimes people can be defensive about their property. I thought I'd leave it there for now, but just as I was walking away, he muttered under his breath, 'You won't be seeing her again, mate.'

I spun around and looked him in the eye. 'Why's that, sir?'

'Ah, just a hunch.'

The whole thing was sounding fishier by the minute.

It isn't unusual for people to make unhelpful comments, such as 'Oh, the fox probably got her,' but in that instance I felt there was something he wasn't letting on about and he wanted rid of me.

I walked away feeling unsettled. I couldn't put my finger on it, but something about him didn't sit right with me.

I reconvened with Zoë and her mum by the bridge to exchange notes and tell them about my discovery. 'I'm not sure about him.' I pointed to the house I'd just knocked at. 'How did you get on?' I asked.

Zoë and her mum said everyone they had spoken to had been very polite and promised they would have a look for Toots.

'Good job, team.'

It was now ten thirty. An hour since we had started, and it was time to head into town. We jumped into the pet-mobile and drove across the river, then along the quarter-mile of open land-scape. I knew we needed to hit the town of Edzell with an impact. I was keen to make sure every man and his dog noticed us arrive and got talking about us in order to spread the word about Toots.

I parked the search car right in the middle of town, as brazen as brazen could be. We all jumped out wearing our orange hi-vis jackets. It was freezing, so I put on my Animal Search woolly hat too. I was conscious that Zoë might suffer from the chill, so I handed her a second fleece to make sure she kept warm.

Zoë and her mum started their door-to-door enquiries in the opposite direction to me. I could tell Zoë was determined to do well – she was keen to make a good impression, but more than anything she wanted to have some news for Sandi about Toots.

If we were feeling the cold, I feared for Toots and worried about how she would be coping. I stepped up my enquiries another gear. We were armed with laminated posters and leaf-lets with our free phone number, as well as grey gaffer tape to stick the posters to lampposts and walls, and in windows. We visited every shop in the high street and gave each a poster to display.

I had arranged for the hotline calls to be diverted from the shed to my mobile. Luckily there was a signal – only two bars, but that was enough.

We kept going, our fingers crossed. I knocked at about a hun-dred doors over the next four hours, a mixture of business premises and homes. As we were half a mile down the road from where Toots lived, it was unlikely she was trapped in a garden or shed there, but we hoped that if someone had heard about a road accident it might shed light on where Toots was.

Unfortunately, our search was fruitless.

'Anything?' I asked Zoë and her mum, when we met up in

the town centre just after two thirty. They shook their heads glumly. I could see that the strain of not knowing if Toots was okay was getting to Zoë.

Suddenly my mobile was singing in my pocket. My fingers were like blocks of ice so I was trying desperately to hit the button before the caller hung up.

'Good afternoon, Animal Search UK.'

'Hiya, I'm ringing about Toots . . .'

CHAPTER EIGHT
THE PLOT THICKENS

My heart leaped. It was the first offer of information we'd had.

'Go on,' I said, urging my caller to deliver, full of hope and excitement.

'There's a golf course in Edzell . . .'

I could hear my heart, it was thudding so loudly.

'. . . and there's a cat's body up there.'

Oh, no. Toots had been found dead and someone had dumped the body at the golf course. My heart sank. I took the caller's name and number. He sounded genuine, so I didn't have any reason to distrust him. 'Where on the golf course did you see it?' I asked.

'As you walk down from the car park to the eighteenth hole there is a hedge along the road, and the cat's body is in it.'

I didn't know if it was Toots, but it might have been.

'What is it?' Zoë asked.

'We need to search the golf course.' I signalled for Zoë and her mum to jump into the car, pronto.

I wouldn't alert Sandi until I had seen the cat for myself: I didn't want to upset her unnecessarily. The golf course was quite some way from the Thoms' house, so it was unlikely that Toots had walked all that way. However, there was a chance that someone had discarded her body there.

We drove quickly to the golf course, which was out of town, in the foothills of the Angus glens. As we zipped along the open road the houses became sparse and the mountains rose into the sky. The atmosphere in the pet-mobile was sombre. Zoë and her mum were upset at the thought of possibly finding Toots dead and I tried my best to calm them. 'It may not be Toots.' I was trying to stay positive, but as we drew closer I was starting to doubt my own words. Whether it was Toots or not, we still had to brace ourselves for seeing the body of an unfortunate cat.

As soon as we arrived I headed over to the golf shop to ask permission to search the eighteenth hole and the surrounding area. I also quizzed the man behind the till about whether he had seen or heard anything. He said he didn't know what I was talking about, but was happy for us to take a look.

The eighteenth hole was some walk away. The icy wind battered our faces. The flagpole was flapping wildly from side to side. We decided to split up and go in opposite directions along the hedge line until we found the body.

Zoë was biting her nails nervously – identifying a body was an awful thing for anyone to have to do. I explained that the sooner we found out if it was Toots, the better it would be for Sandi. It would save her lots of heartache in the long run.

I hunched my shoulders as I pressed into the wind. My nose, cheeks and ears were turning numb. After three hundred yards I caught sight of something black and furry in the bushes. There was no doubt about it: it was a cat's body.

'Stay back,' I warned my recruits, who were now coming

towards me. I didn't want to put them through unnecessary trauma. The poor cat was in a real state and had begun to decompose. I couldn't tell if it was Toots or not. There was no collar. Toots had had a collar, but it might have come off.

I had no choice but to ring Sandi. She might be able to recognize markings we didn't know about.

I dreaded making the phone call. I felt terrible, seeing that poor cat. How would Sandi feel? I had to remind myself that it's better to know than not to know. At least that way you can put your mind at ease and go through the grieving process.

The few rings it took for Sandi to pick up felt like an eternity.

'Hi, Sandi. It's not good news.' I didn't beat around the bush. There was no point sugar-coating it. I explained we had found a cat on the golf course and it had passed away. 'We can't establish whether it's Toots or not. Could you have a look?'

Within ten minutes her white Range Rover had pulled into the car park. She'd obviously driven very quickly. The gravel crackled as her tyres screeched to a halt. Sandi jumped out. She looked anxious and upset.

I prepared her for what she was about to see and she took it well. As we retraced our steps, she appeared to find her strength. She was now focused on discovering whether we had found Toots. We all stood back to give her some space.

Slowly, Sandi crouched over the body. We held our breath as we waited for her to say something. 'It's not Toots!' she exclaimed.

I felt elated and deflated at the same time – relieved that the dead cat wasn't Toots, but dismayed that we hadn't found her. Uncertainty is difficult to stomach.

So it was back to the drawing board. But first I needed to ensure that this poor cat had some dignity. I called the local vet and explained we would drop the cat's remains to them on the way back through town so it could be scanned for a microchip. At least, its owners would get the resolution they would desperately need. It was the right thing to do. We carried on with the search and made sure every single house and shop, every hotel and B-and-B had leaflets.

By the end of the day almost everyone in that town knew about our search for the black and white cat: that was our objective. We had knocked on more than four hundred doors.

The next morning we left for Hereford. It was hard saying goodbye to Sandi and her mum because the last twenty-four hours had been very emotional. I felt Sandi was a bit disheartened that I hadn't been able to find Toots while I was there, but I felt content that we had done everything we could and had significantly raised local awareness about her disappearance.

It was now a waiting game.

'Never give up hope. We don't know whether the next call with news will come in ten minutes or ten days,' I told Sandi and her mum. The search didn't end as we drove away. It finished when we found Toots, or when Sandi gave up, and I knew that Sandi would never give up. Someone who had put her music career on hold and travelled so far to search for her cat wasn't going to throw in the towel. She loved Toots too much.

Zoë had hold of the hotline while we drove back: her job was to manage the calls. It was a much quieter journey on the way down. We were all deep in thought as we drove past the Lake District, Cheshire and Staffordshire, down to Birmingham. We arrived in Hereford at about eleven p.m.

'We'll find Toots, won't we?' Zoë asked, as I dropped her

and her mum at home. She was trying hard not to let her emotions get the better of her, but I felt she was on the cusp of crying.

We hadn't had any calls throughout the eight-hour journey but that wasn't unusual. It might take some time to hear back.

'Yes, we will,' I said. One way or another I was certain we'd do our best to get to the bottom of Toots's disappearance.

Four days later, I was in the shed, a.k.a. our national headquarters, designing posters at the workstation when someone called on the hotline. Every poster has a reference number specific to the pet it features.

'Good morning, Animal Search UK. Can I take your reference number, please?' I ask this because it saves lots of time on the phone: I can check straight away whether or not the animal has already been found.

A Scottish accent said: 'Seven two four nine one.'

That's Toots's number! Tune in. This is it. What's he going to say?

'How can I help?'

The gruff-sounding man said he wasn't going to give his real name. 'Call me Gonzo,' he said.

As in the purple big-nosed character from *The Muppets*? I thought it was strange, but I went along with him because I just wanted to hear what he had to say.

'Is this off the record?' he asked.

'Can be,' I replied.

'You can give up looking for the cat because she's dead.'

Hang on a minute. I'd heard that before, early on in my investigations.

'How do you know she's dead?' I delved deeper.

'I've heard Mr Jones shot the cat because it had killed his birds. He keeps birds on his property, you see. He's buried it at a beauty spot.'

Mr Jones was the grumpy guy who lived nearby. The news struck through me like a lightning bolt. 'Do you know where Toots is buried?'

'All I know is that it's a local beauty spot. That's all I'm saying and I'm not giving you my proper name.'

'Can I give you a call if I can't find the grave?'

I managed to persuade Gonzo to give me his phone number, which was a breakthrough. Unbeknown to him this meant that, if I needed to, I could give his details to the police local intelligence officer. The LIO would be able to establish who Gonzo was and if his phone number was in the database. The informant had said Mr Jones had killed Toots, but that might have been a lie.

I didn't think it would come to that, though, because Gonzo seemed genuine. He said he was ringing because he wanted to put Sandi's mind at rest, which was a decent thing to do. Gonzo said he couldn't prove the allegation, but he was pretty certain. I was sure it was the truth. My police nose told me so. Gonzo had nothing to gain from telling me lies.

For ten minutes I anxiously contemplated how I was going to break the news to Sandi and her mum. Did I just tell them the horrifying cold facts, or should I soften it, saying it might have been a hoax call? It was bad enough passing on a 'deceased call', as the police refer to them, when it's a natural death or a road accident, but killed by someone with a shotgun? How would you word that? I decided honesty was the best policy. I took a deep breath and rang Sandi's mum.

'I've had a call, but it's not good news, I'm afraid.' I sensed her worry and anticipation of what was coming next. 'This isn't confirmed but we have received information that Toots may have been shot by someone living nearby and buried at a local beauty spot. If it is confirmed that Toots is buried there, we'll pass all the information to your local police, including the details of the alleged perpetrator.'

She paused for a few seconds, then quietly replied, 'I knew it. The shot.'

I was taken aback. 'What do you mean, "the shot"?'

'There was a shot the morning Toots went missing. I heard it, but I didn't think to tell you. I didn't think it was relevant. I thought it was just a gamekeeper going about their business.'

The pieces of the puzzle were falling into place.

'Oh, Tom, I didn't know, but I had my fears.' Her voice cracked.

Mrs Thom was very worried about how poor Sandi would react and assured me she would pick the right moment to tell her daughter. She asked what I was going to do and I told her I was going to call the boys in blue. I hoped my years in the force would add some gravitas. If Toots had been murdered, I was going to do everything in my power to see the culprit get a criminal record and ensure justice for Toots.

I rang the nearest police station to Edzell, in Brechin, and asked if they would interview Mr Jones. I went in strong. 'Hi there, my name is Tom Watkins. I run a team of missing-pet investigators. We have a case in Edzell you are probably not aware of . . .'

There was a long pause.

I carried on through the silence, explaining about Toots.

'I've heard about it,' the copper replied. He must have got wind of it from the press coverage.

'Well, I've had some information to suggest that a gentleman who lives nearby to Mrs Thom might have killed Toots with a shotgun and disposed of the body in revenge for Toots killing one of his birds,' I went on.

There was an even longer pause.

'Seriously?' came the reply.

'Yes, I'm very serious. After all, it is a criminal offence to shoot a cat. Would you be prepared to interview Mr Jones formally about the allegation?'

'We'll need a statement from the witness,' the gruff-sounding officer said.

The witness – Gonzo – wanted to remain anonymous. I told him that wouldn't be possible. The copper was reluctant but agreed to speak to Mr Jones anyway, which was a triumph.

It was a long shot, but I had all my hopes pinned on them finding something.

Sadly, the officer rang me back to say Mr Jones had denied all knowledge and there was no sign of fur or blood or shotgun pellets on his property. 'No evidence to go on, I'm afraid.' He sighed.

He was right. There were lots of suspicions and allegations regarding the shooting, but nothing concrete. Without evidence, we didn't have a case. They couldn't charge him.

I spent a day or two chatting to Sandi's mum, trying to locate where Toots's body might be. She drove to various locations, looking for evidence of a burial, but it was a needle in a haystack.

Sandi was devastated. She shut down after that. She posted a message on her blog, which triggered a massive response from well-wishers and was quickly picked up by all the national papers: 'She's gone now. I have to accept that but what I won't accept is that she died at the hands of a shooting. The police have confirmed it is illegal to shoot a cat. However, to enable them to make an arrest, we have to find wee Tooty's remains. All I want now is to find her, take her home and give her a dignified burial.'

My heart was heavy as I read those words in the *Sun*, sitting in my shed. Jenni sensed my sorrow and came in with a cuppa. She placed it on my Animal Search UK coaster. 'Are you okay, love?' she asked.

'Yeah, I did everything I could. It just wasn't a happy ending,' I said glumly.

I tried to look at things in a more positive light. At least we could all feel relieved there had been closure and that we knew Toots wasn't trapped, suffering somewhere. But unhappy endings didn't sit well with me. I'd become a pet detective to see joyful reunions between animals and their owners.

I started thinking of ways I could improve the effectiveness of the search team. What new gadgets could I buy to aid our searches? Good things come to those who work hard and never give up, I thought.

CHAPTER NINE
THE GOLDEN DOOR,
PART 1: CASPER THE CAT

Let me tell you about 'the Golden Door'. In pet-detective language it refers to the door that our missing pet is behind. It could be the first or last house in a street, but the belief that there is a golden door keeps you searching for it.

I was trying to explain my ethos to my latest recruit, Jacob, on the way to search in Redhill, Surrey, for a cat called Casper. Jacob was another friend I'd made at the petrol station. He was a cashier and we'd got chatting every time I'd stopped to fill up the search vehicle. The distinctive markings on my car were always a talking point between the two of us. One day I suggested he come on a search and find out at first hand what it was all about. I filled him in on the telephone conversation I'd had with Casper's owner the night before.

Adele had been in tears, as she'd explained how her long-haired Ragdoll cat hadn't been seen for several days. She'd likened him to a child, saying her baby was all she had in the world. She described how he would greet her at the door when she came home from work by nuzzling his nose into her legs. He liked to lick her hand when she bent down to stroke him. He would cuddle her when she was watching TV on the sofa at night. He was always around her feet, wanting to be stroked. Adele revealed she had made her own posters, which included a reward of four hundred pounds for his return, but had had no response whatsoever.

We'd had a quick chat about Casper's mannerisms. Adele had told me he was lazy and lethargic, a creature of habit that stayed in at night. She said the breed was fluffy, well known for being docile and for spending a lot of time sleeping.

I put my detective hat on.

Casper didn't sound like a cat that would have got lost roaming. He was more likely to have been locked into someone's shed or, being so cuddly, adopted by someone else. I couldn't be sure what had happened to our long-haired friend but it sounded fishy.

The drive to Redhill was a long one, so Jacob and I had to break it with a stop at a pub not too far from Adele's house. Over a glass of Diet Coke, I grabbed the chance to give him a bit of a pep talk to get him into search mode.

'As we approach the house in the search vehicle, we'll be noticed, so we have to be the ultimate professionals. We can't be seen laughing or joking, or doing anything that would make it seem that we're not focused on finding Casper,' I said sternly.

It was great that Jacob had volunteered to be an extra pair of hands on the case, but I couldn't let anything affect my growing reputation as the UK's leading, and only, pet detective.

'Understood.' Jacob nodded. He was keen to impress. He was bored at work and knew if he made a good impression on this search I might offer him a new career. Demand for searches was getting so high I was looking to recruit a team. I couldn't be everywhere in the country at the same time!

As we drove into Redhill I shared with Jacob my plan of action. Adele was out at work so, instead of dropping in on her first, we would drive around the area and get our bearings. As we wove our way around the residential streets in my Ford van – my third search vehicle – I noticed a high volume of 'Missing Casper' posters taped to lampposts throughout the neighbourhood. They had a black and white photo on them, with a handwritten description of him underneath. Adele had clearly put a lot of effort into raising awareness and I was surprised she hadn't had a response in the two weeks since Casper had disappeared. It made me think there was more to the story than met the eye.

First things first: we needed to swap the black and white posters for ours, which had a colour picture of Casper and an eye-catching banner reading 'Missing' across the top.

I noticed it was quite a well-to-do area. The houses were big and, more importantly, so were the gardens. I imagined there were a lot of sheds and suchlike hidden at the back. A lazy cat like Casper might well have gone for a nap in someone's shed and was now locked inside.

I couldn't say how, or why, but I had a hunch this was going to be a good search. And I needed a lift: the murder of Toots still left a bitter taste in my mouth.

Once we had swapped the posters, I parked the van outside Adele's house. It was May and the weather was sunny.

I let Jacob in on my theory. 'Ragdolls are appealing pets. They look pretty and they're docile. There is a high possibility that someone has taken in Casper. So, we need to fly the flag about why we're here. We need to talk to everyone we see, stop people in the street, keep moving the car around to grab people's attention. The name of the game is to make our presence known and for Casper to become such a hot property that if someone is holding him captive they'll be scared into releasing him.'

'Understood,' Jacob said eagerly. He was twenty-one, keen to learn.

We agreed that he would start door-to-door enquiries and I would go down to the local station and hand out leaflets to commuters getting off the trains.

Jacob and I were fully kitted up with our uniforms, and our pockets were bursting with our essential pet detective equipment. We had posters, walkie-talkies and two new additions to the equipment list: microchip scanners and torches. I handed Jacob the cat basket, then jumped back into the van.

I parked the pet-mobile opposite the station so no one would be in any doubt what I was there for. I managed to get permission from the railway staff to put some posters up inside the station, then began handing out leaflets to the many commuters. I'd been there for just ten minutes when my walkie-talkie burst into life.

'Tom, you receiving this? It's Jacob.'

That's quick, I thought. 'Go ahead, Jacob.'

'I've found him!' he shrilled.

What? Surely not! At this point I thought he was taking the mickey. 'Jacob, be serious, mate. Don't mess around, please,' I ticked him off.

'I'm serious, I've found him!'

He's knocked on the Golden Door already? Brilliant!

'Well, where are you?' I asked, as I ran back to the van.

Jacob was on Adele's street.

My heart was racing. How? Why? I was loaded with questions that needed answering. 'Stay there!' I ordered.

As I got into the van, Jacob asked if I could bring the collapsible ladder. It was a piece of equipment I always took with me on searches in case a pet was trapped out of reach. Casper must be stuck in a tree or on a roof, I concluded. 'Roger that, bringing ladder.'

As I started the engine my phone rang again. This time it was Zoë in the office. It was all happening at once! But I had to stay focused on the job at hand and ignored HQ for the time being. I used my satnav to navigate me to the first house on Adele's street, where Jacob had hold of Casper – or so I thought.

As soon as I'd parked, Jacob appeared through the wooden garden gate. 'He's on the flat roof in this garden.' He pointed behind him. He was grinning from ear to ear, delighted that he'd found the Golden Door.

Number ten Albion Road was a massive terraced house, and in the back was a shed with a very fluffy cat on it. Casper was strutting around on the roof, looking calm, collected and in perfect condition as he padded up and down with his tail and button nose held high – not a look you would expect from a cat who had been missing and trapped for two weeks.

I noticed that wire surrounded the shed roof. For the very purpose of keeping cats and squirrels off it. How on earth had he got up there? I wondered. Something didn't seem right about this set-up.

The lady who owned the property appeared from behind us. 'I just spotted him up there and thought I should tell this young man,' she said, referring to Jacob. She appeared a little flustered.

'How long has he been there?'

'I don't know. I've only just seen him,' she replied.

'Thank you for alerting us,' I said.

But I'd clocked the fact that one of Adele's Missing Casper posters with her phone number was still attached to the lamp-post right outside the woman's door.

Two questions were going through my mind. First: how could Casper have been stuck on her flat roof for two weeks and still look perfect? And second: why hadn't she come forward sooner?

I didn't show my suspicions to the woman: I wanted to see if she would trip herself up when retelling her story. Part of your training as a copper is to learn how to read non-verbal communication to work out when someone is lying. Whether you are interviewing someone in their home or at the station there are clear signals to look out for, such as a refusal to look you in the eye, looking down instead of at you, arms crossed instead of an open posture. All of those could mean they are telling a porky.

I watched this woman's body language like a hawk.

'How are you going to get him down?' she asked.

I looked up at Casper, who had now taken a front-row seat, staring down at the three of us. He licked his paw and ran it over his ear, giving himself a casual clean-up while we discussed our rescue strategy. He seemed as happy as Larry up there, having a bird's-eye view of the entertainment.

'We'll place the ladder against the shed, then reach over the wire and grab him,' I said, revealing our plan of action.

'I can't imagine how he got up there.' The woman shrugged.

Jacob held the bottom of the ladder to keep it steady, while I climbed up the side of the building.

'Here, kitty cat.' I beckoned Casper into my arms.

It was a slightly precarious position for me to be in: not only was I balancing on a stepladder I also had my cat allergy to contend with. But Casper needed my help, so what were a few sneezes and a watering eye between friends?

Casper stared right at me with his piercing blue eyes. He then rose to his feet, lifted his big white fluffy tail in the air and pranced to the other side of the roof.

It was an if-you-want-me-you're-going-to-have-to-come-and-get-me look. Not the attitude of a cat that had been stuck for two weeks and was desperately in need of rescuing.

Jacob sniggered as I clambered down the ladder and hoicked it over my shoulder to repeat the process from the other side. This time I was going to use bait. I rooted around in my pocket and pulled out a few loose biscuits, which I always have to hand on cat searches.

I placed them neatly by the edge of the roof and waited for Casper to be lured by the smell. He might have been a pedigree but he wasn't too posh to be tempted by the chicken and duck combo. As he drew closer, I got ready to pounce.

'Gotcha!' I gently scooped the ball of fluff into my arms.

AAAACHOOOOO!

I let out an almighty sneeze as I carried Casper to safety, placed him in the cat basket and shut the door.

Once he was in the cage, Casper became a bit more vocal. I tried to reassure him he would soon be reunited with his mum.

I turned to the home-owner, who was chewing her lower lip anxiously. She seemed rather upset for a woman who had only just noticed a cat on her roof. 'What's his name?' she asked.

'Casper. And he has an owner who misses him very much.'

'Bye, Casper,' she whispered, poking her fingers through the cage door. Casper gave them a sniff and a little lick goodbye.

The lady trailed behind us, as I carried Casper to the van. She then asked about the reward money.

It was yet another red flag. The reward had been offered on

Adele's poster, so she must have read it, which meant she must have known Casper was missing.

I was now convinced this woman would have had no intention of handing Casper over had Jacob not knocked on her door. And now she was trying to cash in.

I told her the reward was at the discretion of the owner, and we would be in touch once we had spoken with Adele. I took the woman's details and left it at that. At the end of the day I had no proof she had cat-napped Casper.

We were just jubilant to have found him, and in disbelief at how quickly we had managed it. It was the first door Jacob had knocked on. I couldn't wait to see Adele's face when we handed him back into her arms. Seeing pets reunited with their owners was what I lived for. But first I needed to attend to Casper's well-being. I gave him some water in a bowl and some more dried biscuits. He took a few sips but this time he turned up his little pink nose at the food.

'Have you lost your appetite, mate?'

Casper twitched his nose, swished his tail and miaowed.

I was conscious that he was in the back of the van on a hot summer's day, so I quickly turned on the ignition to get the air conditioning going. Then I pulled out my mobile and made a very important call.

Adele sounded nervous. People are always predisposed to expect the worst.

'We have a bit of news for you,' I said.

'What's that?'

'We've got him!'

'No way!' she squealed.

'Yep, I'm looking at him in the back of the van as we speak.'

I heard a load more squeals as Adele told everyone where she worked that we had found her boy.

'I'm at work. Would you be able to bring him to me here?'
She was breathless with happiness.

'No problem.'

Adele was a chiropractor and worked just outside town. As we parked opposite her surgery I had butterflies in my stomach. It was near impossible not to be affected by the emotions involved in my job. I was bursting with excitement to witness Adele's reaction when she saw Casper after their two-week separation. And, by the sound of it, Casper couldn't wait to see his mum. He was miaowing like crazy.

'Not long now, boy.' I tried to soothe him.

The receptionist gave us a warm smile as we walked in with the cat basket.

'Ssh.' I held my finger in front of my lips. I didn't want anyone to let on to Adele that we had arrived. Although Casper might have given the game away with his mews! We tiptoed through the hallway and knocked on Adele's door.

The small team of staff had now gathered with excitement and anticipation in the hallway behind us, desperate to see the moment their boss was reunited with her beloved Casper.

'Come in,' she trilled, probably thinking it was a client.

As the door opened, Adele's eyes lit up. 'Casper boy!' She lifted him out and cradled him in the crook of her arm, like a baby. 'I've missed you so much,' she said, closing her eyes and burying her face in his thick white fur. Casper nuzzled his head against her chin, corkscrewing his face into her and purring with delight.

I felt a knot in my stomach watching the emotional reunion. Mission accomplished.

Suddenly, Adele looked up at us and exclaimed, 'He smells of perfume!'

I couldn't take a sniff for fear of my allergy getting out of control, but I asked Jacob to do the honours.

'Yeah, he does,' Jacob confirmed. 'It might be Chanel but I can't say for certain,' he joked.

Adele asked the question I was thinking: 'Why does he smell of perfume?' Then: 'Where did you find him?'

'On a shed roof on your street,' I replied.

'On my street? I posted a leaflet through every single door. And all this time . . .'

'That's what we can't understand.'

'Do you think she had Casper in her house?' Adele drew her own conclusion.

I gave her my best interpretation of the situation. 'It could be a consideration because he wasn't very thirsty or hungry when we found him, which might imply he's been fed and watered elsewhere. He was content and calm, and there's no way she wouldn't have noticed him on the roof if he was stuck up there for two weeks. And then there's the question of how he got up there with the wire surrounding the surface.'

I shared with Adele my theory of why her beloved cat smelt of perfume. 'I think the woman had him in her house all along. She saw us turn up in our uniforms, panicked, and stuck him on the roof out the back.'

'Well, I'm not giving her any money for finding him!' Adele said.

I agreed, but I tried to ease things by pointing out that the woman had given Casper back. It would have been easy for her to keep him hidden upstairs until Jacob left.

There's no excuse for cat-napping, but to a point I was sympathetic: the woman had probably grown attached to Casper over the past two weeks while she'd had him in her home. For all we knew, she was lonely and Casper had brought her comfort at a time of despair. There was clearly something special about Casper that had everyone fussing over him so, something more than his cute fluffy exterior.

As Casper purred like a tractor, Adele asked if we would like to come back to hers for a cuppa before our long drive home to Hereford. We gratefully accepted.

On the way there, she suddenly pulled over and stopped at a cash point. Jacob asked me if I thought she'd had a change of heart about paying the woman who'd kept Casper. We were even more surprised when we arrived at her house and she handed us the four hundred pounds she'd offered as a reward.

'That's for finding my Casper boy!' She smiled, her eyes filled with tears of joy.

Of course, I refused the money. It was too generous a gesture, and we were only doing our job, which we were being paid for. But Adele insisted, thrusting the money back into my hands. I thanked her. I'd use my share of the money to buy new equipment to help reunite more owners like her with their missing pets.

You could tell Casper ruled the roost in Adele's house: there were long white cat hairs in all the most comfy spots, such as the sofa and the armchair. The tartan cat basket under the radiator in the lounge looked unused – Casper clearly preferred expensive furniture!

The Ragdoll followed closely behind his mum as she headed into the kitchen to make us a brew. He wound his body around her legs telling her he came first when it came to refreshments.

'Okay, Casper.' She filled a saucer with special milk for cats and Casper could hardly contain himself. His pink tongue was lapping it up before she'd even placed it on the floor.

As soon as he'd finished, and washed his whiskers, Casper padded past Jacob and me, making a beeline for the sofa, his head and tail aloft.

I could imagine Casper had more of a strut than the neighbourhood cats – he held his head that little bit higher.

'Sorry, did you say tea or coffee?' Adele giggled at her boy's princely behaviour.

A little later we stood up to leave. I asked Adele to stay in touch with updates and photos of Casper. Although the case was closed, it remained open in my heart.

We took off down the road. We kept our professional faces on for half a mile, then Jacob and I spontaneously broke into cheering, whooping and high-fiving. We were jubilant at having found Casper.

It was a three-hour drive back to Hereford and we were laughing the whole way home. I couldn't wait to share the good news with Jenni and Zoë.

Jacob was over the moon. He couldn't wait to do his next search. 'When am I going out again?'

I offered him a permanent job. After all, he'd found the Golden Door on his first knock.

CHAPTER TEN
THE GOLDEN DOOR,
PART 2: RUBENS THE REBEL

Blinking through the torrential rain pounding down on the pet-mobile, I was glad I'd ordered the waterproof Animal Search luminous jackets. The windscreen wipers were on their fastest setting but the road ahead was still a blur. They were far from ideal conditions to do a pet search, but that was part of the job – you didn't get to pick and choose the weather. When an animal was in need of my help, it was my job to get out there, come rain or shine. At least I had a coat: how must the pet be feeling trapped in the wet? Hypothermia was a serious consideration.

I didn't have many details about the search we were about to embark on, only that we were looking for a cat called Rubens and he had been missing for four days.

Rubens's owner was a doctor. He lived in Birmingham, which wasn't too far from Animal Search HQ. I'd find out more when I got there. But, first, I needed to pick up Olivia.

It had been five months since Jacob had found the Golden Door and things were going so well that I had acquired another team member. Unlike my other recruits, Olivia was a former client. She ran a small animal rescue centre and had originally come to me for advice about how to find a cat that had gone missing after she had rehomed it. My tips on where and how to look had proved fruitful and she had found the missing cat. We'd talked on the phone several times so when Olivia asked me for a job I didn't hesitate. She was a pet person through and through, the perfect sort of personality to complement the team. She would work on an ad hoc basis and would be more than happy to cover Birmingham and the surrounding areas.

Unlike with my other trainee pet detectives, I hadn't met Olivia but had liked her calm and confident telephone manner. Also, she'd followed my advice to help find the cat, proving she could listen to instructions and be directed. More importantly, it showed she had faith in me.

I was picking Olivia up in Stourbridge, and I must admit to a prickle of nerves as I parked outside the address she had given me. What would she look like? Would I be able to spot her? I didn't need to worry: she'd seen me coming in the pet-mobile well before I saw her.

Waving to me as she walked down the street, she was in her fifties, beaming as she approached, and wearing practical clothing for the weather conditions, which showed me she had common sense.

'Hello, I'm Tom.' We shook hands. 'Get in – it's raining cats and dogs.' I opened the passenger door for her.

Once we were safely ensconced inside the pet-mobile, listening to the rain fire down at us like gun pellets, we had a proper introduction.

'I'm so looking forward to the search,' she said, combing the wet clumps of hair from her face with her fingers.

'Well, that's good news, considering we've got a storm to contend with.' But, putting aside the weather conditions, I agreed with her – principally because I would be searching an area I knew well. Knowing your terrain can massively increase the chances of a successful search.

As we drove out of Stourbridge, I filled Olivia in with the limited information I had. Being a pet detective wasn't all about finding missing animals. Sometimes I had to do a bit of digging to extract information from the owners.

Ben, the owner, was rushed for time when we had first chatted on the phone, but he said Rubens had gone missing four days ago. He was a three-year-old ginger tom that liked to roam, a bit of a bruiser who was always spoiling for a fight. He had a distinctive scar on his right ear from when he had got into a particularly brutal fight with a neighbour's moggie. Ben was a doctor so he hadn't had much time to look for Rubens but had printed leaflets and posted them through letterboxes in the surrounding area.

He would be at work at the hospital by the time we arrived so, as with Adele, we had to start without meeting him. I didn't have much to go on, although I'd made two comments in the margin of my notepad. First, Rubens wasn't a shy, retiring cat so he might have roamed far from home. Second, he might have been injured in a fight.

Thankfully, the rain had eased off as we turned into the quiet residential street in Solihull. The houses were massive and quite a few had electric gates. I wondered if that would be a problem with our door-to-door enquiries – a lot of the houses had intercom systems. I'd find a way.

'See these big gardens,' I said to Olivia. 'They're a cat's

playground! They're full of birds and other interesting things that could have lured Rubens away from home.' I also observed the many trees that lined the posh street. It meant we had to search both high and low, as the cat might have got stuck up one.

It was time to teach Olivia the dos and don'ts of door-to-door enquiries. I emphasized how important it was to cut to the chase when you were standing on someone's doorstep. 'If I begin, "Good morning, I'm Tom from Animal Search UK", the door will have been shut in my face before I've got the words out because they thought I was selling something. A better approach is, "Good morning, I'm looking for a missing cat, here's a leaflet," and thrust it in their direction.'

Olivia was taking notes. She was eager to learn and I could tell she was a sharp cookie.

'Ask, "Have you seen or heard anything about Rubens?" Now they're engaged with you. You can prompt them by asking questions like "Have you heard any cats fighting?" "Have you heard about any road accidents?" Remind them there's a free phone number. Emphasize they can ring anonymously, twenty-four hours a day, seven days a week.'

I briefed her on the WH questions: What? Where? Who? Why? When? How?

'Pause to allow for a response. Who told you? Where were you? It always amazes me how talkative the public are when they know what you're doing.'

It was just getting your foot in the door that was the tricky part but once you had their attention, people couldn't be more helpful. After all, we're a nation of animal lovers. I'd been more warmly received as a pet detective than I ever had as a copper!

'It's not rocket science. As long as you have a good head on your shoulders, you can do it,' I encouraged Olivia. I told her not to worry: I'd do the first door with her to show her what to say.

'Ready?'

'Ready as I'll ever be!' Olivia took a deep breath.

Even though it had stopped raining, I recommended Olivia wore one of my high visibility waterproof jackets over the orange fleece I had lent her, just to be sure. I was always looking to improve our kit. I now had waterproof trousers too for days like today. I'd also upgraded the torches. They'd cost forty pounds each but they had powerful LED lights and didn't break if you dropped them. They were as good as army-issue ones – fit for my army of trainee pet detectives!

We started our search for Rubens with Ben's next-door neighbour. The house had a white door with a shiny gold knocker. There was also a bell. I'd always been intrigued to know why people had both. I pressed the button and folded my hands behind my back as I waited for a response.

I heard a dog yapping and the shuffle of slippers across wood. The presence of a dog meant it was unlikely that Rubens had entered this neighbour's garden but the owner might know something we didn't.

Slowly, the door opened and an old lady poked her head out. 'I'm not interested in buying anything. Get back, Jasper,' she hissed, tugging at the Corgi's collar.

'Good morning. I'm not selling anything, I'm looking for a missing cat.' I kicked off the proceedings. Olivia was a few feet behind me, listening intently to how I went about my job.

'Just a moment,' the old lady said, shutting the door briefly as she unhooked the safety chain.

As soon as she realized I wasn't dangerous, or selling anything, we couldn't get her to stop nattering. She told me what a delightful cat Rubens was and how he was much bigger than the other moggies on the street. Apparently he made a habit of sitting on the wall and taunting her poor dog. 'It drives Jasper wild. He won't stop barking!'

I was building up a profile of our missing cat. He was confident, mischievous and fearless. I thanked her for her time and asked her to call us if she did hear or see anything.

'Now it's your turn,' I said to Olivia, as we left the old lady's drive.

I'd thrown her in at the deep end, but I knew she'd swim. It was the best way to learn. I crossed the road to make a start on putting up posters, but I kept one ear open for Olivia to make sure she was okay.

My years as a copper had tuned my ears to certain words. But instead of 'urgent assistance', I was listening now for 'injured', 'lost', 'stolen' and 'trapped'. I was hoping none of the above would be used in the case of our missing ginger cat.

As I clipped another picture of Rubens to a fence I realized my idea of hole punching the laminated posters to allow for the cable ties to be threaded through wasn't working. The lamination protected the paper from bad weather, but the holes created a tiny gap for water to seep through. After enough rainfall, the posters looked damp, shrivelled and blurred from where the ink had run. It was back to the drawing board with them, although I'd have to shelve my ideas for now. We had a ginger tom cat to find.

'Any luck?' I asked Olivia.

'Not yet!' she replied. I admired her optimism.

Being positive about finding our missing pet, and about life in general, was half the battle won. And she was going to need it. The sky exploded with an enormous thunderclap. This will test her resilience, I thought.

First it started spitting, and then the heavens opened. At least we had our waterproofs, or we would have been soaked to the bone. I half expected Olivia to run back to the car for cover but she kept going. She was a real trouper.

We must have looked a right old sight when we rang the doorbells, drenched and bedraggled. One lady took pity on me and offered me a cuppa.

'Thank you, but I'm afraid I've got to get on with finding Rubens,' I said.

We had a mission to complete and there was no time for chit-chat unless it was going to shed some light on the case. I couldn't afford to waste a second.

We must have knocked on 130 doors in the pouring rain. A bunch of those residents were out at work, which meant we'd have to try again later that day. Quite a few people we chatted to had seen Rubens but not for a week or so. He was clearly a cat that got about, just not recently. I was starting to fear he might have been knocked down by a car.

My phone was ringing in my pocket. I hoped it would be a tip-off.

It wasn't: Dr Ben was checking up on our progress. 'Any news?' he asked anxiously. He sounded much more stressed than he had the night before. I could hear monitors bleeping in the background and presumed he was on a hospital ward.

I told him we hadn't had any joy so far, although quite a few of the neighbours had seen Rubens, if not for several days.

'My wife's beside herself with worry.'

'Tell her I'll try to get to the bottom of it,' I promised.

You never know which house will have the Golden Door: that's why you have to keep going.

Ben said he was finishing his shift around four o'clock and would be able to help us after that. I was looking forward to putting a name to a face and, hopefully, being able to relieve some of his anxiety. Also I'd be able to interview him properly, which might lead us to new clues.

Olivia was soaking, her hair glued to her face. The last thing I wanted was for her to catch hypothermia. 'I think we should retreat to the search vehicle,' I told her.

But Olivia was having none of it. 'I've got five more houses to do,' she said, striding up the next person's drive.

My admiration for her was growing by the second. She would have made a good copper, I thought.

Olivia was on one side of the road and I was about to knock on a door at the other side – we were now a few streets away from Rubens's home. I dabbed the water from my face with a hand-kerchief. The door was painted racing green and the letterbox bore the words 'No junk mail'. The car in the driveway was an expensive Mercedes convertible. There were several cacti on the living-room windowsill. I saw the upstairs curtain move before I pressed the doorbell. Whoever lived in this house knew I was there.

Thirty seconds had passed and still no response. I rang the bell again.

It wasn't uncommon for people not to answer the door, but I was wet, cold, and determined not to miss a potential clue.

Finally, I heard footsteps and the sound of a key turning in a lock.

'Yes?' The man was in his late forties, balding, and wore a smart blazer and shirt over denim jeans. He held the door ajar, blocking the entrance with his body. I was getting a bad vibe from him. I told him I was looking for a missing cat and when

I asked if he knew anything he dropped his eyes to the floor. 'I haven't seen anything, I'm afraid.' He then hurried me off the step and started closing the door.

I couldn't put my foot in the way, so I had to ask him a question to keep him talking, and quickly. My eyes fell on a toy mouse underneath the radiator in his hallway. A cat toy, no less. 'Do you have any pets yourself?'

The man nervously shifted from one foot to the other. Clearly, he was agitated. 'No,' he replied curtly.

Well, that was a lie because I'd seen evidence of animal life.

'Now, if you don't mind, I have something I need to get back to.' With that, he shut the door in my face.

I was left with a gnawing sensation in my stomach. Why had he said he didn't have a pet when the evidence indicated he almost certainly did? What was he hiding? Could it be Rubens?

I needed to chat to Olivia.

My trainee pet detective was still going strong on the other side of the road. 'I'll just do these last three houses and then we'll call it a day,' she said, battling through to the end. They were the last few on the street and Olivia didn't want to take a break until she had checked them.

Meanwhile, my mind was churning with questions about the man I'd just spoken to. He was lying about something, but I couldn't be sure what game he was playing. At times like these I wished I had a search warrant!

I retreated to the pet-mobile to call HQ and updated Zoë on our progress. She was managing the hotline from the shed. I also wanted to check if Ben was home yet. Five hours had elapsed since we had started the hunt for Rubens.

I was walking back, adjusting a few posters and cable ties on the way, when I heard a cry from Olivia. In her desperation she had forgotten the walkie-talkie protocol.

'Tom! Hurry!' she yelled down the street. 'I've got something!'

I turned on my heels and saw Olivia standing on the porch of the very last house in the road.

'What is it?' I shouted, breaking into a run.

When I got there, huffing and puffing, Olivia put her finger in front of her mouth and said, 'Sssh. If you're very quiet, you'll hear something.'

We pinned our ears to the door.

Nothing.

I prised open the letterbox and we listened again, quietly and intently.

Sure enough, we could hear a cat crying.

And, what was more, he sounded distressed.

I was certain it was Rubens. Happy cats don't miaow like that, I thought. It sounded frantic. 'He needs urgent assistance,' I said.

We looked around us, searching for a way either to get the cat out of the property or for us to get in. Of course it was illegal to break in, so we needed to find a key.

'I'll knock on the neighbour's door again and see if they have a spare.' I jumped over the miniature hedgerow that separated the adjoining properties. Adrenalin was surging through my veins. I was feeling a combination of excitement that we might have found our cat and worry that he might be injured or dehydrated. Rubens had been missing for four days, which was a long while to go without water.

I hoped someone was in. There was no car in the driveway. As I approached the front door, I saw a picture of the missing Rubens in the living-room window. How ironic, I thought. These people must be friends of Ben. I lifted the brass door handle and knocked three times. I stood back and waited, anxiously.

A few seconds passed. Still nothing.

'Can you see him?' I shouted to Olivia, across the little hedge.

'No, just hear him!'

My anxiety crept into my throat. Some part of me wished I could just break down the door and rescue the cat there and then. But I had to follow protocol.

I lifted the door knocker again and rapped loudly.

I breathed a sigh of relief as I heard a woman shout, 'Just a minute!'

The door swung open and she was standing in front of me in Lycra leggings and a hoodie. Her hair was tied back in a tight ponytail. I wondered if she'd been doing one of those home workout videos.

I apologized for disturbing her but said we had an urgent situation on our hands. I explained what we had heard and how the miaows seemed to be coming from a cat in distress. 'Do your neighbours have a cat?' I ruled out the obvious first.

'No, it's a young couple who don't have any pets.' The young lady shook her head.

I was now surer than ever that the cat trapped in that house was Rubens.

'They're away in Tenerife at the moment.'

No wonder they hadn't responded to the cat's cry for help.

I explained what we had heard and asked the neighbour if she had a spare key to the property. Thankfully, she had and ran quickly to fetch it.

Cats can bolt when they're frightened, so the three of us got ready to stop him fleeing. Olivia crouched behind us like a rugby player in a scrum.

As I slowly turned the key in the lock, we still didn't know if the cat was Rubens. 'We're going in,' I announced. I opened the door quietly and steadily.

And there, lo and behold, behind the door was a startled bright ginger cat.

'We've got him!' I exclaimed. Although that wasn't technically true, as we still had to catch him and I had a feeling that wouldn't be a piece of cake: he was dancing skittishly across the floor and swishing his cream-tipped tail from left to right.

There was a flash of pink as poor Rubens started miaowing like crazy. He was frightened, disoriented and stressed. I noticed there wasn't a cat flap and wondered how he had got in. Maybe he'd clambered through an open window upstairs. He'd probably become disoriented by his new surroundings and couldn't work out how to return through the window. He must have been beside himself, frantically looking for an escape route.

'It's okay, boy,' I said, crouching down to his level.

But Rubens was having none of it. One judgemental look in my direction and he scurried down the hallway, his claws tip-tapping on the wooden floorboards, and underneath the table in the kitchen. His fur was on end. His pointy triangular ears were twitching. A hiss erupted from his mouth.

'The poor thing is terrified,' Olivia said.

Rubens's eyes were darting from left to right. His mottled ginger tail was swishing wildly.

I signalled to Olivia to deposit the cat basket to the right of me.

Rubens wasn't docile like Casper: we weren't going to be able to lure him to us with cat biscuits. There was a blue towel folded over the radiator in the kitchen. I pulled it off and opened it up like a parachute. It was hardly high tech, but I'd heard throwing a towel over a frightened animal can be very effective as it plunges them into darkness, enabling you to catch them without being scratched or bitten. This was all in theory, mind. I was about to find out whether it worked or not.

I got down on all fours and started to crawl under the table towards the hissing Rubens with the towel in one hand. Rubens was baring his teeth, his ears flattened. I knew he didn't mean to be aggressive: he was just acting like any cornered animal would.

I shuffled forward.

Rubens edged back. But there was nowhere for him to go except the wall. I had him trapped.

'Be careful!' the neighbour whispered.

'I'm going to do this on the count of three,' I told my audience. 'One . . .'

Rubens unsheathed his claws and swiped the air with his paw. 'Two . . .'

He lowered himself, ready to pounce.

If I'd waited for three, he'd have had my face, so I threw the towel and dived for it. 'Gotcha!'

He was wriggling around in my arms, like a worm on a hook, but I managed to keep hold. I pulled him into my chest and held him as tightly as if my life depended on it.

'Well done!' Olivia and the lady in Lycra cheered.

I carefully placed Rubens in the cat basket and retracted my hands quickly so he didn't get a chance to lash out.

Rubens shook off the towel and reappeared, a little dishevelled but safe.

Just before we left I made a point of asking the neighbour if she would let the home-owners know we had used their spare key to retrieve Rubens. It was the responsible action to take.

We carried Rubens in his protective basket through the rainstorm to his owner's house a few streets away. He miaowed the whole way there, but I kept chatting to him, telling him he'd be home soon. Growing up with Maggie had taught me how reassuring animals find it when you chat to them. Just because they can't have a conversation with you doesn't mean they're not listening. They pick up on your tone, and if you sound happy, it will help to calm and reassure them.

Needless to say, when we arrived at his home, Rubens was dry and we were very wet! Luckily, Ben was there by the time we showed up. 'Hello, Rubens!' he exclaimed, as he opened the door. 'You've had us all very worried!'

Rubens quietened when he heard his owner's voice.

'Come in, come in.' Ben welcomed us into the warmth. I carried Rubens into a very tidy living room and placed the basket on the floor.

It always amazes me how people manage not only to keep their houses spotless but also their cream and white furniture, especially with an adventurous, lively cat like Rubens bounding around the place. I spotted a wedding photo on the mantelpiece.

Ben noticed where I was looking and reiterated how heartbroken his wife had been about Rubens's disappearance and how delighted she would be when she got home from work later. 'I'm going to keep it a surprise,' he said cheerfully.

I let Ben have the honour of opening the basket and welcoming his friend home. Olivia and I stood back to give the ginger tom some space to breathe. Rubens stuck his nose out of the basket and lifted it into the air. He twitched it a few times as he took in the familiar scents. He then let out a little sneeze.

'That's you he's smelling!' Olivia teased me.

'Thanks, Olivia!'

Before we had time to blink he scampered across the room, clawed his way up the back of the couch and came to rest on its arm. He raised a paw, gave it a lick and cleaned his whiskers. By the look of things he ruled the house as well as the neighbourhood.

He seemed happy and content now that he was home. He

kept one eye on me and Olivia, though, from the safety of the couch.

Ben said he couldn't thank us enough for our diligence. He then uttered my favourite words: 'Would you like a cup of tea?'

'Don't mind if I do, mate!'

As we sat at the kitchen table, our cold hands nursing the mugs, there were a few things I needed to clear up. The pet detective in me couldn't rest without knowing *how* Rubens had come to be trapped inside a house a few streets away. Ben hadn't thought to mention that Rubens had a habit of running through people's front doors when they were unloading the shopping from the boot of their car. 'I never thought he'd get stuck inside somewhere!' He shook his head in disbelief.

Maybe the home-owners had been loading their boot with suitcases for their holiday and Rubens had crept past them. It seemed likely to me.

It was another case solved and I felt just as content as Rubens looked while I packed up the pet-mobile, ready for our journey home.

We said our goodbyes to the ginger tom and Ben, then hit the road.

'Job well done!' I praised Olivia for her fighting spirit. She had found the Golden Door on the last knock of the day. We were really lucky that she had insisted on doing the last three houses or we might not have discovered Rubens until it was too late. The rain hadn't put her off and she said she'd be keen to do another search soon. She also hinted at knowing someone who would make a very good trainee pet detective. She would let me know more once she'd had a word in their ear.

I could tell my pet detective agency was on the cusp of blossoming into a real force. It was like being back in the police when I had a dedicated team around me, passionate about doing good and pushing each other onwards even in the pouring rain.

But thoughts of taking over the world had to wait. It had been a physically demanding day and I was looking forward to Jenni's cooking and the warmth of home when I got back.

CHAPTER ELEVEN
THE DEGU

Word had got around the neighbourhood that I was a pet detective. But some people confused my job of finding missing animals with offering sanctuary to animals. I had an unexpected visitor on my doorstep in spring 2010. Animal Search UK's address was on the website. It was a lady holding something small and furry in her palm.

'Do you deal with lost and found pets?' she asked.

Before I had a chance to answer, she opened her hand to reveal a little hamster-like creature. It immediately sat up in her palm, twitching its ears and nose.

'What is it?' I exclaimed.

'I don't know. We found it in our garden,' she replied. 'I think it's a girl,' she added.

The animal swivelled round and the woman snatched it back into her chest protectively. 'I have a cat, so I couldn't just leave her there. She would have been eaten. Can you help me find the owner?' she pleaded.

'Umm . . . er . . .' I hesitated.

Before I could reply, Polly, my daughter, had poked her head out of the door to see what was going on. 'What's that, Daddy?' she asked.

'Well, we don't know, sweetheart.'

The woman unveiled the little creature again and Polly fell in love. 'Can we keep it?' she asked.

It was now two against one. How could I say no? Plus, I couldn't bear the thought of the helpless animal being eaten by a cat. I agreed to take it off the lady's hands and do some publicity in the Kingsacre area of Hereford where it had been found to try to locate the owner. First, though, I needed to find our new friend a temporary home. I told Polly to fetch one of the cat baskets and bring it into the shed. Together we laid some scrunched-up newspaper inside it, then filled a saucer with water and gently placed the animal on its bedding. She stood up on her back legs and blinked at us a few times.

'Do you think she's hungry, Daddy?' Polly, who was now eight, asked. An animal-lover, she took after her mum and dad.

I told her to follow me: we'd see what we could find in the kitchen. I rummaged through the cupboards to see if Jenni had kept the packet of mixed nuts we had been given as a present at Christmas.

Our search had attracted Jenni's attention and she came through from the lounge with Sam in tow. I wasn't sure how I was going to break the news to her that we had acquired a pet. Luckily, Polly was there to do it for me. 'Mummy, Mummy, we have a mouse!'

Jenni looked at me despairingly. Sighed and shook her head.

'It's just until we can find her owner,' I argued.

Jenni, Sam and Polly followed me back into the shed to see how our new house guest was getting on.

We all peered into the cage. The poor thing must have got a fright with four pairs of eyes looking at her. She scurried to the back, where she had already started making a nest by shredding the newspaper. We could still see the tips of her ears and tail as Polly and Sam threaded the hazelnuts through the grille in the door.

We waited patiently to see if she would check out what was on the menu.

Slowly but surely, the little animal crept out from her paper mound. She looked up at us as if to ask, 'Is this kosher?' then scurried towards the nuts and swiped one with a claw, popped it into her mouth and scurried back into her den.

Even Jenni was won over by her cuteness.

'What shall we call her?' Polly and Sam asked.

I wouldn't normally like to name an animal, knowing I might have to return it, but on this occasion I couldn't see it would hurt. 'Let's call her Lucky because she was lucky someone found her,' I suggested.

So Lucky began to make herself at home in the cage in the office while I printed off some posters to put up around the area where she was discovered. I also did some investigating to find out what she was. I tapped her features into Google and it came back with 'Degu'.

For those of you out there who don't know what a degu is, it's a very cute brown animal that looks like a cross between a mouse and a hamster. Degus originate in Chile and lots of people keep them as pets. Unlike mice and hamsters, they are not nocturnal.

'Please, Daddy, can we keep her?' Polly begged again.

It was hard saying no to my daughter, but I had a job to do. There might have been an owner out there who was worried sick about their missing degu. It might have belonged to a child who accidentally let it go in their garden. So I proceeded to put an advert in the local newspaper for a missing degu. This was a first. Sadly, nobody came forward.

Polly had grown attached to Lucky. She cleaned out her cage, fed and watered her. Every day without fail she would come home from school and run straight to the shed to check on her friend. Lucky liked to sit in the palm of her hand and Polly would stroke her for ages, until she wriggled, wanting to be put down.

'Daddy, please can we keep her now? I love her so much. She's my best friend,' Polly asked again.

I looked at Jenni and she gave me one of the smiles and eye-rolls that said, 'Okay, I'll go along with it.' At the end of the day Lucky would be living in Animal Search HQ rather than the living room.

'Yes, you can keep her,' I said. Lucky would be the Animal Search lucky mascot!

Polly rushed up to me and gave me a massive bear hug around my waist.

One thing was troubling me about Lucky, though. 'Shall we get her a friend? She looks lonely.'

Jenni threw her arms into the air and left the room.

'Yes, Dad, let's get another one now!'

So we hopped into the pet-mobile, headed down to the pet shop and asked if they sold degus.

They did, which was brilliant news, although I was quite specific that it had to be a girl. I didn't want to end up with a family of degus in our shed.

Polly picked out her favourite and I turned to the sales

assistant. 'Can you just confirm it's a girl?' I needed to be sure. When the matter was settled we browsed the area that sold cages and bought a nice spacious one that would fit into the shed, and some toys for the girls to play with.

Sam wanted to be the one to name our new degu and he called her Dusty.

Lucky and Dusty weren't the only new additions to the Animal Search team. I had also acquired two new search staff, Liam and Lucas. Both were retired businessmen and entrepreneurs, who had a natural sense of leadership. Liam had come highly recommended by Olivia. Liam and Olivia had been the best of friends for years and Liam had recently been helping Olivia to rehabilitate and rehome some of the rescued cats in her care.

I warmed to Liam immediately. He was a shortish fellow, in his mid-fifties with a big friendly grin. He was ex-forces and had built a company from scratch at his kitchen table, a multi-million-pound one! But, most importantly, he was a pet-lover, in particular dogs. Liam had two German Shepherds called Lady and Freddie.

Lucas had come via the second advert I'd posted at the local job centre. He was a little older than Liam, in his early sixties. He had set up a company that repaired screens for aviation control rooms. So he, too, had been a leader and had come from quite a disciplined background, which was just what I was after. He also reminded me of my dad: not only did they share a birthday, they had a similar personable and professional manner.

Lucas was a family man: he lived with his wife in Hereford and they had a son who was a pilot. But what really drew me to him was that he was a real pet person. Like Zoë, he had his own zoo in his back garden. He had two cats, pigs, chickens, geese and a cockerel. He was a nice chap, clearly clever and competent too, so I didn't hesitate to take him on. He looked like Father Christmas, with his white beard and his smiley face.

Like Olivia, Lucas and Liam would both work for ASUK on an ad hoc basis, whenever I needed extra boots on the ground for a search. At the rate things were going, they'd be looking at a call-out once a week. I was still working for the Highways, and it was becoming trickier to manage my time.

The business was booming, and so were things inside the degu cage, as I discovered, to my surprise, one morning. I unlocked the shed door at the crack of dawn, as usual, and was confronted with an unusual rustling and squeaking.

Lucky and Dusty don't normally make that much noise, I thought, approaching the cage. I peered inside to find seven baby degus squirming in their nest. Dusty wasn't a girl after all! They were still pink and hairless and piled up on each other to keep warm. Mum and Dad were keeping a watchful eye over them, nervously running around, squeaking.

What are we going to do with these little fellas?

Initially I decided I'd have to put an advert in the newspaper, then had second thoughts. I didn't want the baby degus to go to homes where they might live in small cages. The thought of them being cooped up like those dogs in the police kennels nearly brought me to tears. We would look after them and I would build them a bigger cage.

I headed back inside the house to break the news to Jenni.

'*What?*' she exclaimed, her hands on her hips.

I fought my case.

Jenni was endlessly patient with and tolerant of my whims. Being a massive animal-lover herself, she could see where I was coming from. As soon as I got her all-clear, I broke the news to the kids. I knew what their faces would be like even before I told them. Sam, who was now four, and Polly pushed past me as they rushed into the shed to see the baby degus.

Sam squealed with excitement and Polly's heart melted.

'Dad, what shall we name them?' Polly asked.

That was a job for Polly and Sam to enjoy.

My job was to find the degus a bigger cage. And I wondered if the shed was really the right home for them – I wouldn't be able to hear myself think with them scampering around. I decided to build a massive enclosure for them in the garden.

It would be like the office-building project, just for degus. No expense would be spared. Several days later and several hundred pounds worse off, the cage, with a run, spread across half of the garden. Polly and Sam helped me construct an assault course for the degus to keep them entertained. It was fully fitted with rocks, stones, grass, tubes to run through, and puddles to wash and play in. It took a weekend to put together, but I felt proud when I stood back to view my handiwork.

'Well done, love.' Jenni came up behind me, wrapped her arms around my waist and gave me a squeeze.

The kids loved their new playmates, and once we had deciphered which sex they were Polly gave them each a name: Skittles, Cocoa, Tigger, Tank, Sparky, Pepper and Dolly.

I was strict about keeping the girls and the boys apart now. 'Play time' in the run was separated into morning shifts for the girls and afternoons for the boys. It worked nicely for a while. But all my efforts to keep them apart went to pieces when we asked Jenni's brother Harry to look after them one weekend while I took the family camping.

I was pulling the tent pegs out, Jenni was gathering the pots and the pans from around the fireplace, and the kids were playing nearby when my phone sprang to life. I thought it would be someone calling the hotline, as I had my mobile on divert from the shed.

But, no, it was Harry with some troubling news.

'Don't tell Polly . . .' he started. My heart skipped a beat. '. . . but all the degus have escaped.'

For a moment I was lost for words. And then I quickly found some. 'What do you mean they've escaped?' I hissed, walking into the woods and away from prying ears.

'I don't know. I went to feed them and they had all run out.'

He meant that he had left the cage door open when he had last fed them. Fortunately I had moved them into the office for the weekend, so they would be warm and dry. But now nine degus were running around Headquarters.

'I can see one! He's hiding under the cupboard!' Harry exclaimed.

Hell! I thought. I'm going to have to round up these furry creatures without Polly getting wind of what's going on.

I beckoned Jenni to where I was, out of earshot. Her eyes almost popped out when I told her the news. 'What are we going to do?' she gasped.

Ninety per cent of me was worried for their safety and Polly's emotional state if even one had gone missing. The other ten per cent was concerned about the wires and equipment in HQ. The last thing I needed was a degu gnawing its way through my state-of-the-art machinery.

I looked over at the kids playing and hatched a plan. 'How about we drop Polly off at her friend Katie's house on the way home, then try to round them up?'

'Sounds like a plan.' Jenni nodded.

Polly was none the wiser when we stopped off at Katie's. She thought she was having the best weekend away ever – camping followed by fun with her friend! Jenni agreed she would keep Sam entertained while I executed Operation Degu Hunt.

Harry was still there when we arrived, full of excuses. He had a bit of a smirk on his face as he told me they were hiding all over the office.

'Thanks for your help,' I said sarcastically, patting his shoulder.

I was terrified to open the office door for fear of the destruction I might find. I slowly turned the handle and gingerly pushed it ajar so as not to let out any escapees.

Harry was close on my heels.

'Quick!' I whispered. In we went and I shut the door behind us.

I was now about to unleash my detective skills on finding degus!

I told Harry to be deathly quiet and we both stood there for a moment. We couldn't see any degus, but it wasn't long before I heard a rustling noise from behind the wastepaper bin.

I felt slightly ridiculous as I got down on all fours and edged my way forwards.

'I can see him!' I whispered to Harry. The degu was sitting on his hind legs, his nose and ears twitching furiously.

'Well, get him!'

'I'm trying, mate!' I retorted.

It was like catching Rubens under the kitchen table all over again, but this animal was smaller, quicker, and possibly had a nastier bite. I didn't want to find out.

I counted myself down.

Three, two, one. I leaped forward, cupping my hands around the little scallywag. I scooped his tiny body into my hands. He was wriggling like crazy and I could feel his claws burrowing into my skin. I placed him in the cage and shut the door. He blinked at me twice, then scurried off to hide behind his food bowl.

'One down, eight to go! This isn't so hard!'

I'd spoken too soon. We spent the next two hours on our hands and knees trying to catch them. They were hiding in the cupboards, under the cupboards, behind the tumble-drier I had in the office to dry the uniforms. One degu had gnawed his way into a cardboard box where I kept all the new batteries for the torches. It was a nightmare. And they weren't half quick on their feet. Every time you thought you had one, he skittered in the other direction. Harry and I nearly knocked heads under the desk trying to grab one.

Incredibly we found every single degu – which was just as well, for Polly's sake. She was none the wiser when she came home from her friend's house and rushed in to see the degus. There they all were, playing and squeaking away as if nothing had happened.

Meanwhile, I had sore knees from shuffling on the floor for hours. But I didn't give the game away.

'They've missed me!' Polly said, as she pulled Dusty from the cage to give him a stroke.

'Yes, they have. Uncle Harry said they've been as good as gold.'

What's a little white lie if it brings a smile to your daughter's face?

Thanks to my job, I had witnessed at first hand how devastating it can be to lose your pet and the degus' disappearance had given me even greater empathy with the heartbreak the pet-owners I help must experience.

CHAPTER TWELVE
MYSTIC MOG

I've always gone about my work strictly by the book, so when a pet-owner asked if *I* would work with a psychic to help her find her missing moggie, I was a bit lost for words.

Is she having a laugh? was my initial thought. But I quickly realized that Sally was deadly serious. Her precious Ollie had been missing for seven months and she wanted me to give mystic Sarita Gupta in Bangalore a call.

By this point we were a couple of days into the search and Sally was willing to go to any length to find her precious Ollie. I knew he meant the world to her from the moment she called the Animal Search hotline in May 2010. Sally was fighting back the tears as she recounted her last half-year of hell.

Ollie, a white-faced tabby, had gone missing on Saturday, 24 October 2009, and Sally had been looking for him ever since. She said she had put posters up, handed out leaflets and knocked on doors, but with no joy. She hadn't been able to sleep peacefully at night, not knowing what had happened to him. 'It's the not knowing that's the worst.' She choked up.

I lent her a sympathetic ear and tried to calm her. Being a pet detective also demanded counselling skills: a lot of the owners I was speaking to were emotional and needed to unload.

From asking a few more questions I established that Sally, who worked as a nurse, lived alone in a farmhouse in a rather remote location, in the rural Lincolnshire village of Boothby Graffoe. She was very lonely without Ollie at her side.

Even though there weren't many houses to knock on in the area near to where she lived, Sally was still keen for a search team to come out. She was convinced there was more to Ollie's mysterious disappearance than her cat having wandered off. She thought a passing motorist who had thought mistakenly that the tabby was lost might have picked him up. Or he could have been run over on the busy road outside her house. Another possibility was that he had become lost crossing the fields near her home and, disoriented, had relocated, settling down some-where else.

All of these theories were feasible.

I told her I was there to help and would dispatch a search team first thing in the morning.

'I don't mind what it costs,' Sally told me. 'The money isn't as important as getting him back. He's never been away for more than a couple of hours at a time but there's been no sign of him since the day he disappeared. I wish I'd seen your website sooner.' She sniffled. She'd only just discovered my pet detective agency.

'Not to worry, we'll make up for lost time,' I reassured her. I told her to keep faith.

It is harder to find an animal after it has been missing for some time. The brutal truth is that the chances drop after three to four weeks. As with a missing-persons investigation, those first few days are crucial. Saying that, the most unexpected things can happen. Someone might have taken Ollie without knowing he belonged to Sally, and I was confident that if we spread the word further and wider we would get a result.

I'd just finished training Lucas and Liam, so this was the ideal opportunity for them to put their new skills to good use and conduct the largest search Animal Search had done so far in terms of manpower and time.

It was a warm day in May when the three of us bundled into the Vectra estate. We also had a trailer to pull, with four suitcases of luggage and search equipment. What had started out as very basic kit — a cat trap, torches, walkie-talkies and posters — had ballooned into an inventory of everything from a crowbar and a screwdriver to a pair of pliers, a hammer, a chisel, goggles, gloves, waterproof paper to write on and a microchip scanner.

I had recently upgraded again by forking out on better two-way radios with a much longer range, and head torches, in case we needed our hands free to search through barns or farmland.

We had everything we needed to find Ollie and I was going to try my hardest to bring him home. No stone would be left unturned.

It was a long drive, and we arrived in Lincolnshire in the early afternoon. As we approached the village there was nothing but flat farmland as far as the eye could see. It was evident we would have our work cut out for us in terms of the amount of ground we had to cover, so I was glad to have Lucas and Liam on board.

The village of Boothby Graffoe was picturesque, with a

nineteenth-century church and old stone houses. It was small but not small enough that someone might have noticed Ollie. My Golden Door might be waiting for us around the corner.

We passed the local shop and the butcher, and a few seconds later we were through the village and on an open road.

'Gosh, it's busy,' we all commented at the same time. Busy roads made me nervous when I was on a missing-pet search.

'Left here,' Lucas directed, at the next T-junction.

I turned onto a dirt track. The trailer rattled as it bumped over the stones and potholes.

We snaked around a few bends before the narrow track opened into a courtyard. The farmhouse was a big old place, nestled among fields. The landscape was flat but beautiful. As I took in my surroundings and surveyed the terrain my detective brain switched into gear. There were endless fields to the horizon, which meant plenty of room for the cat to get lost or disoriented. Outbuildings? Yes, several within view of the house. Could he be locked inside one?

I noted there was a busy road to the west of the house, which spelled trouble. Somewhere Ollie might sadly have met his fate. Alerting motorists to the disappearance would be critical to our investigation.

Sally appeared from the front door, waving. Her short dark hair caught in the breeze coming off the fields, showing off her sparkly earrings. She greeted us with a friendly smile but I could tell, seven months on, she was still devastated at the loss of Ollie. She was very quietly spoken and her face was full of sorrow; I sensed her life had been turned upside down on the day he had disappeared.

I could only imagine how hard it must have been for Sally to live on that isolated farm. She must have sought comfort in having Ollie on her lap every night. And now he was gone.

All of my searches were conducted with the same level of seriousness with which I would have looked for a missing person, rather than an animal, because I know how devastated I would have been if my beloved Maggie had gone missing. I could empathize with Sally's sadness.

She invited us inside and we congregated in her kitchen. It was big and decorated in a country style with an Aga, a solid oak table and chairs.

We listened intently as she told us Ollie's story. She said he never wandered far and would come inside regularly for food and cuddles. He was last seen prowling around her garden one evening at nine p.m. last October. She'd spotted him through the kitchen window as he walked through the long grass. He'd looked directly at her, then squeezed through the hole in the hedge. She'd thought he'd be back in a matter of minutes for his dinner but she'd stayed up all night waiting for him to return, like a parent waiting for their teenager to come home after a night out. He had never been seen again.

This was an important bit of information for the search because it meant it had been dark when the tabby went missing. The busy road jumped to the top of my list of possibilities. Ollie might have been knocked down and someone rescued, then adopted him from the roadside.

Sally went on to describe how he had come into her life. She had taken on the five-year-old cat after a relative of one of the patients Sally was nursing couldn't take care of him any longer. 'I thought I could look after him,' she said, her voice trembling. She folded her arms protectively across her chest and looked down at the stone floor.

I got up from my seat at the table and gave her arm a gentle squeeze to reassure her. 'You did a very kind thing in giving him a home, so don't ever doubt yourself,' I said, hoping my words hadn't fallen on deaf ears. It's sometimes hard to hear what people say to you when you're in turmoil. Now wasn't the moment to voice my concerns about the busy road. There is a fine line between being honest and being sensitive to people's feelings. I was still optimistic that a whole range of things could have happened to Ollie. I went back to the fundamentals. Cats need three things: food, shelter and water. Most of these things can be found in any housing estate, which is why when cats get lost they will easily re-establish themselves in a new area. A lot of owners have asked me if a cat will walk endlessly and the simple answer is no. Once they have found somewhere that provides them with everything they need, they will stop looking and stay where they are. Same thing happens if a cat has a scare and legs it. He will switch into survival mode and find those three things.

Sally kindly offered to put us up for the next couple of nights, which was incredibly generous. You wouldn't get someone housing a copper for the night. It was another rewarding aspect of my job. I was noticing more frequently now how pet-owners saw me as a friend or a family member, rather than a contractor.

Lucas, Liam and I thanked her profusely, then I launched into pet detective mode as I established what we were going to do.

It was now quite late in the day, after all the travelling, so I decided we would spend the daylight hours that remained putting up posters and conducting door-to-door enquiries. The nearest houses were a mile away across the fields so that was where we would begin our search.

'Can I come with you?' Sally asked.

Normally I wouldn't suggest an owner accompanies us as we conduct our enquiries for two reasons. First, they may find it too harrowing and become upset; and second, people aren't always forthcoming with information if they know the animal's owner is standing on their doorstep. If the home-owner has upsetting news, or perhaps even adopted a missing cat, they may not declare it.

But in Sally's case I made an exception. It would be helpful to have an extra pair of hands putting up posters while we carried out enquiries. In any case, she wouldn't have taken no for an answer.

I unhooked the trailer and we all got back into the pet-mobile. Sally followed us in her car into Boothby Graffoe. I parked in the most prominent place possible – by the village green. In my preparation for the search I had already printed off a map of the surrounding area and now spread it open across the Vectra's bonnet. It was a proud moment to see all of my team suited and booted in their uniforms. Sally, Lucas and Liam gathered around and leaned in.

'Listen up, everyone,' I began. 'We're not going to be spending our time trying to search people's back gardens today because too much time has passed.' Ollie would sadly have passed away if he had been trapped for seven months in a shed and his body would have been found already. 'So, the focus is on talking to people. We need to do door-to-door enquiries, and hand each person a leaflet about the cat. You need to ask them (a) have they heard anything about the disappearance, and (b) have they heard about any new cats appearing in the area. It's pretty straightforward, really.'

Liam and Lucas nodded. I turned to Sally, who was looking a lot stronger than she had earlier. 'Your job is to clip these posters of Ollie wherever you can.' I passed her a pile.

For this campaign we had a close-up picture of Ollie. His sweet face was staring back at us, almost saying, 'Come on, boys, bring me home safely.' He was a very distinctive cat, with a white face and a tiny black speck across his right nostril on his otherwise pink nose.

By the end of play on the first day, we had knocked on 160 doors. No one had seen or heard anything but we still had another 650 to go, so the odds were in our favour.

I made sure I put in a call to the local paper – the *Lincolnshire Echo*. Newspapers are one of the best ways to raise publicity and help find a missing pet. I've been a natural at generating press attention ever since I'd called the radio station, told them I was a pet detective and that I would find the missing Afghan Hound. Perhaps it stemmed from my time as a copper, when I had to negotiate my way out of sticky situations. Who knows? Anyway, I have the gift of the gab, as Jenni likes to say.

The reporter loved the line about it being Animal Search's biggest investigation.

We all hit the hay early that night, as we were tired from our drive and investigating. The next morning I came down to breakfast to find Sally had already been to Tesco and bought us all fresh croissants. She had also picked up a copy of the local paper. 'Have a look at this,' she said, smiling broadly.

It was the first time I'd seen her really smile since we had arrived. 'Look at this, boys!' I called Liam and Lucas over.

We had the front page. *Detectives in Hunt for Missing Moggie.*

Lucas let out a roar of laughter. ' "The search is being done on a scale that dwarfs many police investigations . . ." ' He read out his favourite line.

'Good, eh?' I lifted my eyebrows.

It was exactly the kind of publicity that would help us find Ollie. Sally was over the moon that the paper had decided to give us top coverage. I double-checked my phone to see if the volume was on loud. Now we just needed the calls to come in.

I took a final slurp of my coffee, placed the mug on the kitchen table, and peeled my luminous jacket off the back of the chair. 'Ready?' I said, zipping it up.

'Ready, boss,' Lucas and Liam echoed.

It was time to find Ollie. We had 650 doors to knock on and every minute counted.

It was a warm May day, and you can probably imagine how quickly we heated up under our jackets, with all the equipment we were lugging around. We had radios, microchip scanners, leaflets, pens, pencils and torches sprouting from different pockets. I'd mastered the knack of spreading my tools between my combat trousers and my inner and outer jacket pockets. If you didn't see us coming, you'd hear us with all our jangling!

We parked the pet-mobile in the heart of the village again and got cracking. I could see Sally's mood was dropping after her initial high at the newspaper front page, so I tried to lift it by recounting some of my success stories.

I was so intent on giving her hope that I even mentioned how one particular family who had registered their missing cat on the Animal Search UK website had worked with a psychic and had had interesting results. Sally's ears pricked as I recounted how Mrs Roberts from Birmingham had contacted a psychic from Bangalore in India to find her cat, Frankie.

The psychic had told Mrs Roberts that Frankie would be in an area where children play. 'And, sure enough, the cat was in a Wendy house in a back garden in the owner's street.'

Sally stopped dead in her tracks. 'You're kidding?'

'No, I'm not.'

'Mystic Mog', I'd nicknamed the case, when Mrs Roberts rang me up to tell me the cracking news. I don't have much faith in psychics, but it clearly worked for her. The moral of the story was never to give up hope.

Stories of my success had the desired effect and seemed to give Sally a spring in her step. She followed Liam to another part of the village, which we had still to blitz with posters, while I carried out door-to-door enquiries on Oak Road.

Six hundred doors later we still hadn't heard a thing. Lots of people had read the story in the *Lincolnshire Echo* but it hadn't jogged any memories. Not even one sighting of Ollie strolling through the village last autumn.

I was surprised. He was a memorable cat, with the distinctive black freckle on his pink nose.

I dabbed my brow and stared despondently at the map of the village. I knew better than anyone that information could come in days after the search, but it was always nice to get an instant result.

Suddenly the mobile in my pocket sprang into life. Someone was ringing the hotline.

'Hello, Tom Watkins, Animal Search UK. Can I take the poster reference number, please?'

The line was bad. It was crackling and hissing.

'Say that again – I didn't catch it.' I strained to hear the information. 'What? You've seen a cat like the one in the paper?'

It was a hair-tearing-out moment. The caller had a tip-off but I couldn't hear it.

Suddenly the line went dead.

I wanted to yell at the phone with frustration. But instead I coolly and calmly took a moment, hoping the caller would ring back.

A moment turned into a minute and soon five minutes had passed. I had no other choice but to crack on with my investigation.

As I was making my way up the paved path to the next house, the phone started singing again.

'Sorry about that, we've had engineers in, tinkering with the electrics,' the familiar lady's voice chirped. 'Now, where was I?'

She sounded elderly. As a copper I'd had to be quick to pick up such things.

'I shouldn't really be saying this,' she went on, 'but I saw a cat just like the one in the paper at the bungalow in my road.'

It turned out my good Samaritan was grassing up her neighbour. I wasn't sure if she had the right cat until she mentioned the moggie she'd spotted had a black dot on its nose.

We've got him! I thought. My heart was pounding with excitement.

I thanked the lady for her tip-off and got straight on the walkie-talkies. 'I've got something. Over.'

'What's that, chief?' Lucas responded.

I was conscious not to alert Sally yet. I needed to suss out the situation, as I didn't want to give her any false hope.

I told them to carry on with their enquiries while I made a beeline for the bungalow.

It was quite possible that Ollie had become lost crossing the fields behind Sally's house and relocated here, I thought, as I walked up the tarmacked driveway. The front door was wooden, with a circular stained-glass window. I pressed the bell. It was one of those ear-piercing high-pitched ones that went on for ever.

I took a step back and examined the porch. There was a small shrub in a red pot and a rolled-up copy of today's local paper.

This home-owner clearly hadn't read about us being in town, I thought.

I heard some movement on the other side, and what I thought was a faint miaow. The door opened and on the other side stood an elderly man.

I launched into my well-rehearsed lines. 'Hi, I'm looking for a missing cat.'

The elderly gentleman was a little hard of hearing, so I raised my voice a notch or two. It was obviously a delicate situation, which had to be approached sensitively. I explained that a cat that looked like Ollie had been spotted on his property and that Sally's beloved tabby had gone missing.

'I've had Felix for five years now,' the man cut in.

He seemed genuine but only by seeing Felix would I know for sure.

There was still a glimmer of hope. Again, it was going to take diplomacy to get around it. I asked if he would be kind enough to show Felix to us. If I knew what Felix looked like, I could rule him out if anyone else happened to call in with a sighting.

He kindly agreed to introduce us to his cat. He called Felix's name, and a few moments later the cat appeared in the hallway. That was the first clue that he probably wasn't the one we were searching for: he was answering to his name.

As the tabby drew closer I saw what a doppelgänger he was for Ollie. He even had the black speck on his nose. But, although similar, he wasn't the cat we were after.

Felix rubbed his head against his owner's leg.

'Hello, mate!' I greeted him. Felix miaowed and wove himself in a figure of eight between his owner's legs, purring, tail aloft.

I needed Sally to see this cat so that if she got calls in the future she knew that a lookalike was prowling the area and what features he might have to distinguish him from Ollie.

The old man was a real gent and agreed it was fine for Sally to meet Felix, so I radioed for Liam to bring her over in the search car. Just as it was a sensitive situation to question the man about his cat, showing her a cat that reminded her of her beloved Ollie also needed to be handled with care. I could imagine she might hold on to the glimmer of hope that the man was not telling the truth and his cat might be hers. She might have been holding on to that hope when she approached the house, which was why I needed to intercept her.

As soon as I saw the pet-mobile roll up outside, I dived in.

I opened the door for Sally and whispered, 'I don't think it's Ollie. It's a very similar cat, though.'

She gave me a nod, but I could tell she hadn't given up hope. After seven months she must have been yearning to see a cat that reminded her of her boy.

As we approached the man on the doorstep, he picked up the lookalike and held him gently under his arm. I checked on Sally. Her eyes became wide and dewy. Her bottom lip quivered as she reached her hand out and tickled Felix under his chin.

'He has different markings,' she said, with a lump in her throat.

She managed to fight back the tears. She gave Felix one last stroke, then pulled away. She looked glum, but hopeful at the same time. In a funny kind of way we were making progress. Painful progress, I guess you could call it.

I took down the old man's phone number, just in case someone called Sally and said they had seen Ollie in such and such street. Sally could immediately get on the blower to this man and ask if Felix was with him. If he came back saying his cat had been indoors all day, Sally would have hit the jackpot.

It was good to connect to home-owners in the community: speaking to them in person significantly increased the chances of them noticing or hearing something in the future.

After that it was back to the grindstone, knocking on doors in the village and putting up posters everywhere we could think of. We were all exhausted by the time we got back to Sally's that evening. Despite a long, emotional day, she cooked us dinner before our drive home.

She barely took a bite of her jacket potato and beans, though. She was deep in thought. Suddenly she blurted, 'I don't want this to be the end of the search.'

I explained to her it was just the start in terms of the coverage we had achieved: we just had to wait for a phone call. 'When we leave today the search doesn't stop. We're with you, supporting you until Ollie comes home.'

'Never give up hope' was my motto – lots of people have, then been surprised. But Sally wanted to reach out that bit further. She said, 'Can we ask the psychic in India if she knows where Ollie is?'

CHAPTER THIRTEEN
PSYCHIC SARITA

Psychic Sarita from Bangalore had seen a vision of Ollie. His owner, Sally, was breathless with excitement as she recalled what the mystic had said to her. 'Ollie is either stuck in a building with a tin roof or in a drain nearby connected to that building.'

There must be a lot of those in the Lincolnshire countryside. I was taken aback by how vague the description was. It had been four days since I'd seen Sally and she seemed in much higher spirits. Although I was sceptical of how helpful a psychic could be, I didn't want to dampen her hopes. Plus, I knew that a pet search with a psychic involved would rekindle media interest.

'So do you know of any buildings near you with a tin roof?' I went along with it.

Turns out Sally had already done a recce of all the sheds nearby. 'Yes! About half a mile from my house,' she trilled.

I wasn't expecting that.

'It's a derelict building with a tin roof.'

'What about the drain?'

'There's a drain next to it.'

I was astounded. I took a slurp of tea, as my throat had become dry with excitement. It was evening and I was working late in the shed.

'Have you looked down the drain?' I asked.

'The lid's half on, but it's too heavy for me to move on my own. And it was too dark for me to see down there.'

My mind was already whirring with a list of the tools I would need to search the drain – torches, head torches – before she even asked me to come up and take a look.

Then I had a eureka moment. 'Maybe you could get Dyno Rod to take a look with one of the cameras they use to inspect sewage drains.'

She jumped at the idea.

We'd both been so excited by the prospect of a break in the case that I hadn't thought to ask if the psychic knew whether or not Ollie was okay. How long had he been trapped in the drain? I broached the question with Sally. She didn't have the answer but she prayed he was alive, that he had gone roaming again from wherever he had been living for the past seven months and got stuck on his travels. Maybe he'd been trying to find his way home.

'Even if Ollie has been stuck down there the whole time at least I'll get closure,' she said bravely.

I agreed. Knowing was better than not.

I was bubbling with excitement at the thought of searching the drain, being able to help Sally. And the other half of me was thinking, *This is a load of rubbish. A psychic can't be right.*

I told Sally to leave things with me. I'd be up once I'd made the preparations. I also wanted to address the issue of the busy road while I was up there. We hadn't had enough time to cover it in our last search.

I suggested to Sally that we didn't pin all our hopes on Sarita, and said I would bring up a sign to put on the busy road near her house in case a driver had seen something. It would be bright, luminous, with a picture of Ollie and read: 'Missing. Drivers, have you seen anything?' with our free phone number underneath. But first I needed to put in a call to Dyno Rod. They thought it was a wind-up.

'Say that again?' The guy at the other end chuckled.

'Seriously, I want to search for a missing cat down a drain.'

'How long has it been missing?' the Dyno Rod guy asked, still in shock.

'Seven months.'

There was a long pause on the phone. 'Are you for real?'

It was in the last days of May that I retraced my route back up to Lincolnshire. This time I was going it alone.

Sally looked significantly more upbeat when she greeted me in the driveway this time around. She gave me a hug and invited me in for a cuppa while we waited for the Dyno Rod guy to turn up.

As she nursed her mug between her hands, she told me she was prepared for the worst. The not knowing had been the most painful part of the grieving process.

I told her not to pin her hopes on the mystic but agreed that the coincidence of a shed, drain and corrugated roof near her home was remarkable.

Suddenly a flash of bright orange passed by the kitchen window. The wait was over. It was the Dyno Rod van. We rushed to the front door.

A man in his mid-twenties jumped out of the driver's seat. He looked a bit grubby from working all day but he was a friendly chap. He had a clipboard in one hand and lifted the top page, checking for the job details. 'So, where's the blockage?' he asked.

Clearly the bloke I was chatting to on the phone hadn't told this man the job description. 'It's not a blockage, mate, but a missing cat in a drain,' I explained.

The guy blinked a few times in shock. 'Ooo-kay, so where's the drain?' He looked confused.

'We don't really know. Next to a building with a tin roof.'

'Come off it!'

'No, for real, that's what the psychic in India said.' I went on to explain the unique situation. He might have thought he was on *Candid Camera*.

After he'd got over his surprise at the unusual situation, he was on board with our mission. He said he was a pet person himself and would see what he could do. The plan was that I'd go with Sally in the search car and Mr Dyno Rod would follow in his van.

We parked by the roadside in the middle of nowhere about half a mile from Sally's house. There was nothing as far as the eye could see, except fields and one derelict farm building with a tin roof.

It was kind of eerie-looking.

'What do we do now?' the drain guy asked.

'We find the drain,' I said, loading my jacket with a torch and the other essentials I might need. The contractor grabbed his equipment from the back of the van – a long, flexible rod with a camera attached – and the three of us took off across the fields, wading through the long grass, in the direction of Mystic Sarita's premonition.

Sally had marked the drain with a traffic cone so we had no problem finding it. We all got down on our hands and knees and peered into the black abyss. We must have looked a right sight to anyone who was walking their dog nearby.

Sally and I watched with trepidation as the drain guy threaded the rod through the hole. The small computer screen lit up and we could see inside. Sally was biting her nails nervously. My heart was in my mouth. Was Ollie down there?

It was muddy and the walls of the drain were laced with a green fungus. It was not the sort of place you'd want to get stuck.

We were now on tenterhooks.

'Anything?' I double-checked for signs of life.

'Nah, this place hasn't seen life for years,' the Dyno Rod guy said.

The screen was plunged into darkness as the camera reached the end of the drain.

'It's soiled up from here on in. Nothing would have got past the mud.'

I felt a wave of relief. I didn't want Ollie to be found down there: it would have been like being buried alive.

We clambered back to our feet and brushed off our knees. Even though I was still thinking the psychic's premonition was probably a load of rubbish, I didn't want to leave without inspecting the derelict building, just in case.

The Dyno Rod guy was keen to help with the search. I switched on my torch and told my new team to follow me.

It was dark and musty inside. I shone my torch around, lighting up nooks and crannies. We cautiously took a few more steps when suddenly something rose out of the darkness.

We all jumped back with fright as a pigeon nearly sliced our noses off with its wings. It flapped wildly into the air and came to rest on one of the overhead beams, staring down at us with its beady eyes.

'That nearly scared me to death,' Sally said, clutching her chest.

'There's nothing here. Time to head back to base.' I'd had enough of this circus. I wanted to get back to some detective work.

After I'd thanked the Dyno Rod guy for all his efforts, I got to work on alerting motorists along that busy road about Ollie's disappearance. I dug a hole in the grassy verge and inserted the wooden post with the board. It was similar to what you would find outside a house, only it had a picture of a cute tabby cat instead of a 'For Sale' notice. 'That should do it,' I said, dusting my hands together. Anyone travelling along that road would be alerted to our search. It might jog a memory, or someone might have seen a cat like Ollie in a neighbouring village. I hadn't given up hope.

Neither had Sally, thankfully. As I said my goodbyes I sensed that she wasn't going to give up until she had closure.

She said she was glad she'd followed through with the psychic's premonition because, you never knew, it might have led to a discovery. She was tired after all the highs and lows but she was hopeful we might get a response. It was still early days in our search, after all. Most of all, Sally was at peace: she had done everything she could to find her boy. 'At least I won't lie awake now thinking I didn't try to help him. That would have eaten me up,' she said.

I gave her a hug.

It was the saddest I'd felt since I'd started my job. Every

owner I had met had been devastated by the disappearance of their animal, but it had troubled Sally for so many months. I wished I could wave a magic wand and make it all better for her.

I was looking forward to getting home. It was hard not to let my job get to me sometimes. Being quite a sensitive bloke underneath, I took everything very much to heart.

Later that night, back at the shed, I was going through some paperwork. It was past midnight. Jenni and the kids were fast asleep inside the house, but I couldn't switch off. I glanced at the map of England above my desk — the map of unsolved cases. I reluctantly pinned a picture of Ollie to Lincolnshire. 'We'll find you one day, mate,' I said.

There were always going to be cases I couldn't solve, same as when I was a copper. But I vowed there and then I would do everything in my power to help these owners continue their searches.

I would never give up on Ollie, or any of the other pets out there who needed me and my team to find them.

CHAPTER FOURTEEN
BLUES AND CLUES

I was still feeling down in the dumps about Ollie, so I visited my dad for consolation. After a cuppa and some words of wisdom, Dad asked if I would drop his recycling off in the centre of the village on my way home. 'No problem,' I told him. I must have had my car door open for three minutes, if that, while I walked over to the bins, and when I got back in I saw I'd acquired a passenger.

Sitting on the seat next to me was a cheeky ginger and white cat. 'Rufus!' I exclaimed. He was still up to his old tricks. The stowaway was grinning at me in the way only cats can and gazed up at me with the self-assured look that told me he was very pleased with himself.

I kept my door open, suggesting he might want to get out, but Rufus was having none of it. 'Go on, then. I'll give you a lift home.'

Rufus was purring as I drove him up the hill back to his mum's house, curiously peeping out of the window with one paw on the glass to steady himself. He clearly loved riding in cars.

I parked up and turned to my new friend. 'Come here, you,' I said, scooping him into my arms. What was an allergy between friends?

He was still purring as I carried him down the driveway and knocked on Emma Webster's door. She was delighted to see me and broke into fits of giggles when she saw what I was carrying. 'Delivery for you,' I said, between sneezes, holding the furry bundle in my arms.

'Rufus, you naughty boy!' Emma pulled him to her chest.

I told her she needed to keep a close eye on his antics or she'd be calling on me again soon. It was nice to catch up with her and see how Rufus was getting on. Cases were never closed once I'd said goodbye: I kept a place in my heart for every single one of the pets I'd helped find.

The morning's excitement put a spring in my step and a renewed burst of enthusiasm for growing my company into the world's best detective agency. So much so that, later in the day, while I was patrolling the motorways around the West Midlands, I spotted something that would make a perfect addition to the team: it was big, white, had flashing lights, and had once been used to save lives.

The old ambulance was rotting in the St John's yard just off the M5. With two searches on average a week now, which could be anywhere in the country, it was becoming increasingly apparent that we'd soon need a bigger fleet of pet-mobiles, and preferably large ones in which to store the equipment and from which we could co-ordinate an investigation. What would make a more perfect mobile information unit than a converted ambulance?

I imagined myself driving up and down the motorway

with the Animal Search UK logo emblazoned along the sides for all to see. It would be just like in *Ghostbusters*, only the old American Cadillac Miller-Meteor they had converted had once been a hearse.

Finally I would have a vehicle large enough to take all of the team and the equipment and I could even wire it up so we could have a printer in there too. That way, if we were ever caught short of posters on a search, all I'd need to do was jump into the back of the ambulance and, hey presto, another hundred posters would materialize.

I had to snap myself back to reality. *Calm yourself, Tom!* I didn't even know if it was for sale.

As soon as my shift finished I got on the blower to St John Ambulance and tentatively enquired as to whether any of the vehicles in their depot that were looking a bit tired and shabby were for sale. I suggested they could use the money to help them buy a new vehicle to save lives.

Incredibly, that was all it took. They suggested I call at the depot and have a look at what was on offer.

Within a week I had arranged for a tour at the depot in West Bromwich. An old guy with white hair and a grey beard met me at the gate. He was wearing blue overalls covered with oil smears. He pulled a well-used cloth out from his pockets and gave his hands a wipe before offering to shake mine. I guessed he was the mechanic who kept the ambulances in trim.

'So, what have you got for me?' I said cheerily.

'Follow me,' he said, in a gruff Midlands accent.

The mechanic led me past row after row of ambulances, lined up like dominoes. He explained that they were either being serviced or past their sell-by date – which I learned was after fifteen years on the road. It was like an ambulance graveyard.

The one he had in mind for me was right at the end of the courtyard.

'I took delivery of this one eighteen years ago,' the mechanic reminisced as we walked. He revealed that it had been donated by a member of the public when it was brand new. 'Here she is,' he said, patting the side of the clapped-out vehicle as you would a horse.

It looked more knackered than my old shed had. The back window was smashed in. All four tyres were flat. You could barely make out the white paintwork for the green mildew and rust streaking down the sides. The wheel arches were rusted through.

And that was just the outside.

He wrenched open the back doors and we were hit with an unpleasant cocktail of mould and surgical spirit. I plugged my nose with my hand as I stepped inside. The interior had suffered over the years – the fabric covering the benches was torn and moss was creeping around inside the windows. However, despite its dilapidation, I imagined the hundreds of people who had been stretchered in and out of it over the years. The lives it had saved. It was a humbling moment.

It was a mess, but I could tell it had potential.

The big question was, would it start? After three years of being battered by the wind and rain, I was guessing not.

Sure enough, the battery was as flat as a pancake.

We were going to need some jump leads to spark it into life. The mechanic went off to fetch them while I drove the pet-mobile close to it. When the man got back, we lifted both bonnets and connected the old engine to the new.

I was doubtful a jump lead would get the rust bucket going. But, amazingly, it started first time, which was a miracle considering it hadn't been touched for three years. The Ford V6 2.9 engine roared: I loved the sound of it. What I loved even more was the thought of how many pet lives it would help me save.

I decided there and then that I wanted it. The next question was, how much did he want for it? I thought he'd say a few grand, because even though it was in poor shape, it had done just thirty-seven thousand miles, a really low mileage. He rubbed his chin with his thumb and forefinger as he thought it over. Finally he put me out of my misery. 'Three hundred and seventy-five quid, and it's yours.'

I nearly fell over. I tried to hide my surprise, though, as I didn't want him to increase the price. 'I can just about scrape that together,' I replied.

We shook hands to cement the deal and that was it. I was the proud owner of an ambulance and a stretcher. Now I had to work out how I was going to get it home. The old ambulance wasn't drivable, with the flat tyres, the smashed window and no MOT, so I called on a company called Auto Support to collect and deliver it to my house, seventy miles away in Hereford, a week later. That gave me seven days to sweeten Jenni up and get her used to the idea that an ambulance would be parked in our driveway from now on.

Jenni wasn't alarmed by the news. I would go so far as to say she was quietly pleased for me, although I didn't describe quite how run-down it was. She had a bit of a shock when the pick-up vehicle turned up with it that Friday evening.

The kids rushed onto the driveway, but Jenni stood there in

disbelief, her hands on her hips. 'What have you gone and done now?' she said, staring at the clapped-out ambulance.

She wasn't the only person to give me an odd look. As you can imagine, there were a few raised eyebrows among the neighbours, too.

The couple next door came out to watch the unloading. I could lip-read them saying, 'Oh, no!'

'Have you been down the junkyard again, Tom?' Malc from over the road asked me.

I responded with pride: 'No, that's my new mobile incident unit, mate. Welcome to the future of pet detection!'

He grinned and wished me luck. He sometimes gave me a hand when I needed to wash the pet-mobiles.

The kids were over the moon about the latest addition to the Animal Search fleet of vehicles. Sam tugged at my leg, wanting me to lift him into the driver's seat. He and Polly took it in turns to sit behind the wheel and pretend they were ambulance drivers. They honked the horn a few times, which made Sam giggle. We tried to get the siren going but the electrics had packed up – although that was probably a blessing: the neighbours wouldn't have been best pleased with the noise and flashing lights.

'What's it for, Daddy?' Sam asked.

I explained how the ambulance that used to save people's lives would now be saving pets. Jenni flashed me a smile.

For the next five months, when I wasn't out on searches or patrolling the highways, I was restoring the ambulance to its former glory. It was a painstaking process because the vehicle was in such bad shape, but I found it incredibly rewarding to see the transformation.

First things to go were the old green and yellow ambulance stickers. They broke and snapped when you pulled them so I had to use a solvent to dissolve the glue and three days' worth of elbow grease.

Five new tyres were needed, which set me back £250, almost as much as the vehicle had cost, but I saved on the replacement of the smashed window by using a local merchant in town. I also made a little back by selling the old stretcher on eBay to an undertaker.

For luck, I kept the original stickers that were on the dashboard, which read 'blue lights, horn, auxiliary power'. Power points were already installed in the back, ready for us to plug in laptops, chargers and my printer.

I had the engine serviced, then had the vehicle MOT tested. To my delight, it passed first time. It was a huge boost to my spirits that nothing was seriously wrong. She was now fit to be transformed into an Animal Search vehicle. This was the fun part.

I called on my mate Jason, who had helped me lay the patio for the shed. He was very handy when it came to DIY. We sat with a cup of tea in the shed, and drew up a plan of what we were going to do. I wanted benches down the side with padded cushions. Storage wasn't too much of a problem because there were already overhead cupboards, but I asked Jason if he could design the seating so there was space underneath to store the cat baskets, a dog rescue cage, the waterproof jackets and fleeces and an emergency food supply just in case we broke down somewhere. Rations included Mars bars, Rich Tea biscuits and bottles of water. I always like to be prepared for the worst-case scenario.

'And can I have a pull-out board in there too, which we can turn into a bed?' I asked Jason. That would solve the staying-overnight issue.

It was a real team effort. Jason got to work sawing and

welding, Jenni helped sew together the cushions, while I rolled up my sleeves and power-washed the outside, scrubbing away the mould and mildew.

I then went to the local discount shop and bought dozens of boxes to store the equipment. Everything had to be labelled and have its rightful place. The ambulance was a far cry from the glove compartment in which Ace Ventura had messily stored his cat treats. I had cans of tuna stacked neatly in the overhead compartments. There was a red box for dead batteries and a green one for charged batteries – that way there would be no mix-up. The last thing you need on a search is for a torch to die at a crucial moment.

The final, and best, touches were the markings. I dropped off a plain white vehicle with Roger, the sign writer, and two days later I picked up a Missing Pet Information Unit. That was the name I'd settled on after much discussion with the team.

It looked magnificent, as if it was brand new, with bright yellow and orange stickers and the writing in red along the sides. People would see us coming a mile off.

I'd been to Roger's to pick up a number of cars by now, but this was something else. I can't tell you how incredible it felt to drive home. Everyone was pointing and staring – I felt like a celebrity as I cruised along the streets of my estate.

The kids and Jenni were waiting on the drive at home. Sam was jumping up and down, with his arms outstretched above his head. 'Yay, pet search!' he cheered.

Jenni wore a broad smile. 'Well done, Tom. It looks amazing!'

'Thanks, love.' I gave her a kiss for her continued support.

Polly ran her hand over the writing along the side, from one end to the other. It was at that moment that I decided I'd nickname the ambulance 'Polly' after my daughter because I cherished it just like I did my family.

The Missing Pet Information Unit was so impressive I even fooled the neighbours into thinking it was new. This time, rather than looking horrified, the couple next door congratulated me on my latest purchase. I felt an enormous surge of pride as I told them it was the same vehicle as before.

'Okay, everyone, jump in!' I told my family. It was time for the inaugural trip.

Sam insisted on riding in the back, so Jenni jumped in with him and Polly kept me company in the front. I turned the keys in the ignition and smiled as I listened to the engine purr like a cat. 'Here we go!'

We did a lap around the estate. It was surprisingly quick due to the powerful engine but turning the wheel was like wrestling with an elephant because there was no power-steering. It was big and cumbersome, but I didn't care – I was just so pleased with it. I'd successfully resuscitated the ambulance so it could save more lives – the lives of furry creatures.

CHAPTER FIFTEEN
NO BONE LEFT UNTURNED

Do you remember the missing dog in the woods? You're probably wondering if I managed to find him.

It was my first big canine search and it was like looking for a needle in a haystack. We'd been combing the undergrowth of Bourne Woods in Frensham, Surrey, for hours when Olivia found Cody's red collar hanging from some brambles. We weren't sure if the two-year-old black and white collie-cross was dead or alive.

I shone my torch into the gloom, wondering how we were going to find him.

'Keep going, troops!' I urged my team on. We had a ditch to climb out of first.

It was 6 January 2011 and the cold and damp chilled us to the bone. The rain was lashing against our faces.

A former high-ranking British Army officer, Mike, Cody's owner, was used to challenging conditions. He had joined our search in the woods while his wife, Debbie, gave a hand with door-to-door enquiries and putting up posters in the surrounding villages.

Mike had a very confident manner – he was now the chief executive of a company that ran prisons – but the disappearance of his beloved Cody had clearly got to him. As we trudged through the mud, he confided that he and Debbie felt responsible for Cody's disappearance. The dog-walker had lost Cody in the woods the previous evening, but they felt guilty for not walking him themselves. 'It's hard when you have work commitments,' I said. 'At least you thought about Cody's well-being and arranged for him to go out.'

'I guess so,' Mike mumbled, looking at the ground sombrely.

Despite his downcast mood, you could see why Mike would have risen through the ranks in the army. He was proactive and keen to do anything to aid the search. He'd come prepared – he was wearing army-style boots and gaiters around his shins to stop water seeping into his trousers. He'd also brought a compass and an Ordnance Survey map with him, which was far superior to the one I was carrying – it showed the gradient of the terrain we were tackling. He folded it out in the pouring rain and balanced it on his raised knee.

We could see from the map there was still a huge amount of ground to cover. All we could do was continue to make our way in the sweeping motion you see police officers following in murder investigations. That way, if Cody was stuck in the undergrowth or caught in a prickly bush, we would find him.

I rang Olivia to see if she'd had any luck at her end.

'Nothing.'

I shook my head glumly to the team.

We splintered into formation again, doing our best to hold the line. There were about fifty yards between me and Mike, Mike and M, M and Liam.

Hard on the heels of another missing pet. In the hot seat on the hotline. 'Hello, Animal Search UK …'

Who needs DIY SOS? Animal Search UK HQ here we come

Polly, the pet search information unit, gets a bath and scrub up

Pet-mobiles ready for deployment

Walkie-talkies: an essential piece of kit for keeping in touch when out on a case

Cheeky Rufus reunited with his owner Emma. On to the next case!

Out in Polly on the look out for Spencer

Got him! A rescued
Spencer ready to be
returned to Terry and
Trish

Terrier, Camera and Action! The reconstruction of the theft of
Toby the terrier

The press gather to cover the event

Toby is found by a young man and the hunt for his owner begins

Getting away with it – the thief takes Toby from the unsuspecting youth

Chairman Mao back home safe and sound with Sophie

The roadside sign used to track down missing moggie Oliver

M – short for Matthew Marshall – was my latest recruit. He'd joined three months ago, thanks to an introduction from Liam. Matthew was tall at six foot one, a down-to-earth type of guy. He still worked part-time as an electrical and mechanical engineer. He had no experience of pets but he was very much a people person – he met dozens of new clients each week through his job. People warmed to him instantly so he had no problem with getting them to let him search their gardens and sheds.

I now had a strong team behind me at my pet detective agency, but I could have done with double the number on this search. There was too much terrain to cover and not enough boots on the ground.

Just as the rain started to ease off, the mist descended. A vast blanket of grey swallowing every tree from its base, coupled with the worry of finding Cody, it was suffocating. It was even more imperative that we stayed in line. I radioed through to the others.

'Liam, stay within sight of me so that we can make sure no ground goes unchecked. If you see a coin on the ground I want you to check under it!'

'Received. No problem, Tom.'

'M, you okay?'

He was to my right, beating the brambles down with a stick. 'All good, Tom, going steady on my line.'

I wanted them ready for when we changed course.

'Another two hundred yards and then we sweep to the right,' I instructed.

'Roger that,' they replied in chorus.

Mike was a real trouper. Despite being upset, he was calm and unflappable. It was nice working with an ex-forces person: we were on the same page.

We trudged onwards.

Mike told me a little bit more about Cody and Debbie. He said that, because he spent a lot of hours away working, Cody took over as man of the house and gave Debbie comfort in his absence. The dog's disappearance had hit her hard. Mike had to leave for work again on Monday and he didn't know how she would cope. By then we had to have found Cody.

I liked his military we-must-succeed-at-all-costs frame of mind. I could relate to that. Even though I love all animals, I'm a dog person at heart.

I explained the major difference between a dog search and a cat search: dogs can run a lot further in a short space of time, which means we had a lot more ground to cover. They also behave more frantically when they're separated from their owner. Unlike cats – who gravitate towards shelter, food and water – dogs will run around haphazardly, desperately trying to find their owner.

'So what does that mean for Cody?' Mike asked.

'It's a good thing we aren't near any busy roads that he could run headlong into without thinking.' I tried to see the positives. Just then we had no option but to look on the bright side and keep moving.

Suddenly we emerged into a clearing. There was a single bench, an oasis of calm hidden deep in the woods. I imagined on a summer's day it would be a romantic picnic spot. Looking up at the dark sky, I couldn't think of anything worse right now.

We huddled together to look at the map again. And that was when we heard the noise. It was so faint at first I wondered if it was the howling of the wind through the trees. But then Mike heard it too.

'Sssh!' I held my finger to my lips.

There was no doubt about it. It was the sound of a dog barking.

Mike started shouting Cody's name, cupping his hands around his mouth.

'It's coming from over there.' I pointed to the other side of the clearing. Our boots squelched as we ran through the muddy grass. My heart was in my mouth – I was hoping, praying, we'd found Cody.

We saw a pair of white ears and a fluffy head bouncing over the fern and brambles. 'Cody!' we all shouted.

The dog yapped wildly and excitedly.

But the barking was followed by the shrill note of a whistle, then the appearance of a dog-walker. 'Here, Poppy!' The guy called his dog to him.

She could have been Cody's double. All our hearts dropped as quickly as they had risen.

Why anyone would want to walk through the woods in those weather conditions was beyond me. The dog-walker seemed a little intimidated by our high-visibility presence.

'Afternoon,' I said.

'Afternoon,' the man replied apprehensively, clipping his dog back on its lead.

With our bright orange uniform and powerful torches, the poor bloke probably thought we were conducting a murder investigation.

'Have you seen this dog on your walk?' I held up the soggy poster of Cody.

The guy unzipped his well-worn waxed jacket and wiped the raindrops from his glasses on his jumper. He pushed them back up his nose and squinted at the poster. 'He looks a lot like Poppy,' he exclaimed. 'But, sorry, haven't seen him.' He added that he hadn't seen a soul until he'd come across us.

I checked on Mike to see if the news had hit him hard. If he was upset, he hid it well behind a wall of steel and professionalism.

I hadn't given up hope, but I honestly didn't know where Cody could be. It was back to the drawing board.

I pulled out a pair of binoculars from the pocket in my combat trousers. It was the latest piece of equipment I'd invested in. They were army standard and if I had been on the battlefield I would have seen the enemy coming from miles off. In Bourne Woods, despite the mist, I spotted a squirrel in a tree and two magpies playing tug of war with a twig.

'Okay, guys, let's get back into line,' I instructed. It was all we could do – that, and hope for the best.

Suddenly my mobile was dancing in my coat pocket. Fumbling with cold wet hands, I nearly dropped it into the mud.

The screen read: *Olivia Search Team*. She had news.

'Yes . . . Right . . . You're kidding!' I exclaimed.

Everyone stared at me with bated breath.

'Good news, lads! We've found him!' I yelled.

Suddenly the cold, the wet and the exhaustion were forgotten. We were buzzing.

I'm a football fan: finding a missing dog or cat is like thinking you've lost a championship match and suddenly your team turns it around to win the cup. The extremes of emotion leave you exhausted but elated.

It turned out that Cody had run out of the woods and into someone's front garden. The home-owner had seen one of our posters a matter of minutes earlier and called the hotline. Debbie and Olivia were collecting the dog as we spoke.

We were all laughing and whooping as we made our way back to the car park. This time we got to take the track rather than the bramble route.

Mike was grinning from ear to ear, chuffed at the news. I couldn't wait to see the two reunited. There's nothing more moving than watching an owner reconnect with a pet they'd lost or even thought might be dead.

Olivia had taken the pet-mobile for door-to-door enquiries, so we all bundled into the back of Mike's BMW. We were so damp that the windows misted up in seconds.

Five minutes later we were pulling into Mike and Debbie's driveway. And there, waiting to greet us, was a wet and bedraggled but clearly jubilant Cody. His white tail was wagging hard and he was pulling against his collar, his front paws cycling through the air, desperate to greet Mike after their separation.

It's funny to see how an animal can reduce even the toughest of men to jelly. As soon as Mike caught sight of his dog, all formality and protocol went out the window. He jumped out of his car and dropped to his knees.

It must have been hard for Debbie to release her grip on Cody, having only just got him back, but from one look at Cody's face, you knew he wasn't going anywhere. When she let him go, he came bounding across the driveway, his ears flapping. He planted his muddy paws on Mike's chest and licked the entirety of his face.

'Hello, boy.' Mike tickled and ruffled behind Cody's ears. 'We love you, yes, we do, we do. Where have you been, pal?'

The reunion nearly brought a tear to my eye. It had been such a long, exhausting search. After we had all given Cody a stroke, and taken pictures of the family reunited, Debbie invited us in for a cuppa and a slice of cake.

It was music to my ears.

By the time I finally got home I was knackered. But no sooner had I walked through the door than I was handed my next case file.

Zoë had left the notes in a manila folder on my desk.

Missing: Jerry.

Owner: Jill.

Jenni popped her head around the shed door. 'Are you going to eat something, love?' she asked, concerned with my energy levels.

'I'll be there in a jiffy. I just need to take a look at this first.'

Jenni sighed.

I might have solved one case that day, but now another owner needed my help.

I looked up at the map of the UK, with its scattering of pet pictures. My unsolved cases were haunting me. I couldn't rest until I'd solved them and all the others that were coming in.

CHAPTER SIXTEEN
JERRY AND JILL

When a pet goes missing, there is often more going on in the owner's life than meets the eye. I'd worked on a number of cases now where the disappearance of the animal added to the turmoil that was already unfolding behind closed doors. Recently, I'd helped a family whose estranged son had returned home the day their dog disappeared. Luckily I managed to find Pebbles, so there was a happy reunion all around.

My detective nose smelt something amiss in the case of Jerry and Jill. First, Jill was so upset on the telephone that she could barely speak. She had trouble explaining what had happened to her ginger Burmese cat, Jerry. The words were choked in her throat, so I tried to calm her down, saying there was no rush, that I was there to listen whenever she was ready.

My tea was getting cold but Jenni would understand. This took priority.

Little by little, Jill opened up and shared with me her loss. She had recently returned to the UK after living for many years in

Germany. *Why had she left?* I wondered. And from the way she described packing in a hurry, it seemed she had made a snap decision to leave. I was intrigued as to what had prompted her swift departure.

Jill had reluctantly left Jerry with a friend in Cheltenham while she frantically hunted for a house to rent in the same area. Her friend had absent-mindedly left a window open, allowing Jerry to escape into the alien suburbs of Gloucestershire. He'd been missing for two days.

'Jerry is lost in a place he doesn't know.' Jill sniffled. 'He'll be lost for ever.' She broke down in sobs.

She was devastated that he had been lost while in someone else's care, someone she'd trusted to look after him. Jill revealed she didn't have any kids and that Jerry was her 'boy'. 'He's the only thing that's been solid and loyal to me over the years.' She wept.

Another red flag went up in my mind. *Loyal over the years?* It sounded like a loaded phrase.

I reassured Jill that even though Jerry was lost on 'foreign soil', cats need three things wherever they are – food, shelter and water – and since he had gone missing in a suburb those three things could be found close by. It was very unlikely he had wandered far. At least we knew why he had gone missing. That was good. It wasn't as if he had disappeared from a family home out of the blue. He had escaped from a near-stranger and was lost – it gave us a good starting point.

'Do you think you can find him?' she pleaded down the phone.

My heart went out to her. Clearly she had been through more than the disappearance of her cat and needed plenty of reassurance.

She cheered up a little once I explained how I could help find

Jerry with my search team and our tried-and-tested methods of pet detection. If we conducted door-to-door enquiries and displayed posters with photographs, the chances were that someone would have seen him.

'Jill, if anyone can find Jerry, we can,' I said confidently.

It was a bold statement, but our success rate was something to be confident and proud of. And I had a secret weapon up my sleeve. I would be taking a new piece of equipment on the search that I hoped would reunite more pets than ever with their owners.

I was excited to make the big reveal when we arrived in Cheltenham. But first we had to get there. We drove in convoy to Gloucestershire, with Liam and M following, just in case Polly the ambulance broke down.

Halfway there, we stopped at a motorway service station to check Polly: it was the first long journey we had done with her. After popping the bonnet and checking the oil and the water, I was pleased to discover that all was well. I clambered back into the ambulance and, with the roar of her engine, we curved along the slip road, merging into the throng of cars zipping down the motorway. Coming through! The other drivers quickly made way for our ambulance.

Those hours on the road gave me time to reflect on Jill's words. I wondered what state we would find her in. I knew the situation had to be handled sensitively. I was concerned she might feel a little overwhelmed with three men in her living room, so I had to come up with something less intimidating.

It was my first time in Cheltenham, and my first impression of the place was that it was dead posh. The leafy suburbs had big houses with manicured lawns and hedges. Even though it was winter, they still took time, or employed gardeners, to keep their gardens in tip-top shape. As a car enthusiast, though, I was more distracted by the motors in the driveways. Everything from Land Rovers to Bentleys to Jaguars.

The place Jill was renting until she found somewhere to buy was on a more modest street, although the terraced houses were still fancy. We parked outside hers, which had a white door.

Liam wound down his window and I stuck my head through. 'Okay, chaps, Jill is very upset about what's happened so I think it would be best if I just take Liam in with me. M, are you okay using the time to map out the areas we need to search?'

Liam had been working with me for a year now and knew the score. He was good on the doorstep, calm, pragmatic, sensitive.

Jill opened the door as I was reaching for the bell. 'You must be Tom,' she said, staring over my shoulder at the giant ambulance parked in front of her house. It was pretty unmissable.

She was in her forties, smartly dressed and well spoken. But her eyes were red and puffy from crying, and she looked exhausted, which wasn't surprising. She held out a hand, which felt fragile and limp in my firm ex-policeman's grip.

She led Liam and me through into the living room, where we took a seat on her brown sofa. She was too anxious to sit still so she stood at the doorway, leaning against the frame. She tucked a strand of blonde hair behind her ear as she tried to find the courage to speak.

I helped Jill find the words by asking some simple facts about Jerry. How old he was, what sort of cat he was – inquisitive? A night owl? A cheeky chap or shy and retiring?

Jerry was a five-year-old pedigree with a typical ginger personality – fiery and mischievous. Jill cracked a smile as she told us how he liked to jump on her lap and knead her finest cashmere jumpers with his claws. 'It should drive me mad, but I only love him more for it.' She had been in the UK a matter of weeks. I couldn't imagine how hard it must be to adjust to a new life at the same time as losing your beloved cat.

She told me Jerry meant the world to her and now she had nothing left. 'Have you ever lost someone you love, Tom?' She looked me directly in the eye.

I thought about my Maggie. 'I lost my dog when she was seventeen. She was my best friend.'

Hearing my pain seemed to soothe hers. We were comrades in arms.

She was on the cusp of revealing why she'd had to leave Germany so suddenly. But she wasn't quite ready to do that and opted to make us a cup of tea instead. I've often found that owners brew the wrong drink because they're so overwhelmed by grief. Liam and I politely accepted our mugs of coffee and I made up for the biscuits Liam couldn't eat, him being diabetic. I can never resist a chocolate Hobnob.

Jill returned to her spot in the doorway to the living room, warming her hands with her mug. Suddenly the floodgates opened. Tears were streaming down her face.

'Please find Jerry. My life in Germany was destroyed when I found out my husband was having an affair with his secretary.'

Liam and I weren't expecting that revelation. Liam shifted awkwardly in his seat.

'Jerry is my closest friend now, and I'm scared I'll never see him again.' She wept.

It was heartbreaking to watch. I put my hand on her arm, giving it a gentle squeeze to reassure her that we were there to help. 'Don't worry, we'll get Jerry back.' The amount of pressure and responsibility I was taking on my shoulders was huge but I didn't know what else to do or say.

She wiped the tears away with her sleeve and managed a little smile. 'Thank you so much for coming. What do we do from here?' She sniffed.

I showed Jill the thousand leaflets we had printed of Jerry and explained we would start the distribution where he had gone missing and work outwards in a circle, covering as much ground as possible. I would park Polly the ambulance at various locations where there was a high footfall. The main one would be the local shop. Why? Most people visit their corner store at some point in the day, so it was the perfect place to publicize Jerry's disappearance.

And then I pulled out my secret weapon. 'Can you fetch Jerry's favourite cat biscuits for me?' I asked.

Liam flashed me a quizzical look.

Jill disappeared into the kitchen and came back with a packet of Whiskas Dreamies, liver and chicken flavour. I dug my hand into my trouser pocket and pulled out a piece of electronic equipment. A Dictaphone.

Liam looked surprised.

It was an idea I'd come up with the other day when I was in the garden and overheard my neighbour calling her cat. Why hadn't I thought of it sooner? If we had a recording of an owner calling their pet's name, we could play it while searching back gardens and sheds. Add the sound of an owner shaking the pet's favourite dinner treat and it might just coax the animal out of hiding.

I placed the Dictaphone on the glass coffee table and asked Jill to call Jerry and rattle the biscuits. She was a little self-conscious at first, but I told her to go for it. 'Here, Jerry, good boy, here, Jerry,' she trilled.

It was a good effort, considering how upset she was. I took a few recordings, then placed the Dictaphone in one of the compartments of my combat trousers.

'Can I come with you?' Jill asked.

I was very confident Jerry hadn't been stolen due to the circumstances of his disappearance, so I was happy for her to accompany M on his door-to-door enquiries. If there had been any hint of Jerry having been stolen, I wouldn't have allowed it. Why? Because witnesses would be cagey about saying things with the owner there for fear of recrimination.

I glanced at my watch. Time was ticking by and we needed to be out there searching. 'Come on, then, let's go and find your boy,' I said.

She managed a smile. I could tell she was reassured because it was clear that we cared. We certainly gave two hoots about her and Jerry.

'Go and get your coat, your keys and anything else you need,' I said, heading for the front door. People can forget the simplest things when they're beside themselves with grief.

A couple of minutes later Jill jumped into the ambulance with me and we drove the short distance to her ex-friend's house. He was now 'ex' because she couldn't forgive him for being so careless with her cat.

She seemed immediately to perk up, probably because she knew we were on the case and determined to find Jerry for her. She also commented on the fact we were in an actual ambulance! At least it created a talking point and a momentary distraction from the crisis.

Jill wasn't the only one to comment on Polly. I parked her outside the nearby shops and she attracted a lot of attention from the locals. While Jill helped M put up posters and Liam carried out door-to-door enquiries, I proudly stood next to the ambulance, handing out leaflets to interested residents.

I was certain Jerry was close by and that, if we asked enough people, eventually we would find him. As always, the public were very receptive when they found out we had a missing cat to find. In fact, it can be a bit of a job to stop them talking once they've started. *What's it like being a pet detective? Have you seen* Ace Ventura? *What is the most unusual animal you've had to find?*

Even the shopkeeper joined in, nicknaming me 'Ace'! He was so impressed with our good cause that he said I could park right outside his shop on the tarmacked area all day long. That was a real upgrade from across the road. Especially as there was a steady flow of people coming and going. Similar to the Golden Door, there was the 'Golden Person' – a term I'd coined for the one passer-by who might know something.

Jill's friend's house was a stone's throw away from the hospital, and a short walk from the famous Cheltenham racecourse, so the people I was chatting to were a variety of locals, from horse-racing enthusiasts to families visiting their loved ones in hospital. I remained in constant radio contact with the rest of the team, asking M and Liam for updates. They had covered a lot of ground, but had had no bites.

Frustratingly, although we knocked on about a thousand doors over the next couple of days, we still weren't any the wiser about the whereabouts of Jerry.

I knew we were close, though. Why? Because I was confident he hadn't strayed far and it was just a matter of finding the 'Golden Person' who could lead us to him. I couldn't let Jill lose Jerry, not after everything she'd been through already.

It was Thursday afternoon. I was outside the shop again, handing out flyers, when my radio started crackling.

'What's that, Liam?' I said.

'We think we've seen him!' he boomed.

'Where?'

'Albert Road.'

'I'm on my way. Over.'

I stuffed the posters into my pocket and yanked open the back doors of the ambulance. I jumped in, grabbed the cat basket jumped out and legged it down the street. Albert Road was around the corner. The icy winter air burned my throat as I puffed my way up the street.

'Where is he?' I shouted to Liam.

'Over there, on the porch.'

Liam pointed to a tubby ginger cat that was sunning himself in the winter sunshine. It was hard to tell whether he was Jerry or not. I needed to get a closer look. I inched forward, cat basket in one hand, Dictaphone in the other.

I straightened up from my semi-crouched position as soon as I realized the cat wasn't the least bit wary of me. He was giving me a look through his squinty eyes that spoke volumes. 'Hacked off' would be the polite way to put it. I think he was trying to tell me to get out of his sunshine and hurry up about it.

The recording of his mum's voice would be a decider.

Meanwhile, Liam was on the blower to M and Jill – we needed Jill to identify the cat ASAP.

I pressed play on the recorder.

'Here, Jerry, good boy, here, Jerry!' Jill's voice called.

A mum pushing a pram past gave me a hard stare, then crossed to the other side of the road.

I played it again and this time the cat stirred. He rose onto his paws.

This is it! I thought. *We've got him!*

But the cat didn't come forward. Instead he stretched his

front legs, arched his back and let out a giant yawn. He wasn't the slightest bit interested in what I was up to.

Just as the tape stopped playing, Jill arrived. 'That's not Jerry!' she exclaimed.

'I know.' I sighed, tucking the Dictaphone back into my pocket.

It was the second time we'd been fooled by a doppelgänger.

After a flare of adrenalin and excitement we were all feeling the come-down. It had been a tough three days and the ginger lookalike had been our first lead.

'How are you doing?' I asked Jill. She would be feeling the disappointment more than anyone else.

'I'm scared we won't find Jerry alive – it's nearly a week since he disappeared.' Her voice cracked.

Liam, M and I all tried to console her, promising the search wouldn't end when we went home.

It's the hardest thing for pet-owners to understand – that it can take a few days for the publicity to seep through the community. Jill, like many I'd worked for, was expecting instant results.

My heart felt heavy as we said goodbye that evening. Jill was crying and in desperate need of reassurance that we would find Jerry. How do you walk away from a person in need? With serious difficulty, that's how. It was at times like these that my job as a pet detective blended into friend and counsellor.

I told M and Liam to go back to their families while I sat and had another cuppa with Jill. I nibbled biscuits while she poured out her heart, telling me stories about Jerry. How, when they'd lived in Germany, he'd had his own cushion on the sofa where he would bask in the sunlight streaming through the plate-glass windows. She said it was hard moving back to England, as she didn't have many friends left after years abroad.

I was grateful for hugs and kisses from Jenni and the kids when I got home. There's nothing like hearing about someone else's heartache to make you appreciate what you have.

Jill was in touch a lot over the next couple of days. I'd chat to her on the phone while putting together poster campaigns in the shed.

She was losing hope, but I was still confident Jerry would show up.

Five days after we had first visited Cheltenham, a week since Jerry had disappeared, a mobile hairdresser called me on the hotline. 'I've been cutting the hair of an old gent who doesn't get out much,' he said. I had the phone pinned between my ear and my shoulder, as I used my hands to stack up posters coming off the printer.

'Go on,' I encouraged him. The bloke was calling from Cheltenham.

'Well, while I cut his hair, he told me he'd befriended a ginger cat.'

I stopped what I was doing. The hairdresser now had my undivided attention. 'Go on,' I said.

'He doesn't leave his home much, so he wouldn't have seen your flyers, but the picture on it looks exactly like this ginger cat.'

The old man lived in the area we had been searching, but probably hadn't answered the door when we'd knocked. The mobile hairdresser kindly gave me his address and told me he was called Dennis.

I wanted to jump for joy, but I'd been stung by a doppel-gänger before, so I had to play it cool. I needed to alert Jill, but

I had to warn her not to get her hopes up. I couldn't have a repeat of what had happened the other day – it would break her.

So I trod cautiously, but acted quickly.

Jill picked up the phone on the third ring.

'Don't get too excited, but I think we may have found him,' I said.

She let out a squeal of joy.

I explained what I knew and suggested that she went round to the old man's house and had a look. I told her to take a cat basket with her just in case. I reiterated that it might not be Jerry.

But in my heart I knew it was. All the circumstances seemed to add up.

I put down the phone and waited anxiously in the shed for Jill to call back, hopefully with good news.

Twenty minutes passed, and I was nervously biting my fingernails. Jenni stuck her head around the door, wondering if I wanted to watch *Coronation Street*.

'Just waiting on a call, love.' I told her I wouldn't be too long.

Another twenty minutes passed and I was pacing up and down the shed. I was staring at the phone, willing it to ring.

My heart nearly stopped when it burst into life.

'Hello, Animal Search UK.'

It was only Zoë, asking what time I wanted her in the office the next day.

I put the receiver down, only for the phone to ring again.

This time it was Jill. I couldn't tell at first if she was happy or sad, she was so tearful.

'Is it him? Is it Jerry?'

'It's him, Tom, it's my boy!' she cried. She had him in her arms.

I nearly broke down in tears too.

The old gentleman had been feeding Jerry and looking after

172

him since he had turned up on his doorstep miaowing for help. I felt sorry for him – there is often a casualty in cases like this, especially when the person who has adopted the missing pet gets attached to their new friend. Sad as it was, though, my job was to return Jerry to his rightful owner.

I could hear Jerry miaowing between her little sniffles and sobs.

'He's fine. I've just given him some food, and then we're going to watch my favourite box set,' Jill said.

It sounded like my kind of relaxing evening.

I slept well, as the weight had been lifted off my shoulders. I struggle with sleepless nights just as much as a worried pet-owner. I've been known to wake up in a cold sweat from a nightmare about all the missing pets out there that need my help. My biggest fear is not getting there on time.

I was touched when a thank-you gift from Jill arrived in the post. It was a box of Cadbury's Roses – my second favourite treat after Hobnobs. No sooner had I ripped off the cellophane wrapper than Jenni swiped them, protesting that they weren't good for my waistline. I was allowed one or two after tea. I couldn't argue with Jenni – she wore the trousers in our house.

CHAPTER SEVENTEEN
CHAIRMAN MIAOW

You know when a cat is named after a Chinese Communist leader that he's going to be trouble. Having been a police officer, I wouldn't normally condone trespassing, but in the case of the missing Chairman Mao, there were exceptional circumstances. I'll explain later.

The black cat, who was named after the Chinese dictator because his 'miaow' sounded like 'Mao', had been missing for three days before his owner, Sophie, rang to ask if I could travel into central London to find him.

Jacob and I drove in wintry conditions for four hours to reach the scene of the disappearance. Flurries of snow swirled through the air, hitting the windscreen and melting. The interior heater was blowing on the highest setting and Jacob had his now obligatory energy drink in hand, ready for the five cold hours ahead of searching for our latest AWOL moggie.

When the search car passed Big Ben, we knew the journey was almost over. Polly the ambulance drank fuel, so we couldn't take her everywhere. Jacob had got lucky with the Golden Door on the case of Casper the cat, so I was hoping he would bring the same magic to this search.

I was pleased Sophie lived in a busy, close-knit community in Lewisham, south London, as that increased the chances of someone having seen her little dictator. Thanks to a brief chat with her on the phone, I already had an idea about Chairman Mao's personality. He was a homebody that liked his food. So much so, he had been known to rummage through the bins in the street. One thing that stood out in my mind about this greedy chap was that he could use a cat flap and would let himself in and out of the house during the night. I shared that piece of information with Jacob, who was always ready to brush up on his detective skills.

'If he's familiar with how to use them, he may have entered the cat flap of another house,' I hypothesized. Looking to fill his belly, no doubt. 'We should bear that in mind when we do the search.'

'Gotcha,' said Jacob, enthusiastically.

Sophie's road was busy. She saw us arrive and handed us a parking permit, which she had organized for the day. Jacob parked and prepared the posters and equipment (torch, spare batteries, Dictaphone, microchip scanner, cat basket and cat food). I had just added another item to the equipment list – a pet first-aid kit, a green pouch that attached to your belt containing bandages, swabs, disinfectant wipes and a foil blanket to keep the pet warm and snug. I hoped we would never have to use it, but I liked to be prepared for every scenario.

Meanwhile, I got chatting to Sophie. She was in her late

forties and worked as a teacher in the nearby secondary school. Like many of the owners I meet, she looked exhausted. Her shoulders sagged. Her eyes were puffy and red. She was very despondent. 'Chairman has never done this before. He must have been killed or stolen.' She'd forecast the worst.

I followed her into the warmth of her small living room, which had an eclectic mix of furniture – much like the shed! There was a paisley print 1970s sofa, a second larger sofa, a brown carpet and a black-tiled fireplace. Light was streaming through the big bay windows that looked onto the road.

'Don't worry, it's not always the case. Cats go missing for a number of reasons.' I launched into my list of typical explanations, such as Chairman having got lost, locked in somewhere, adopted. 'If he's been run over, we can find out what happened and give you closure.'

Sophie recoiled with horror. 'I dread the thought of him dying because I wouldn't have anyone left,' she said, her eyes looking over the family photographs on the mantelpiece above the fireplace. Chairman Mao, she said, had been her rock. He had helped her through the long, lonely nights. 'He's supported me through some very tough years.' Sophie's eyes welled with tears.

I knew at that moment it was vital we brought her black cat back to her, if at all possible. At the very least, we would find out what had happened to Chairman Mao so she could have some sort of peace.

At this point my detective nose didn't have any clear leads. I was worried about the traffic in Lewisham: had Chairman Mao met his end on one of the busy roads? However, the cat flap clue was pointing me in the direction of a possible lock-in, inside someone else's property.

I needed a few more clues. I asked Sophie if she would be kind enough to give me a run-down of Chairman Mao's last-known movements and an even better idea about his personality. Jacob joined us just as I was pulling out my notebook.

'What's his normal territory?' I probed.

'I'll show you,' Sophie replied, asking us to follow her upstairs.

It was a spacious three-bedroom terraced house that clearly hadn't been altered in years. Miniature oil paintings of landscapes and seascapes hung along the staircase. The three of us stood in her bedroom staring out of the sash window into her snow-dusted back garden. We got a bird's eye view into the neighbours' gardens as well. Sophie said Chairman Mao used to venture into the two adjacent ones. 'That's about as far as he went.'

That was good news for us because it meant we were covering a small search area. But I never put all my eggs in one basket: there was a chance he might have been spooked and legged it further afield.

'Does he roam around at the front of the house as well?' I enquired.

'No, not normally.'

That put the focus back on the garden, which I would describe as being the size of the penalty area on a football pitch. It was very presentable, with a patio and a white metal table and chair set.

I had more questions for Sophie. 'Can he climb fences?'

'Yes, easily.'

I jotted *Harry Houdini* in my notebook. I noticed some flats to the right of her house with the windows and back door wide open. *The occupants will be worth speaking to.*

But first a few final questions. How long did he usually go out for? Did he go out during the day and at night? Had he ever not returned home before? Did Chairman Mao, to her knowledge, go into other people's houses? Did he wear a collar? Was he microchipped and, if so, were his details up to date? Was he taking any medication?

We'd established that Chairman Mao hung around at the back mainly; he could climb and use a cat flap; he was fit and healthy, didn't stay out at night and didn't venture far.

All the clues were pointing to a lock-in somewhere close by.

Before we got started I asked Sophie if she would be kind enough to pose for a photo that I could give to the local paper. A story there would raise awareness tenfold.

She picked up a silver-framed picture of Chairman Mao from the mantelpiece and clutched it between her hands. The moggie had a very distinctive marking under his nose that looked like a white moustache. I could tell he was a distinguished chap from the way the corners of his 'tache curled upwards as he grinned for the camera.

'Thanks for doing that. I know it was hard for you, but it could help you get your boy back.'

I then asked Sophie to make a recording into the Dictaphone. Her voice croaked with her choked-up tears. 'You're doing really well,' I told her. Jacob chipped in then, telling her she was brave, and once this was out of the way, we could get on with finding Chairman Mao.

Sophie had hired us for one day only, so I was determined to solve the case before darkness fell. It was a race against time. I would take the house to the left of Sophie's property and Jacob would knock on doors in the opposite direction.

As I loaded my pockets with the necessary tools and equipment, I put in a call to the news desk at the *South London Press*. They were as keen as mustard to cover the story of a pet detective and a cat called Chairman Mao, so I rang Zoë and asked her to craft a fact-filled press release.

The first door I knocked on, nobody was in. The letterbox received a carefully folded leaflet with two pictures of Chairman Mao. The second house was divided into three flats. A lot of these London terraced houses have been converted, which is great for the landlord but makes our job trickier. It can be tough reaching all the tenants.

I was most interested in chatting to the owners of the ground-floor flat, as its garden was adjacent to Sophie's. But nobody was at home.

I rang the buzzer for the next flat.

A woman answered the intercom, but I couldn't understand a word she said.

'I'm looking for a missing cat,' I repeated.

There was a long pause, then the sound of the automatic locking system opening. I yanked the front door open and marched inside.

The woman at the other end of the intercom poked her head around the door. Ironically, she was Chinese and didn't speak much English. When I mentioned the name Chairman Mao, her eyes widened.

'He's a cat.' I miaowed for her.

She looked at me as if I was crackers.

But as soon as I held up the poster with a picture of the black cat, she suddenly clicked on to what I was after. 'No, sorry, no cat.' She shook her head.

Just as I was about to leave her with a leaflet, she appeared to remember something. 'Come, come.' She beckoned me to follow her.

She knocked on her neighbour's door, the one I'd tried minutes earlier.

'Cat, cat!' she said with urgency.

'In there?'

'Yes, cat!'

I wondered if she was trying to tell me the neighbour had a cat of their own. But it soon became apparent that that wasn't the case. We both pressed our ears to the wooden door. The noise was faint, but there was no mistaking it: it was a miaow. And, what was more, it didn't sound as if it had come from a happy cat but from one that was trapped.

It was a cry for help.

I needed to investigate the situation, and quickly.

As I radioed Jacob, the Chinese lady did her best to explain that the neighbours had gone on holiday, which made it even more likely that the miaows were coming from Chairman Mao.

The problem now was how were we going to get inside the property? Unfortunately, it wasn't like the case of Rubens, where the neighbour had a spare key. We were well and truly locked out.

It was as if Jacob had handed the lady a can of Red Bull: she was suddenly buzzing with energy and enthusiasm to help us work out this conundrum. She followed us into Sophie's house where I explained to Sophie how we had acquired our new friend. Then we all walked through to the other side of the house together.

All four of us were now shivering in Sophie's back garden, crunching our way across the snow, searching high and low to find a way to look into that flat and confirm whether the trapped cat was actually Chairman Mao.

'What about over here?' Sophie pulled away the vines and thorny brambles hiding a rickety old wooden gate that led onto an alleyway between the two properties.

'Nice one,' I said, yanking it free and scratching my hands in the process.

Jacob, Sophie and the Chinese lady followed me through.

That was one obstacle down. There was one more to go.

'How are we going to get over the fence?' Jacob asked.

As I mentioned earlier, I wouldn't normally condone trespassing, but this was an extreme situation. Whether the cat inside the flat was Chairman Mao or not, the fact remained that it sounded distressed and in desperate need of our assistance. I couldn't wait for the home-owner to return. At the end of the day, what I was doing wasn't strictly legal, but I knew the mitigating circumstances would outweigh the offence, in the unlikely event that I was questioned about it. I was willing to take the chance to save a cat's life.

There was a gap in the fence, which had been covered with chicken wire.

'You can't do that!' Jacob remonstrated.

'Already have, mate,' I said. It hadn't taken much to tug it free. I crouched low and squeezed through. I peered over my shoulder at my gawping audience. 'Wait here, you lot, I won't be a moment.'

Speechless, they stood glued to the spot.

As I dusted off my mucky knees I adjusted my eyes to my new surroundings. It was a small garden, all of which was grass. It wasn't one of those backyards with a door that opens onto it, so we couldn't see inside from where we were standing.

The troops followed me with their eyes as I made my way along the side of the property until I reached the back door. To my joy, I was greeted with a cat flap.

I called to Sophie, 'He could be in here – you never know your luck.'

Sophie started flapping her hands excitedly.

We all had our hearts in our mouths. Even our new friend was rooting for us.

There was no window on the back door for me to look through, so I had to use the cat flap. I got down on all fours and pushed the small square door inwards. I stared through the port-hole into the neighbour's house while the troops cheered me on from the sidelines. I must have looked ridiculous with my bum in the air!

'Chairman Mao,' Sophie called, from across the fence.

'Is it him?' Jacob yelled.

'I dunno, mate.'

There were a few seconds of silence and then the wait was over. Who should come slinking around the corner? Chairman Mao.

'Miaow,' he said, walking up to the cat flap. Then he sat down and stared at me with his big green eyes. The poor chap probably couldn't quite understand why a pair of eyes was gawping at him through a hole in a door.

'Hello, mate!' I introduced myself.

'Miaow,' he replied, twitching his white moustache.

'I've got him!' I yelled, over my shoulder.

'Oh, my baby!' Sophie exploded with happiness, and there followed a round of applause.

My theory about his disappearance had been correct. Chairman Mao had entered the neighbour's property, looking for food, I'm guessing, but unfortunately the cat flap had been set to open only one way so he'd got trapped inside. Owners often use the one-way locking system as a means of keeping their own family cat in overnight.

He was clearly in shock. I gave his little head a stroke through the hole in the door. Meanwhile, Jacob went to fetch a cat basket.

For a moment I wondered how I was going to get Chairman Mao out but, with some gentle encouragement, he gingerly put one paw, then the other through the cat flap.

I gently guided him inside the basket and locked the door. I always make a point of closing the basket properly because we don't want any repeat performances on the way home! On a serious note, if a traumatized cat were to escape while in transit, it could be even harder to find it again: felines can run long distances when they're in shock.

As soon as we were safely back in Sophie's garden, Chairman Mao's mum lifted him into her arms. She had tears in her eyes as she buried her face in his thick black fur and kissed his head. He hadn't eaten or drunk anything for four days so he was thin, weary and shaky on his paws.

Sophie rushed back into her house so she could give Chairman Mao the care and attention he needed. Meanwhile, Jacob and I took our time tacking the chicken wire back across the hole I had squeezed through. Once we were done, it looked as good as new.

And then came the most important bit: celebrating our success. We high-fived each other. It was a brilliant result because we'd been only forty minutes into the search when we'd found him. Even the Chinese lady joined in, cheering and whooping, and we high-fived her too.

It was almost time to say goodbye to Sophie and Chairman Mao, which can be either a jubilant or sad moment at the end of a day's searching. For Sophie it was a happy ending. Only forty-five minutes earlier she had been convinced she would never see her beloved boy again. She had used those very words. And now she was practically skipping in her living room for joy. We'd done that! We had transformed her, and it felt amazing.

Chairman Mao was out of the cage and sitting at the top of the stairs, looking imperious. It was like he'd never been away.

Before we could start to say goodbye, though, Sophie spoke the magic words: 'Would you like a cup of something?'

'It would be rude not to,' I joked.

Chairman Mao let out a miaow of agreement. He proceeded

to lick his paw, then gave his whiskers a good old wash and his ears a groom.

'He's a very proud cat. He likes to look after himself,' Sophie remarked.

'Good man.' I dipped my head to him.

I wouldn't expect any less from a cat with such a ... distinguished name.

CHAPTER EIGHTEEN
SNIFF! ONLY I COULD FIND HIM

I was about to interview a new member for my search team. But the candidate wasn't a person. Oh, no, the prospective recruit was a dog!

Max the German Shepherd was officially the world's first dog trained to track other dogs. His owner, André, had rung the office, out of the blue, suggesting I might need his services on my pet searches. We had common ground to get us chatting: André explained he had worked as a special constable at Stourbridge police station a year or two after I had left the force. His story piqued my interest and I'd agreed to meet him the following weekend at Animal Search HQ, a.k.a. the shed.

I wasn't sure quite what to expect. A dog that finds other dogs? How does that work? All was quickly revealed when André showed up at my house. He was driving a very muddy people-carrier that looked like it had been through the wars, with a big scratch down one side. As he reversed into the drive I was met with the sight of a friendly German Shepherd peering out of the back window, his big tongue sticking out as he grinned with excitement.

'Morning, Tom,' André greeted me. We shook hands, then he opened the boot of the car. André was a handsome chap, with dark hair that was cropped in such a way as to make him look like an army squaddie. He was thirty-two, but looked a lot younger. Max sprang out of the boot with high energy onto my driveway. He wagged his bushy tail enthusiastically and charged at me like a rocket.

'Hello, boy!' I said. As I reached down to stroke his head he stuck his snout into the palm of my hand and snuffled.

After I'd wiped my hand on my trousers we went to the shed. Luckily I was wearing some old combats, as I'd been washing the ambulance prior to André's arrival. 'Come through to the world headquarters. Mind your head,' I said.

We both ducked as we entered the shed.

'Have a pew on a swivelling chair, mate.'

André sat down and Max flopped at his feet, resting his chin on top of André's foot.

'When he's not on search training, he's very relaxed.' André explained Max's chilled-out behaviour.

Two cups of tea later, and plenty of reminiscing about people we both knew in 'the job' – the police force – we got on to why we were meeting. It turned out that, just like me, André had had an affinity with the stray dogs in the kennels when he worked in the force. And, also like me, he had woken up one day and decided that he wanted to be the best in the world at something.

'It's a niche profession you've chosen there, André,' I

commented. 'What made you train Max to find other dogs rather than people?'

He explained that no one else was doing it and he hoped he would be able to corner the market, helping owners find their missing dogs. 'That's why I thought we'd work well together,' he said.

I was dying to know more details. Like how long he had been training Max, and how he had gone about it.

Max yawned. We heard him sigh deeply as he rolled onto his side, stretching out his long legs. He'd clearly heard this bit before.

André explained that he had been working with Hereford and Worcester Animal Rescue. He would borrow a helper and one of their stray dogs for an afternoon. The volunteer would take the dog for a walk and hide out of sight. After a quick phone call to say they were ready, André would let Max off the short lead and attach a much longer one to his collar for the hunt. 'He finds them in less than ten minutes,' he boasted.

André had spent the past six months finely tuning Max's nose to sniff out dog rather than human scent. It was pretty remarkable stuff.

'Can Max find cats as well as dogs?' I asked.

'I haven't tested that, but I feel confident he could with some further training.'

That was music to my ears. To have a dog that could sniff out cats would cut search times down by half. We'd been missing a sniffer dog from the team. I could see it now – uniforms, search cars and Max, nose to the ground weaving in and out of back gardens. We were looking more and more like a police squad by the day. But before I got carried away I needed to see if Max was as good as André made out.

We agreed to meet at a countryside location André sometimes used for his training. He knew the owner of an orchard on the outskirts of Hereford. The apples were harvested for the world-famous cider-makers, H. P. Bulmer. The fruit-filled orchard measured about fifty acres, with plenty of hiding places – perfect for getting lost.

When I got there I waited for André to arrive. He pulled into the layby in his beaten-up people-carrier with his German Shepherd barking and whining in the back. Max knew it was business time, and he couldn't wait to be let loose.

André opened the boot door, and not one but two dogs leaped out onto the muddy verge. It was like Little and Large.

'Who's this little fella?' I crouched to meet a sandy-coloured Staffordshire bull terrier crossed with some other breed that made her a lot smaller than she would have been as a pure Staffy. She was adorable.

'That's Biscuit,' said André, explaining how the Hereford and Worcester Animal Rescue Centre was looking to find her a loving home. He'd borrowed her for the morning to help with our training. How anyone could have abandoned that dog was beyond me.

'Hello, Biscuit.' I reached down and gave her a scratch behind her little floppy ears. She leaned into my hand, enjoying the attention. I could tell we were going to be friends. 'So, how does this work?' I asked André.

He said it was pretty simple: Biscuit and I had to leg it and after about fifteen minutes Max would hunt us or, rather, Biscuit, down. I was usually the one finding pets and now a pet was finding Biscuit and me.

'You ready for this, mate?' I asked my partner in crime.

'Woof,' Biscuit replied, wagging her tail.

Max was pulling hard on his lead, itching to be let off.

I turned to André. 'Happy hunting!'

With that, I clambered over the stile while Biscuit squeezed under. She looked up at me with her big doe eyes, waiting for further instructions. 'Come on, girl! Let's make this a real test,' I said.

With that, we ran off into the trees. We were ducking below the branches, doubling back, zigzagging through the orchard until we were both dizzy. Biscuit was loving it, savouring every moment of being away from the kennels. She bounded along beside me as if her legs were on springs. If I hadn't thought Jenni would hit the roof I would have been tempted to take Biscuit home – I could see the little dog becoming quite a good companion.

After about fifteen minutes and a route that even the SAS would have had trouble following, we found a little wooded area at the corner of the orchard.

'We'll hide in here,' I said to Biscuit. She wagged her tail in agreement.

After a quick call to André to tell him to unleash Max, I took my coat off and spread it on the floor for us both to sit on. Biscuit was panting heavily. We must have run and walked about a mile, and I had annoyingly forgotten the dish for her to have a drink. But I did have a bottle of water in my pocket so I cupped one hand and poured a little stream of cold, refreshing water into it. Biscuit lapped with enthusiasm and made quite a mess on my trousers, sloshing water everywhere.

I dug deep in my pocket, hoping I had some treats stored away for times like this. 'It's your lucky day.' I grinned, pulling out two Digestive biscuits.

Biscuit, true to her name, was now 110 per cent focused on my little snack and started to dribble as I bit into the first. I spoke with my mouth full to my new friend. 'Do you want the other one?' Biscuit's tail started wagging and she licked her nose.

'There you go.' Biscuit gently took the crumbling Digestive

from my hand and snapped it in her jaws. She half fell to the ground, as she crunched the bit she had in her mouth. I picked up and fed her the second piece.

'You're a gentle little thing, aren't you?' I stroked her head. 'Right, we've got to be quiet now. Will they find us?' I chatted away as I used to with my Maggie.

I sat, legs outstretched, with Biscuit lying next to me, her head resting on my thigh. It was as if we'd been friends for years. I hoped she'd find the lovely home she deserved.

After ten minutes, I heard André's voice: 'Find her, boy, find her . . .'

My heart started to race. It was like being a convict on the run. André and Max must have been belting along to get within earshot so quickly.

'Good lad, find her, find her.' André's voice was closer now.

We were tucked around a corner out of sight. Biscuit stood up and her tail wagged furiously.

'Sssh!' I signalled to Biscuit with one finger on my lips. I don't suppose she knew what it meant, but that's what fugitives do in the movies, isn't it?

Next, I heard Max panting and the sound of running feet, as André tried to keep up with his sniffer dog. We were seconds away from being caught.

'Good boy! Good boy!' André cheered, as Max rounded the corner and discovered us both.

Biscuit was bouncing up and down on the spot – excited that friends were joining our picnic.

'Well done, Max, good boy,' André said, as he patted him firmly on his head, then unclicked his harness and threw Max's favourite ball for him to have as a reward. I let go of Biscuit's lead and she sprinted off after Max. The two dogs had a good old run around, tussling each other to the ground and chasing one another through the trees. They were the best of buddies, even though they had only just met.

'Outstanding, mate,' I said to André. 'We took a really obscure route so you did very well.'

We took our time heading back through the orchard to the car so Biscuit could get a good run around. I didn't want to say goodbye to my new friend – we were getting on so well. I lifted her back into André's boot and gave her a cuddle goodbye. She whined a little, making it known she'd miss me too. It was like saying goodbye to the dogs in the police kennels all over again.

I closed the boot and two wet black noses pressed up against the window.

'Have you got the number of the rescue centre to hand?' I asked André. I tapped it into my mobile so I could give them a call later that week. I wanted to keep tabs on Biscuit. Just like the pets that go missing, I needed to know she was all right and being looked after by a loving family.

'So, what now?' André asked, as he opened the driver's door.

What we needed now was a real lost dog to find. We agreed we'd test Max's detection skills on the next canine search that came along. Little did we know then that it was going to be the largest search in terms of manpower and duration I'd ever undertaken and Max would really be put to the test.

CHAPTER NINETEEN
SHERLOCK BONES

'Okay, listen up everyone,' I said, zipping up my high-visibility jacket. 'It'll be most effective to comb the local area by taking a village each.' I traced my finger across the map.

I felt a pang of apprehension. Not only were we about to embark on Animal Search's largest case to date in terms of manpower and resources, but we were also being filmed for a Channel 4 *Cutting Edge* documentary. I couldn't let the fact I was going to be appearing on national TV go to my head, though. I had a job to do and that was finding missing Shetland Sheepdog, or Sheltie, Spencer.

'This is Spencer,' I said, holding up the mug shot.

My team of eight leaned in to have a better look. The cameraman zoomed in. I began debriefing them on our emergency call-out. 'Spencer has been missing for twelve hours . . .' I explained that our search was of the utmost urgency. The Lassie lookalike had disappeared at Strensham Services, near Junction 8 of the M5, one Friday afternoon in May 2011. He'd just been adopted by Trish and Terry from a family who could no longer look after him. Terry was making the two hundred-mile drive with Spencer to his new home in North Wales when he had stopped for a break at the service station in Worcestershire. Spencer, who was most likely disoriented by his journey, had slipped his collar and legged it. Terry had spent hours trying to find him but with no joy. I'd got the call for my pet detective skills late the night before.

Poor Terry was devastated that he had lost their new friend before his wife had even had a chance to meet him. Both he and Trish had driven back the hundred-odd miles from their home to join me for the search.

I glanced across at the heartbroken couple. Trish had tears in her eyes as I explained to my team all the hazards Spencer was facing out there alone.

Terry was chewing his thumbnail. I could tell he was weighed down with guilt. He'd known Spencer for just a couple of hours but I could tell he had already grown attached to the two-year-old dog and was feeling bad for letting him slip away.

'It's not your fault, mate,' I told him. 'Spencer hadn't got to know you as his owner. It could have happened to anyone.'

Terry looked at the ground. Trish squeezed his arm tenderly. In my job it is hard not to get emotionally involved. The thought of Spencer being scared and alone almost brought a tear to my eye, but I had to stay strong. All those years as a copper on the beat had forced me to toughen up. I had to stay focused on the facts, two of which were troubling me more than anything else: the motorway and the weather. Both were equally dangerous. One wrong move and Spencer could end up in the path of a speeding car, and the heatwave we were having meant it wouldn't be long before he was facing dehydration.

I cleared my throat and started on the procedure. 'I suggest we all buy maps from the local service station to mark out the areas we have to cover. Lorna, would you go with Terry and Trish to a village and help search for Spencer there?' I asked.

Lorna was the newest addition to the team. She'd been on four missing-cat cases, but this was her first dog search.

'Yes.' She nodded, joining the couple.

Terry and Trish seemed relieved to have been handed something to do. It was clear that they wanted to do whatever they could to help.

'Speak to as many people as possible. Everyone from a dustbin man to a paper boy to the local vicar,' I went on. 'Search every field, barn and back garden. This dog has to be hiding somewhere.'

I felt like a general readying his troops for battle. We were going to fight tooth and nail to get Spencer back safely.

I had a mountain of equipment to help us with the search. We were armed with hundreds of posters I'd printed off as soon as I'd got the call the night before. They had the usual eye-catching red banner running across the top and a photo of Spencer underneath. Even though he looked cute and cuddly, he came with a warning in the small print. I described the black, brown and white pooch as friendly, but members of the public should be aware that he would be scared and might lash out in fear.

I glanced at my watch. It was eight a.m. already. It looked like it was going to be a clear, sunny day, but in my job I've learned you have to be prepared for anything. 'Can we have the waterproof posters to go outside?' I directed the team, just in case the weather turned. 'And can you put the clips on them before we get going, please?' I asked Liam. I was a stickler for procedure.

A lot of the crew, like Liam, M and Lucas, were part-timers, called out as and when I needed extra boots on the ground, so they wouldn't necessarily know all of my formalities. I sometimes forgot that I wasn't on the police force any more and had to have a word with myself about not being too tough on my troops.

'The paper posters are for inside, like shop windows,' I said. It sounded obvious, but you get the best results if you keep instructions clear and simple.

'We're going to need lots of Blu-tack for the posters, so check you have some in your vehicle. Lorna, you should have that.'

Lorna gave me a nod to indicate she was on the case.

My team now had a list of at least fifty things they needed to check before going on a search: we've been caught out by the silliest thing at a crucial moment. I make sure everyone has two pencils in case one breaks, and a pencil sharpener. Pencils are preferable to pens, as they still work in the rain.

Now it was time for the facts.

'Spencer was last seen at four thirty p.m. on Friday on a country road that runs parallel to the motorway.' I drew my finger along the map.

Even though we were currently standing in a busy service station, which hundreds of people passed through each day, we were surrounded by acres of deserted farmland. Our only advantage was that the terrain was flat, which meant it would be easier to spot Spencer.

My description suddenly prompted Terry's memory. 'He headed off down there,' he blurted out, pointing to a country lane. 'I ran after him for as long as I could see him, but he was just too quick for me.' I could hear sadness in his voice.

He didn't look like the sort of guy who would be emotional. In fact, he looked like the kind you wouldn't want to get into a fight with. He was almost six feet tall, well-built, with a shaved head and stubble. But that was the magic in my job – I got to see how animals brought out the softie in even the toughest people.

'Thanks, mate.' I patted Terry on the back. Being a pet detective is sometimes just as much about offering support and giving confidence to the owners as finding their missing animals. I told Terry not to lose faith. 'My motto is, although it can be desperate at times, don't give up hope, because you can be amazed by what can happen.'

Terry feigned a smile. I could tell he was putting on a brave face for Trish.

It was now time to dispatch my troops to the local villages. I paired everyone off, then made my way to my pet-mobile – Polly the ambulance. A big case like this called for the big motor. Polly would attract a lot of much-needed attention, which could help us find Spencer.

The cameraman clambered into the passenger seat next to me. He pointed the lens at my face and I suddenly felt hot under the collar as he recorded my every move. Channel 4 were calling the documentary *The Pet Detectives* and would be featuring Animal Search UK alongside two other characters – a man who dealt in finding missing exotic animals, and Colin, who specialized in more 'messy' animal cases. When I say messy, I mean disputes over ownership, when a couple breaks up or gets divorced – something I steer well clear of. This was a golden opportunity for me to shine. I had to put my best foot forward.

'The major factor in this search is how dangerously close we are to the motorway,' I disclosed to the cameraman, as I turned the keys in the ignition and got going.

Admittedly, dogs were much easier to find than cats, but I'd never had to carry out a search in such a precarious location. The longer Spencer was missing, the more scared and disoriented he would become. He might end up bolting straight into the path of a speeding car.

'And let's not forget the heatwave we're having. Poor Spencer will be thirsty. Time is of the essence,' I warned.

I'd never been on a search where the dog didn't know the owner. Spencer had known Terry for just a matter of hours before he'd slipped his lead. Terry's voice would be of no comfort to the poor thing.

'Are you hopeful you'll catch Spencer?' the cameraman probed.

That was an easy one. 'Yes, I am.' I wasn't going home without him.

My thoughts on how I was going to nail the case spun in my head as I pulled up in the nearby village, which was approximately two and a half miles from the services. I reached inside the glove compartment for my walkie-talkie.

'Tom calling Sandy, are you receiving? Over.' My voice crackled through the radio. Sandy was a volunteer from Sheltie Dog Rescue: she'd jumped on board as soon as she'd found out we were looking for a Sheltie.

'Sandy receiving, over,' came the reply, a few seconds later. She'd used walkie-talkies before and knew the jargon.

I reported my findings: 'There is no sign of Spencer on the road where he initially escaped. I'm now going to start door-to-door enquiries in my allocated area.'

'Roger that. Over.' Sandy signed off.

Our teams spent the next eight hours handing out a thousand leaflets, putting up posters, knocking on doors and speaking to every man and his dog, quite literally.

'Have you seen this dog?' I said, holding up our Missing poster. 'He looks like Lassie but is darker than Lassie, and he's a bit smaller,' I explained to the occasional puzzled member of the public. It's not often you come across a man in uniform, looking for a missing pet.

We stopped horse-riders, walkers, delivery drivers, shop-keepers, landlords, vicars, anyone in the rural community who could possibly have any information about Spencer. Sadly, no one had spotted him. We headed home exhausted – and disappointed.

It was hard breaking the news to Terry and Trish. I had the same feeling in the pit of my stomach as when I used to be a policeman delivering bad news on the doorstep. I tried to find the silver lining, though. 'No news is good news,' I told the couple.

Trish wiped a tear from her eye. She looked exhausted from our day of searching and they still had another hundred miles to drive before they were home.

'We'll call if we get any news. Try to get some rest.' I smiled reassuringly.

But poor Terry and Trish had to endure three more sleepless nights without any good news. We'd combed the area from back to front but without even one sighting of Spencer. I was starting to despair. What else could we do? I was using every resource possible.

The couple seemed so distressed I couldn't bring myself to tell them the truth – that the chances of finding Spencer alive were quickly running out.

Spencer would be very vulnerable after four nights without water during a heatwave. I just hoped he'd found somewhere safe to rest and conserve his energy rather than be wandering around panic-stricken.

By the end of the fifth day, I'd almost given up hope.

I radioed through to the team that I was going to take a final sweep of some disused farm buildings, then call it a night. My feet were on fire from the miles I'd covered and my heart was heavy.

The radio crackled loudly. I swivelled the knob to turn it down – and then the magic words came through.

'We've had a sighting of Spencer, over.'

Finally, a breakthrough! A member of the community had notified one of our team that they had seen him that morning in a field only four hundred yards from where he'd first gone missing.

I crunched Polly's gears into reverse and turned back down the country lane. The engine was purring loudly. My heart was pounding wildly. The clock was ticking and I needed to make use of every daylight hour left.

Now there had been a concrete sighting, it was time to call on our secret weapon: to unleash the UK's first ever dog trained to track other dogs.

'Hello again, mate.' I greeted André and Max at the location where Spencer had last been seen. Sadly the documentary team were busy getting footage of the others. They were about to miss out on what I hoped would be the first ever dog-finding-a-dog footage.

Everything was riding on Max finding Spencer.

And Max couldn't wait to be let out of the boot. He was yapping and bouncing around, eager to get on the scent. He bounded out of his cage onto the scorched earth. He came to say hello to me and licked my hand. His big ears were pricked and alert, and after days of disappointment I felt a flutter of excitement that we might find Spencer alive.

André crouched down and held out Spencer's collar. Max edged forward gingerly, sniffing the leather. His head cocked to the side and then he nose-dived into the grass. He sounded like a truffle-hunting pig as he hoovered through the undergrowth. He looked up at us both as if to tell us he'd found Spencer's scent, and then he was off. Max bolted across the field with André, holding on to his lead for dear life, and I was puffing behind.

'We're on to something here,' shouted André, as I tried to keep up.

'I think you might be right, mate,' I yelled excitedly, hurdling the fence.

Max screeched to a halt as we entered a wooded area, almost sending me tumbling into the back of André. He lifted his nose into the air, had another good sniff, then charged off through the trees.

It was like a circus. We couldn't always go where Max ran. He was on a long lead, but we often had to let that go, dash round the obstacle, and quickly catch him again. We ran through brambles and hedges, our legs and arms cut to pieces. Max was hungrily following something, and we were confident we would find Spencer in a shelter or a hideaway or injured somewhere. Suddenly Max began yelping with excitement. We were certain we had struck gold.

'We've got him now,' hollered André, as we bounded out into a large field of corn stubble.

'Hang on a minute, mate.' I folded double, gasping for breath. We'd been running for two hours, possibly the most exercise I'd had in ten years. I looked up, but there was no sign of Spencer, just a massive field the size of six football pitches.

'Where is he, boy?' André held out Spencer's collar to remind Max of the scent. Our little tracker took another whiff, trotted a few yards through the stubble, then started wagging his tail. The trail had run cold.

My heart sank.

'I really thought we had him then.' André sighed.

Still trying to catch my breath, I puffed out a few positive notes. 'Spencer must have been here recently or spent a lot of time in the area,' I concluded.

We'd left Sandy back at our Missing Pet Information Unit. She had been surveying the fields with the binoculars while we'd been sprinting across them.

'Nothing to report here, Sandy, over.' I called through the disappointing news on the walkie-talkie.

It was nine p.m. by the time we headed back, and we could barely see where we were treading for lack of light. The sound of the motorway helped guide us to our meeting point, but it was also a gruesome reminder of what might have been poor Spencer's fate. I wasn't sure if we were going to find him alive, or find him at all now.

CHAPTER TWENTY
BARKING UP THE WRONG TREE

The next morning I instructed the team of eight to meet me near the cornfield as it was the only lead we had. I was sitting in the ambulance, eating a sandwich as I waited for the troops to roll up, when I saw a black blob on the horizon.

'That's him!' I spluttered, through a mouthful of BLT.

I thought I was seeing things. It was a roasting hot day, and the black dot was shimmering like a mirage, but when it moved I was certain it was Spencer.

'We've got him,' I belted down the walkie-talkie. 'Are you receiving? Over.' I was so excited I'd forgotten the formalities.

A glimpse through the binoculars proved I was right – it was Spencer. The poor chap looked traumatized and disoriented as he stood wavering in the middle of the field. He'd been without food, water and contact with humans for seven days: he was bound to be panicking. The stubble was clearly hurting his paws as he kept licking his pads. My heart went out to the poor thing. If only he knew we were trying to help him. This was one of those moments when I had to steel myself against rising emotion.

I had to think practically instead: now we knew where he was, how could we catch him? I rang the team again, urging them to get down to the meeting point, pronto. I thought through my strategy as I was waiting and decided our best chance of catching Spencer was to herd him into a corner, then pounce on him.

'I'm going to name the sides of the field one, two, three and four,' I said, pointing to the vast expanse in front of us. 'So, if I radio through that I'm going to side one, we'll all know where I'm heading.' The team nodded in agreement, then paired off to their allocated positions.

Spencer was crouched in the centre of the field, watching our every move. He was panting heavily, which was a sign of distress. You'd think we would be able to catch him, but he wasn't responding to his name, and every time we were within retrieving distance, he legged it the other way. I knew he was running because he was frightened but he wasn't making it easy for us.

'He's a real nuisance,' I said in exasperation. 'Tom calling Lucas, are you receiving? Over.'

It was time to reel out the traps.

Lucas had three dog traps in the back of his vehicle. They are big cages designed to catch canines safely and humanely. The contraption works much like our cat baskets: we put food inside, the dog is lured in, treads on a little platform and then the door closes behind it. It's like a guillotine motion, but slow enough not to hurt the dog if it is caught underneath. Lucas spaced the traps evenly over the vast field, then drove across the stubble, depositing a trail of meat that would lead back to the cages.

Spencer didn't fall for it, though. He wouldn't go anywhere near the bait, or us. We were running out of ideas.

As night crept in, we retreated to the ambulance for a debrief. I put the kettle on the gas stove and warmed everyone a much-needed cup of soup. We put our feet up in the back of the van and reflected on the day's events.

'The problem is this field. It's too big.' I sighed. 'Every time we get close to him, he scoots off in another direction. What we could really do with is a motorbike! If there were two of us on the bike, one with a net trying to catch him . . . he wouldn't be able to outrun that!'

Liam, M and Lucas agreed. It was food for thought, something to add to the search equipment wish list. I proudly told the team I once represented the police force in cross-country bike competitions and would love to get back in the saddle.

'What we need is a tranquillizer dart,' Liam chipped in.

'Good idea, Liam. If you could look into how we could go about hiring someone to do that for us tomorrow, that would be great,' I said. I let out a yawn. It was getting late and we were all beyond exhausted. Goodness knows how Trish and Terry were feeling. Waiting by the telephone for news can be as exhausting as doing the legwork.

The three of us took it in turns to check on the traps every thirty minutes, desperately hoping that Spencer would take the bait. He had been crouched in the same spot for the past three hours, panting heavily. He was clearly scared and traumatized, and I was afraid he wouldn't last much more than a day or two without water.

We were so worried that Lucas slept in the makeshift bed in the back of the ambulance that night and I checked into a bed-and-breakfast at three a.m. so I could be within a stone's throw of Spencer if need be. I woke up feeling incredibly anxious.

It was the crack of dawn. We were back on Spencer's tail and the camera crew were on mine.

'This has become extremely serious,' I spoke into the camera.

Lucas was driving Polly this time, so I could be ready to spring out at any moment. The Channel 4 team followed close behind in convoy. I had no idea how I was coming across on TV, but at that moment I didn't care: catching Spencer was all that mattered.

'Try turning in here, mate.' I pointed to a layby near the field where we had last seen Spencer.

Suddenly, out of nowhere, the Sheltie broke through the hedge onto the country road. Lucas slammed on the brakes and we skidded to a halt. From the smell of burning rubber, the TV crew had done the same! I had to think on my feet as I had just seconds to catch him. I spotted a sausage roll in the side pocket – dogs can't resist meat. 'Get as close as you can, mate,' I yelled. Adrenalin was pounding through me.

I chucked the pastry out of the window, hoping it would take Spencer's fancy for long enough to pounce on him. But Spencer was having none of it and ran the other way. He still had a lot of spring in his paws despite having been on the run.

'Get him,' I yelped. Lucas crunched the gears and reversed up the road while I bounded out and hid behind a large rock. Spencer was now nicely sandwiched between us. He wasn't getting away from us this time.

He stopped in his tracks. He lifted his head and sniffed the air.

'C'mon, Spencer, you can do it,' I muttered under my breath, willing him to walk towards me.

My wish was granted – Spencer started trotting along the country lane to where I was hiding. *Hang on a minute – I've no equipment to hand. What the hell am I going to do when he gets near me?* I panicked. My plan was to wait until he passed and just dive on him. Not the most sophisticated technique, but I didn't have much choice.

As Spencer got close to the rock, I peeped out. He looked in my direction. I quickly ducked down.

I've got him! My heart was racing.

Spencer was now only five feet away. He was so close I could almost touch him. I saw the whites of his eyes as he stared at me, and I gazed back at him. He then gave me a look as if to say, 'Not yet, mate', turned around and legged it.

'You little beggar!'

Spencer scampered through the hedge into the enormous field we had been staking out. It was pointless chasing after him: we were back to square one.

The fiasco had been caught on camera. *At least it'll make good viewing*, I thought.

The troops arrived and I told them the bad news. Liam had been out that morning to get some fluorescent netting that looked like something you might find at the back of a football goal. We draped it across the hole in the fence with the intention of shooing Spencer into it.

I peered through the binoculars to get a closer look at the dog's condition. The poor chap was suffering. His legs were wobbly. His head was drooping. He would stand up, walk a few yards, then collapse onto the stubble. I signalled to the team to close in on him. Hopefully this time he would be too weak to run away.

'Sandy, hold your position,' I urged.

'I'm holding my position, over,' she replied, from across the field to my right.

'Liam's coming to me. Lucas is going to the road closest to the service station,' I explained. 'Lucas, can you get M to run to Sandy and then towards me? So that's M to Sandy, then back towards me, over.'

I crouched, like a big cat stalking its prey, as the others herded Spencer into the net. 'Come on, boy, that's it . . .' I coaxed, under my breath.

Spencer started running towards me.

'That's it, Spencer, into the net.' My heart was in my mouth.

'Get him!' I yelled. The team charged like the cavalry.

Spencer bolted into the netting. His legs became tangled, he toppled onto his side, and we all dived around the edges to keep him contained.

'Gotcha!'

Poor Spencer didn't even wriggle, he was so exhausted. I hugged him like my life depended on it; I wasn't letting him go until he was in the back of the van with the door securely locked.

I could tell Spencer was relieved to be saved. He looked up at me with eyes that said, 'You got me. Thank you.' The poor dog had been eight days and seven nights without shelter, food or water. It was a miracle he was still alive.

I slipped a lead around his neck and gave a gentle tug in the direction of the ambulance. I didn't have to ask Spencer twice, he traipsed behind obediently. As I led him away I was greeted with a round of applause from the TV crew and some local dog-walkers who had stopped to watch the commotion.

'You're safe now, mate.' I chatted to him along the way. He blinked at me several times and licked his chops – his way of telling me what he needed.

He was so weak I had to lift him into the back of the ambulance. 'Here you go, boy.' I put a big bowl of water under his nose and gave him a rub behind his ears. He lapped it up within seconds.

As I closed the back doors I felt a massive surge of relief. It could so easily have gone the other way.

The job wasn't over yet, though. There was something very

important left to do. I peered through the window at Spencer as I dialled Terry and Trish.

'Hello?' Trish answered anxiously.

'I've got some news for you,' I announced.

'What's happened?' Trish gasped, her voice wobbling. Poor Trish had already braced herself for the worst. She must have thought I was calling to say Spencer hadn't made it.

Moments like this were pure gold. They made all the hard work worth while.

'I'm looking at Spencer as we speak.'

'You're not!' she gasped, in disbelief.

'Yup, we've got him,' I said proudly, with a Cheshire Cat grin on my face.

Trish burst into tears and I had a lump in my throat. It was a very special moment I'll never forget.

Next came a tidal wave of questions. She was asking everything from how Spencer was doing to when they would be able to have him home. I explained to Trish we would be sending Spencer to the vet for a once-over and would deliver him to her door the following day.

As I got ready to drive off, M turned up, waving a newspaper. 'We've made the paper!' he shouted. He passed me the copy of the *Worcester News*. 'They've likened our search for Spencer to a major manhunt because of the number of men we had out in the field and the fact we even had a dog chasing through the forest after him.' He chuckled.

'Next time we'll be on motorbikes, though!' I said.

I was already thinking of ways to catapult my pet detective agency to another level.

CHAPTER TWENTY-ONE
CAT-ASTROPHE

I'd overstretched myself. One minute Animal Search UK was flying high with multiple press and TV appearances, the next I was £15,000 into my overdraft and struggling to pay the bills.

I was on such a high from watching Animal Search grow that I didn't factor in all the money I was spending to keep it running. I'd shelled out too much on equipment. I'd hired too many staff. I'd converted too many pet-mobiles. I also had the rent to pay on a new office I'd opened in Hereford town centre. I still had the shed, but we couldn't all fit into it now.

The biggest problem, though, was that I'd left my traffic officer job at the Highways Agency, thinking I could manage on one income.

Sadly, I was wrong. I needed my salary to keep afloat my family and the business I was passionate about.

I'm sure anyone who's had money problems can sympathize with me when I say it can be incredibly derailing. My stress level skyrocketed. I couldn't switch off. I was constantly thinking about the business – when I was in bed, when I was driving the car, when eating a meal with Jenni and the kids or while watching telly. It was becoming unhealthy.

Something else that was unhealthy was my diet. I started to comfort-eat, bingeing on pastries, croissants and toast with lashings of jam. My weight ballooned from seventeen stone to nearly twenty in a matter of months. I felt lethargic, out of breath, and generally tired but wired. The GP gave me a check-up and said my blood pressure was through the roof. Not surprising, really, considering I was working fourteen-hour days seven days a week. He prescribed some pills that I was to take daily to lower it.

I took on board the doctor's warning, but it was hard to control my worry. I would stay up late into the night thinking of ways I could improve the business model, make it more profitable. I was trying everything so I wouldn't have to sack my staff. They had become my friends and I would be devastated if they had to go.

When I wasn't bickering with Jenni over money, she was worrying about my health and well-being.

'Put your phone away, Tom.' She sighed deeply as I rolled over to check my messages for the umpteenth time. I tucked my mobile under my pillow only to pull it out ten minutes later. The glow of the screen lit up our bedroom. Jenni huffed, turning onto her side.

'I'm sorry, Jen, just one more minute,' I said, furiously tapping away, making some notes. It was now past midnight and my brain was in overdrive.

I thought of all the ways I could save money without saying goodbye to the team. With deep regret, I decided I had no choice but to sell my most prized possession.

'Please, Daddy, don't sell Polly,' Sam begged.

Polly the ambulance had become one of the family. Not only had she been invaluable during our searches but we had also taken her away with us for camping holidays. She was the only one of the search vehicles I could get some decent money for – a grand, if we were lucky.

'I'm sorry. I have to, kids, but one day we'll get an even better one and go on more holidays together,' I promised them.

We were sitting at the table having tea.

Even Jenni, who had been pushing me to save money, was in shock.

'She'll make a lovely campervan for someone.' I smiled weakly. I'm a glass-half-full kind of guy – I had to see the silver lining in that moment so it wouldn't become too sad.

Jenni put her knife and fork down and cupped her hands around mine. She looked me in the eye and said, 'Tom, we've worked so hard to get this far. We can't afford to lose the organization. Polly is lovely, and it will be sad to see her go, but if it saves the business then that's what we've got to do.'

I loved Jenni: she always said the right thing when I needed her most. To lift the mood, I suggested we had one last ride in the old ambulance together.

'Right now?' Jenni asked.

'Yup, come on, let's go!' I rounded up everyone for our treat.

Sam sat in the front with me, and Polly jumped in the back with Jenni. We went to Lock's Garage on the Abergavenny road. They do wonderful ice creams there with a chocolate flake. We ate them in the back with the doors open looking out onto the fields. We talked about the good times we'd had with the ambulance over the past year or so. It was a bubble in time away from all the stress that had been going on.

The next day, Malc from over the road washed Polly for the last time in our driveway. After a clean and a polish she was looking perfect for her photo shoot. I reluctantly pulled the small digital camera out of my pocket and snapped away from every angle.

Every shot held a different memory: the front, from which we'd removed the blue lights; the back, where we'd replaced the smashed windows; the sides, where we had carefully designed and affixed all the stickers and the ASUK logo; and the cab, where we'd celebrated many a success on the way back from an intense and tiring search.

I then loaded the photos onto eBay, where I put her up for sale. The starting bid was ninety-nine pence and there was no reserve.

In the write-up I couldn't help but mention what she had been used for – that 'she has some tales to tell' – partly because I thought it might spark interest, but also because I was so proud of how I had transformed her. She had certainly had a colourful history – first saving people, then pets.

The mileage was still low, which was a selling point. The only thing I may have left off the description was that she did just ten miles to the gallon! She drank fuel like it was going out of fashion.

On day five of the auction the price had risen to six hundred pounds, which was okay, but not quite what I wanted, so I held out. On day seven it had risen again to my target of a thousand.

Then the price suddenly jumped to twelve hundred. Five minutes later it was at fifteen hundred.

'Jen, come and have a look at this,' I shouted.

She rushed over with Sam and Polly in tow. They all gathered around the screen and we watched with amazement as all these people started bidding on Polly. The price was going up and up. With three minutes left to go before the auction closed it had risen to an almighty three thousand pounds.

I nearly fell over.

Jenni and the kids were so excited they were jumping up and down. I couldn't quite believe my eyes.

'This is brilliant! It's really going to help the business!' Jenni squealed. She was right: three grand would pay the staff wages for a month. We'd gone from feeling really low to being on a high within minutes.

After exchanging a few details with the buyer, the kids asked where the old ambulance's new home would be.

'Is it so someone can go on holiday, Daddy?' Polly asked.

I told her I didn't know, as you only have a limited amount of information to hand on eBay. I was very curious myself.

'Can we see her go?' Sam and Polly asked.

I told them not to worry, I'd arrange for the ambulance to be picked up when they were both at home.

The buyer, who was called John, probably wasn't expecting the whole family to be there when we picked him up in Polly at the station a couple of days later. He spotted us immediately, for obvious reasons, although he stood out himself. He had long blond dreadlocks and was wearing tie-dyed clothes. He was about forty-five, and I wondered if he was a New Age traveller.

We shook hands and I drove us home so we could sign the paperwork.

John was an interesting chap who had had a colourful life travelling all over the place. Since the ambulance was such a quirky vehicle it seemed only right she was being passed on to someone equally unusual.

We had a cup of tea and some biscuits around the kitchen table and I couldn't help but relive all the wonderful search stories that had involved Polly. I recalled how nearly a year ago I had lifted Spencer into the back after rescuing him from near death. I told John that the ambulance had been on TV for a *Cutting Edge* documentary, which he was impressed with. I spoke fondly of the process of finding her in the St John's yard and the restoration project.

'So what are your plans for Polly?' I asked. I was hoping he wasn't going to say 'to travel around Europe' because I'd have to break the news that she might not make it, being twenty years old.

When he told me he would be taking her to a few music festivals, I breathed a sigh of relief.

Although it was sad, it was a nice send-off. When it was time for John to go, we all stood on the drive waving Polly off as if she was a good friend we weren't going to see for a while. Sam was tearful. He reached his arms up to me, so I picked him up and gave him a cuddle. We watched as she went over the speed bumps and disappeared into the distance, to her new life.

The sale kept the wolf from the door, but despite massive cost-cutting and endless hours of staying up late to find ways to make the business more efficient, I was forced to let go of one of our team.

I spent hours agonizing about it, but there was no way around it. What was even harder was that the guy was a really good mate.

'How am I going to break the news, Jen?' I asked. She told me

just to be honest and direct. It was like pulling off a plaster –
better to do it quickly, for everyone's sake.

The next morning my boots felt like lead as I made my way
from the car park to the office. After making myself a cup of tea,
I approached the workstation. 'Could we have a word in private,
mate?' I asked Jacob.

From his expression, I think he knew what was coming. We
disappeared around the corner to the little sectioned-off area I
had in my new office. I closed the door so we could speak pri-
vately. We both took a seat but I couldn't look him in the eye, I
felt so ashamed. I took a deep breath and pushed out the air
through pursed lips.

'Jacob, I'm really sorry, mate,' I started, 'but we're just not
getting the work we need to keep you on.' What made things
worse was that I knew he'd given up a decent job to work for me
full time.

Jacob looked really sad, which was heartbreaking. He admit-
ted the job hadn't been entirely what he had thought it would
be, though. That he was hoping he'd be helping me more with
searches rather than the admin side of things.

'That was where I went wrong. I should have made clearer
what the job would entail.' I took the blame. It was my fault for
taking him on full time instead of whenever I needed him for a
search.

I told Jacob I'd pay him a month's wages upfront and there
was no need to stay: he could use the time and money to find
another job. It was the least I could do. I hated leaving a friend
in the lurch. 'I don't want to do this, Jacob, but if I don't, Animal
Search will go under.'

'Okay, no worries, I understand,' he said glumly. Without me prompting him, Jacob stood up and said, 'I'll get my things together and go.'

The office fell silent. Everyone pretended to stare at their computer screens as Jacob made his way back to his desk. Once he'd filled his bags with his belongings I followed him out to the car. He put his bits and bobs on the back seat, then turned to me with an outstretched hand. 'Don't be a stranger,' he said, as we shook. It was a kind thing to say, considering how he must have been feeling. Before he could get too upset, he got hurriedly into his car and drove off.

I felt awful. Nobody wants to see their mate upset like that.

I went back inside and sat by myself for half an hour in the reception area, gathering my thoughts. I was relieved to be free of the financial burden but very sad that Jacob wouldn't be working with me any more.

I hoped he would find another job easily so there would be no hard feelings.

And I hoped all the heartache had been worth it and that I'd done enough to save the business.

CHAPTER TWENTY-TWO
WAGGY TALES

I tapped my pin number into the cash machine. It was six thirty one morning in 2013. I was on my way to drop off some posters at Liam's house for a search and had stopped to get some cash. I'll never forget that moment for as long as I live. The statement on the screen told me I was ten pounds in credit. Only a year earlier I had been overdrawn by fifteen thousand. I had thought this day would never come.

The boost of cash from the sale of the ambulance, along with letting Jacob go, had been the injection I needed to ease the financial pressure. Gradually, bit by bit, month by month, work picked up again and I dug my way out of the overdraft.

I celebrated by buying a croissant and a coffee from a café in Bewdley, Worcestershire. I savoured every sip and crumb, knowing I'd bought the treats with my own money. I'd been given a second chance. The gods must have been smiling down on me as, not long after, I was given a high-profile case to work on.

When I say high profile, I mean a celebrity: a supermodel to be precise.

It was Wednesday, 21 August 2013. I was driving the old pet-mobile towards Birmingham, going through Bransford, a little town near Worcester, when my mobile bounced into life. I pulled over into a little garage forecourt to take the call.

It was the office.

'Tom, you'll never guess who's just registered their missing cat on the website!'

'Go on.' Zoë sounded really excited, so I guessed it was someone famous.

'Abbey Clancy and Peter Crouch!' she exclaimed.

Being a footie fan I knew of Stoke City player Peter Crouch, a.k.a. Crouchy, but I'd never heard of Abbey Clancy. I don't get much time to watch TV or follow celebrity gossip columns. 'Who's she?' I asked.

'Only a famous model! She's going to be starring in *Strictly Come Dancing*.'

That was a show I had heard of. Jenni was partial to watching it with dinner on her knee on a Saturday night.

Zoë went on to say that Abbey had lost her family cat three days ago from her home in north London. She wanted to hire a search team as soon as possible. She'd give me a call tonight to chat through the costing and what it involved.

I felt a flutter of excitement. Not only was I going to be chatting to a glamorous lady but this was just the kind of publicity we needed to catapult Animal Search back into the fast lane.

There was one very important fact I needed before I could chat to Abbey. 'What's her cat called?'

'Maggie,' Zoë replied.

I liked any pet that shared its name with my beloved dog.

That evening I was in the shed office. I decided to look into the case in preparation for my phone call. I tapped Maggie's case number into the website admin area and there she was, a long-haired Tortoiseshell with a lovely white fluffy tummy, and several black and ginger patches on her upper body and back. She had an adorable raccoon-like black mask around her eyes. She was so pretty my gut instinct immediately told me she might have been adopted. Abbey and Peter were living temporarily in London while she filmed *Strictly Come Dancing*. Because Maggie hadn't lived long in the area, I thought a neighbour might have taken a shine to her and adopted her, perhaps assuming that Maggie was a stray as they hadn't seen her before. As I scrolled through Maggie's details – age seven, no collar, missing since Sunday, 18 August – the phone rang.

'Good evening, Animal Search UK, Tom speaking.'

'Hello, I was talking to someone earlier about my missing cat.' The woman had a Liverpudlian accent.

'Is that Abbey?' I always use first names, as it softens the conversation. We're not a formal business like a bank – we're a family business dealing with other families.

'Yes, hello,' Abbey replied.

'You're ringing about Maggie, I presume?'

As soon as I mentioned the name of her beloved cat, her voice became quiet. 'Yes,' she answered.

I asked her what she had tried so far in her search for Maggie, and Abbey described how she had put up dozens of posters but the summer showers had destroyed most of them. She had rung the local vet but they hadn't seen Maggie or heard anything of her. 'We've called her and called her but there's just nothing . . .' Abbey's voice trailed off. She sounded upset. A house move to a completely new area, a busy work schedule and a young daughter to look after (which I discovered thanks to an internet search – it's amazing what you can discover at the touch of a button), then Maggie going missing: it was bound to be a real strain on anyone.

I sought to reassure her and lift her spirits. 'Don't worry, we deal with dozens of cases each day. We're very good at getting family members, like Maggie, back home where they belong.'

She booked a two-man search there and then.

The pressure to perform was sky high. My alarm clock went off at five the following morning, although I needn't have set it: I was already wide awake. I was buzzing because I was about to embark on one of the biggest celebrity searches I'd done in Animal Search history. I was at the hands of the UK media. If something went wrong, if I missed a detail, the backlash could be catastrophic, enough even to destroy our hard-earned reputation.

Jenni sensed my anxiety. Even though she was still half asleep, she gave me some positive thoughts for the day. 'Just be yourself, Tom. That's all anyone can ask for,' she croaked. She knew the strain I'd been under and didn't want me pushing myself too hard.

She was right. I was letting my fear of the paparazzi overtake what really mattered – finding Maggie. Reuniting Abbey and Maggie was my primary and only objective.

I gave her a kiss to tell her I loved her, then jumped into the shower, had a shave, put on my freshly ironed white shirt and my black combat trousers, then tiptoed downstairs. Polly and Sam were still asleep.

I'd asked Big Noah to come on the search with me and he was as keen as mustard to meet a model. Big Noah was Lucas's son. He was a trained pilot and had recently got his 'wings'. While he was looking for a job I'd asked him if he wanted to do what his dad did – help me out with the odd search on an ad hoc basis.

On the way down to London Noah and I chatted about the

case and discussed strategies. I'd already surveyed the terrain on Google Maps. The houses in Belsize Park, north London, were big, which meant they were likely to have gardens to search. My initial feeling was that Maggie had either got lost because she was in an unfamiliar area or had been adopted.

But there was another possibility. 'Someone could know she belongs to Abbey Clancy and Peter Crouch and has taken her for money,' I suggested to Noah.

'She's being held for ransom?' he said, astonished.

'Quite possibly. They might be waiting to see how much of a reward Abbey will offer to have Maggie back.'

It was a horrible idea, but there are people out there who will do anything for money. It was essential that we didn't make any mention of Abbey and Peter when we conducted our door-to-door enquiries.

As we approached Belsize Park we could immediately see it was a built-up area, which meant lots of people to speak to. We were greeted by tall, three-storey houses, with basements, roof terraces and gardens – countless places Maggie could be trapped or hiding. It was going to be an intensive search.

Not surprisingly, there was nowhere to park outside Abbey's house. I was conscious that we had two minutes before we were scheduled to meet her, so I told Noah to go and introduce himself while I found a parking place.

'Okay,' Noah said nervously.

'Here, show Abbey these.' I thrust the posters in his direction.

Noah grabbed his walkie-talkie, scampered up the steps and knocked on the door, which had big white colonnades at either side, while I drove off around the corner. He had probably been inside the house for five or six minutes when my radio crackled. 'Noah to Tom. Receiving. Over.'

'Go ahead, Noah,' I replied.

'I've met Abbey.' His voice rose an octave. 'I'm going to come and collect my clipboard and kit.'

I told him I was parked behind Abbey's house. As Noah turned the corner, I'd never seen him look so red and bashful before. 'I've just met Abbey Clancy!' he said, flustered. He was clearly star-struck.

I smiled and told him to pull himself together – although I wondered if I, too, would fall under her spell. Now it was my turn to introduce myself, find out more about Maggie and get the all-important recording of Abbey's voice on my Dictaphone.

As I made my way up the steps to the vast four-storey building, the front door opened and I was greeted by the lovely Abbey Clancy. She was a beautiful lady, but looked anxious. She didn't have any make-up on and was wearing a long baggy jumper and leggings.

We shook hands and I asked if I could come inside to put a few questions to her.

'Sure,' she said, and welcomed me into her home. It was very clean and tidy and full of designer furniture. It looked like something straight out of a *Hello!* magazine photo shoot. The kitchen was very well equipped, with lovely solid-stone work surfaces and a gleaming tiled floor. I noticed the kitchen because I had immediately spotted its balcony doors, which looked onto the garden. Had Maggie disappeared out the back?

My hunch was right. Abbey revealed that her beloved cat had gone missing when the cleaner had let her out of the patio doors in the basement.

'What time of day was that?' I launched into my investigation. I was relaxed in Abbey's company because I was a bit longer in the tooth than Noah. Why was I asking that? Because the chance of a road accident was higher at night. The chance of Maggie being locked in a shed, or getting stuck up one of the many scaffolding structures that surrounded the house, was higher during the day.

Abbey recalled it was around three p.m. She also said that Maggie wasn't an adventurous cat: she would rather curl up with the family than go out exploring.

She opened the patio doors and we both stood on the first-floor balcony, looking out over the garden. The sun was streaming over on our faces.

'The cleaner thought she ran that way,' Abbey said, pointing to the right.

'I see . . .' I took notes. 'And when she did go out in the garden, how far would she go?' I asked.

Abbey told me Maggie went into the gardens at either side of the house, but no further, as far as she knew.

'Is she taking any medication?' That question always throws owners, as I guess it's the kind of thing you would ask about a person. But pets are like miniature furry people.

'No, she's fine at the moment,' Abbey said quietly. She looked anxious. Her young daughter had flu and was lying with a blanket wrapped around her in the living room. Abbey confided that she was having a tough time, with Maggie missing for five days and her daughter unwell.

'We've had Maggie for almost seven years, you know. I was apprehensive about bringing her down from our home up north,' she said. She didn't cry: she was holding it together well.

My heart went out to her. She clearly loved her cat.

It was easier said than done, but I told her to try not to worry. We would do everything we could to bring Maggie home. I promised I'd look for her as if I was searching for my own pet. 'How long have you lived here?' I carried on with my questions, doing my best to sound less officious and more caring.

'Only a couple of weeks.'

I had a horrible flashback to Toots. She, too, had gone missing after relocation to a new place. I wasn't going to let this case end in the same way, though. This could be a simple case of Maggie losing her bearings. We just needed to find her quickly.

I asked her how she would feel about getting a story about Maggie into the press. I explained there was a chance it could lead us to someone holding her to ransom, but it would more likely prompt a witness to come forward or to make Maggie such hot property that the person who had her would feel pressured into releasing her for fear of repercussions. 'Maggie will light up the eyes of newspaper editors, as you must be aware.'

Abbey didn't think twice about her answer. 'Anything you can do to improve the chances of finding her, just do it!' she exclaimed.

This led me to ask if she could help me with the Dictaphone recording. Abbey called Maggie's name six times and rattled her food bowl with biscuits.

I didn't want to waste a moment more so I told her Noah and I would crack on with the enquiries and report back soon.

'Oh, one last thing,' I said, just before stepping out onto the porch. 'Does Maggie have a favourite treat? Something I can give to her when we find her,' I said optimistically.

Abbey disappeared back into the house and reappeared with two packets of biscuits, one for me and one for Noah to carry around in our pockets.

As I walked through the large front doorway and down the steps to the pavement I knew that Maggie's future lay in our hands. I always felt the pressure on searches. The pets we were looking for were integral parts of the families who called upon us for help. They were children's playmates, adult companions or sometimes a child for those who had none.

I called Noah on the radio. He had been preparing the

equipment, making sure there were new batteries in the torches, ready to search in and under sheds and in cellars, and marking out our routes on a map while I'd been chatting inside.

We agreed to go in opposite directions from Abbey's house.

'I'll go to the right, you go to the left, cross the road after ten houses and return back in the other direction, meet you in the middle. These are big houses, and if they're turned into flats try to get a resident to let you into the communal area, then door-to-door every flat, rather than leave a bundle of leaflets in the foyer. We need to speak to every man and his dog.' I put my detective hat on.

'And every woman and their cat!' Noah joked.

'Yep – them too.'

I noted several houses with scaffolding wrapped around one or two sides of the building. They were similar to Abbey's, three to four storeys, and in some cases they also had cellars or basement flats too. I called to the builder above me on the scaffolding.

'Are the owners in? Or is it unoccupied?'

Why was I asking that? An unoccupied building, which tradespeople frequently went in and out of, could be just the sort of place Maggie might be trapped in, if she'd snuck in there while the door was open.

'It's vacant, mate. What you after?' he asked. He was a big burly guy, with stubble, and he was wearing a white helmet.

'We're looking for a missing cat. Can I give you a leaflet with a photo, please?'

'Yeah, sure,' shouted the builder, who started to come down a ladder from the first-floor level. He was covered with dust – he'd been chiselling render from the side of the house. You'd think that builders, busy to finish a job, wouldn't care about someone's missing moggie. Far from it: the reaction I encounter from most people, anyone from the homeless to teenagers to a businesswoman rushing to work, is largely positive and restores my faith in community spirit.

The builder took the leaflet, which had a red Missing banner and two photos of Maggie. He paused for a minute, rubbing his chin with his thumb and index finger, as if he might know something. He then shook his head and said, 'Nope, sorry, pal, haven't seen her. She's pretty, isn't she?'

'Yes, and we're on the case until she's found. We're not giving up.'

I'd learned that if I laid it on a bit thick about how big a search I was conducting and the enquiries I was making, word that Animal Search was on the case spread quicker. So, anyone who had information on Maggie's whereabouts would feel under pressure to declare what they knew. Or if someone was indeed harbouring her, they might release her, knowing we were hot on their heels.

The builder looked bemused. 'What's this, then? A council thing?' he said, examining the leaflet. 'I've never heard of a pet-search company.'

I put him right. 'We're a small private organization. People hire us to conduct enquiries,' I said, glancing upwards at the scaffolding again. 'Could I ask a massive favour? I was wondering if the cat we're looking for is stuck either inside or at the top of the scaffolding. Could you take a look right to the top, just in case?'

The builder let out a little chuckle. 'Whoever's hired you must love their pet!' he said. 'Yeah, sure, I can look at the top. How long has she been missing?'

I explained since Sunday. The builder told me the property hadn't been accessed since last Friday. That was good news: it meant it was unlikely Maggie was trapped inside.

'But I'll check the top now,' the builder said, climbing back up the ladder.

'Cheers. Do you mind if I search the back garden too, in case she's stuck or injured somewhere?' I called after him.

'Yep, no worries, but mind yourself, it's a bit of a bombsite.'

He wasn't joking. As I made my way along the side of the large property, I had to clamber over and weave around the debris. There were boards, half a door, a cement-mixer, planks and piles of rubble dotted here and there. At the back of the garden there was a tumbledown shed. The wood was rotting. The windows were hazy, coated with green mildew on the outside and cobwebs within. As I approached the shed, I pulled out my torch.

The boards creaked and slid around under my boots. Anyone could have heard me coming. My heart jumped as I heard a faint noise from inside the shed. It sounded like a plastic plant pot being knocked over.

Could Maggie be trapped inside?

Was she injured in there?

I needed to investigate further.

CHAPTER TWENTY-THREE
MAGGIE THE MOGGIE

I squeezed my fingers into the hole in the rotting wooden door and tugged it open. It got stuck on the ground, so I scraped away the debris with my boot to allow it to open fully. There was another clatter from the back of the shed. Something inside was moving. I shone my torch into the darkness and the light caught something.

Two eyes were staring back at me from a sea of black. Was it Maggie? I was holding my breath, as I tried to get a better look. Then, like a sprinter launching off the blocks, the owner of the eyes leaped towards me in a bid to reach the door.

'Whoaaaaaa!' I shouted, as the sudden movement made me jump. A fluffy black and white cat scuttled through my legs. It jumped over the planks, like a frog leaping across lily pads, clambered up the wall and was gone.

That cat certainly wasn't injured and it wasn't Maggie. I sighed. I thought I'd better check the remaining areas of the shed just to be sure. I found a hole at the back, which the occupant had been using as a cat flap, but, alas, no sign of Maggie.

After a thorough look in all the nooks and crannies remaining in the garden, I scrambled back to the front where the builder was just stepping down the ladder to the pavement. 'Nothing from top to bottom, boss,' he said.

I thanked him for his help and pulled out my walkie-talkie, hoping Noah had good news for me.

Nothing.

I continued the search up the road. Anytime we came across a poster with Abbey's writing on it we replaced it with one of ours.

As the day wore on something wasn't sitting right with me. Nobody had seen or heard Maggie. Not one person. Which was unusual in such a built-up area. I'd expected at least one sighting from the neighbours.

The possibility that Maggie had been cat-napped was now in the forefront of my mind. 'It feels like a bit of a waiting game now, to see what comes back,' I said to Noah.

I was going to have to report back to Abbey just to keep her up to date. I picked up the phone rather than turn up on her doorstep. Why? Because occasionally owners think, mistakenly, you have found their pet if you ring the doorbell unannounced. My aim was always to avoid unnecessary heartache.

'No good news, I'm afraid, Abbey,' I said, into my mobile phone. 'But I'll see you in a few minutes with a full update.'

Abbey had the door open and was standing on the porch, waiting for me as I crossed the road. I followed her inside and broke the news. 'Nobody has seen Maggie,' I said. I shared my theory that she had either been cat-napped, was locked in somewhere or had been adopted. I reassured her that our door-to-door enquiries, the presence of our search vehicle, and the call I'd made to the newspaper for press coverage would hopefully mean that if someone had adopted her they would get cold feet and let her go.

'Does that really happen?' she gasped, shocked that someone would steal her cat.

'Unfortunately when a new cat appears in an area, some people are inclined to think it's a stray and take it in.'

'No!' Her eyes widened.

'It's not the right thing to do, but they think they're doing a good deed. Mostly when that happens, though, the cat is well cared for by the new owner, and when they discover it isn't a stray, they almost always give it back, without a problem. So don't be disheartened. If that's happened, we'll do everything we can to get her back.'

As I turned to go on with my enquiries, Abbey patted my shoulder. 'Thank you, Tom, that's good news.'

I could tell she knew I was doing my best and, more importantly, that I was sympathetic to what she was going through.

I spent the next two hours speaking to passers-by and putting up posters in high-footfall areas such as the entrance to the Tube station and the corner shop, while Noah did more door-to-door. Most of the gardens we searched were tidy and well kept. Others were overgrown with weeds, brambles and nettles. The trees were full of foliage and I made a mental note that I would have to find a device that would help me search them more thoroughly. In the last hour we really pushed to speak to everyone, stopping anyone who was coming back from work.

Suddenly, out of nowhere, two men on motorbikes tore past me. One cut in front of me, screeching to a halt. The man, dressed all in black, lifted up his visor, pulled out a long-lens camera and pointed it directly at my face.

Click. Click. Click.

The flash was blinding.

I crossed my arms in front of my face to protect my eyes from the glare. I'd asked for press attention, but not this intrusive kind. I wanted a story about Maggie, not to be papped. 'Leave it out, mate.' I waved off the attention. I couldn't imagine how Abbey handled this day in, day out.

The photographer calmed down his trigger finger and I managed to chat to him about the real story. 'Here, take this back to your editor,' I said, shoving a poster in his direction. I was glad they were going to cover it: after a five-hour search we were still none the wiser about Maggie's whereabouts.

I was wary about leading them to Abbey's front door, so I decided Noah and I would drive straight to Hereford and I would debrief Abbey from Animal Search HQ. Both of us felt downbeat as we made the journey through the city and back to the countryside. As much as I knew not to expect results on the day, it was disheartening. I didn't look forward to putting in the call later that evening.

Not surprisingly, Abbey sounded a bit despondent when we chatted. I explained that we had handed out hundreds of leaflets, searched dozens of gardens and spoken to countless residents. 'Very often if we don't find the pet on the day, we will find them in the following week,' I said. As with a medical emergency – if a patient receives treatment within twenty-four hours, they're likely to survive – if I search for a pet within twenty-one days of it going missing, I'm likely to find it.

'The search doesn't end here,' I said. 'Hang on in there. I'll be in touch soon.'

'Okay, thanks, Tom.' Abbey rang off.

The next day the story was all over the papers. Coupled with Abbey's messages on Twitter, there couldn't have been many people left in the UK who didn't know about Maggie's disappearance.

Every day that passed without news, I looked up at the map of England with its pictures of unsolved cases. I refused to add Maggie. I was convinced this case would end happily. The cat's picture was everywhere. She had become hot property. If someone had adopted or cat-napped her, they would be struggling to keep her a secret.

I was right. Exactly two weeks to the day after Maggie had first vanished, I took a phone call. It was to my home line, not the hotline. It was Sunday afternoon. I'd just finished having lunch with the family and thought it would be my mum calling.

There was no hello, or hi, simply a statement: 'I think I've found Maggie,' the guy at the other end blurted.

He'd caught me unawares.

'Sorry, did you just say you've found Maggie?'

'Yeah, I've got her with me now,' he said.

This is a bit strange, I thought. Why is he ringing me on my house phone for starters? That wasn't the number I'd put on the leaflets and posters. I didn't beat around the bush. 'Where did you get this number from, mate?'

The guy explained he had seen the poster, but he couldn't remember the free phone hotline number, only the name of Animal Search. He'd googled the company and my home number had appeared. That was a plausible explanation.

'Where is Maggie now?'

She was in his living room. The guy was as cool as a cucumber.

'And can you please send me a picture of Maggie?' I didn't want to get Abbey's hopes up unnecessarily. If he was a hoaxer, that would put him off, I thought.

'No problem,' he chirped.

I gave him my mobile-phone number and took down his details. He was called Pete. 'By the way, where did you find her?'

'She was wandering in the street outside my house. She looked a bit lost and lonely so I took her inside, and then I heard about your search.'

Pete lived in Camden Town, which was some distance from Abbey's house. Maggie had travelled a few miles, which was rare but can occasionally happen if a cat is scared and disoriented.

With that he rang off to take a picture. Meanwhile, I stood in my garden, looking at my phone screen, anxiously waiting for the big unveiling. *Be Maggie, please be Maggie*, I prayed. I had no idea if he was telling the truth or was just some weirdo making a prank call.

A few seconds later my phone screen lit up. *One message received.*

I clicked it open and there was Maggie on the screen, looking lovely, stretched out on a carpeted floor. I yelped with joy. I immediately rang Abbey.

She picked up straight away. After two weeks without her beloved cat she would have been desperate for news. 'Are you sure it's her?' she gasped, with a mixture of disbelief and delight.

'I'm ninety-nine per cent certain.' I told her I'd send her the picture and the address.

'Okay, I'll speak to you later!' Abbey wasn't hanging around. She put down the phone and must have raced around to Pete's house.

A couple of hours later Abbey called me back. She sounded like a different woman. She'd always been a bit serious and business-like in her manner, but now she was happy as Larry. 'Tom, it was her, thank you so much. She's fine. My daughter is ecstatic,' she said.

'That's what we're here for.'

We said our goodbyes, and a few hours later Abbey tweeted a cute picture of herself cuddling Maggie, saying, *Maggie has been found in Camden miles from our house safe and well. Sooo happy. Thank you for all your prayers x* Later, she added a special shout-out for us: *Would definitely tell anyone who has lost a pet to register with @animal-searchuk to help find your pet. It worked for us.*

She added another picture of Maggie stretched out on the floor, looking happy, content and completely oblivious to the fright she had caused. That's cats for you!

The pictures went viral and the next day Animal Search was all over the papers. We were everywhere from the *Daily Mail* to the *Sun* to mentions on TV and radio. I was as pleased as Punch with the publicity, but more than anything, I was relieved it had been a happy ending. I couldn't have handled another unsolved case.

Jenni came into the shed to give me a congratulatory kiss. 'I'm proud of you.' It had been some turnaround for Animal Search: one minute we were nearly going under, the next we were headline news. 'I can't wait to watch *Strictly* this weekend,' she chirped.

For the first time ever I was looking forward to spending my Saturday night watching the show. I'd be able to watch Abbey Clancy doing the foxtrot with the spring in her step that I'd helped to put there.

CHAPTER TWENTY-FOUR
ELEMENTARY, MY DEAR WATKINS

It was my first big stolen-dog case. That was what Ruby the Lurcher's owner suspected, anyway.

Mrs Fitzpatrick was in a state of great distress when she called me one Sunday. She had wasted no time getting in touch after her seven-year-old rescue dog had escaped through a hole in the fence in her back garden. Ruby had run onto the road behind her house. 'I could hear her barking for me, but when my son and I reached the road a few minutes later she had vanished,' recalled Mrs Fitzpatrick. 'What should we do? She'd had a hard life before we rescued her. We love her dearly and want her back.' She was close to tears.

'I understand what you're going through, Mrs Fitzpatrick.'

'You can call me Valerie.'

'Do you think she was stolen, Valerie?' It's not often I ask that question, but it was unusual that someone hadn't come forward with information in three days. She'd gone missing in a busy suburb; she was microchipped but no one had contacted the vet yet; and she had vanished within minutes of leaving Valerie's garden, which could be seen as suspicious.

It was a good thing I was an ex-copper and used to dealing with theft.

Mrs Fitzpatrick lived in the wealthy suburb of Farnham in Surrey, but she described the residential area behind her house as being a bit 'rough'. 'I fear the worst,' she spluttered. 'There are a lot of ruffians on the estate behind my house and I do hear through the grapevine that they sell dogs for money. Would you search those areas as part of your enquiries?'

'Absolutely,' I said. 'We'll cover every road in your vicinity, as thoroughly as we can.' It was my job to investigate all avenues but not to point the finger at anyone. It was a less wealthy area but that didn't mean it harboured a dog thief.

When Valerie sent me Ruby's picture, I could instantly see why she loved her so much. She was a cute, dainty Lurcher, fawn-coloured, with scruffy hair and big eyes gazing up through dark lashes.

I asked if she had any distinguishing marks we could publicize on the posters. Valerie told me Ruby had a few war wounds. She had several scars along the side of her body caused by jumping over barbed-wire fences and an old bite wound from another dog she'd encountered in the park. She also had a stitched ear.

Valerie wanted a two-day two-man search. M, Lucas and Liam were already working on cases so I needed to call for back-up. I had just the person in mind for the job. Someone with whom I'd recently rekindled my friendship but who hadn't worked with me for two years.

Jacob jumped at the chance to help me find Ruby. He had always liked that part of the job much more than dealing with office work and answering the phones. He was happily settled in a new career working as a Sainsbury's delivery driver, but that didn't stop him occasionally hankering after his pet detective days. He had a week's holiday he needed to use up and thought, Why not?

'You never know, Jacob, you might find the Golden Door again!'

We loaded the Astra with everything we needed, including a dog trap, leads and food to lure Ruby into the trap, then set off for Farnham.

Valerie's house was a 1960s bungalow in a cul-de-sac. It had a nice front garden and some plant pots lining the driveway. A car enthusiast, I was quick to notice the Porsche in the garage, half hidden under a canvas cover.

Jacob and I were greeted by a few dogs jumping up at our knees. They were wagging their tails and licking our hands.

'Oh, don't mind them,' Valerie said, pulling them back. In her mid-fifties, she had a lovely welcoming smile and gave off an aura of warmth and kindness. It didn't surprise me when she told us all her dogs were rescues.

If Ruby had indeed been nicked, time was of the essence. 'First things first, why don't you show us where Ruby escaped from?' I launched into my investigation.

Valerie locked the other dogs into the kitchen and we followed her through her house and into the back garden. She crouched by the gap in the hedge and fence, pointing to where Ruby had escaped. I peered through the porthole onto the road.

'I'm concerned for Ruby, as that area over there is a gypsy area. And I know that gypsies like Lurchers,' she said.

From my experience as a police officer and a pet detective, I'd learned that was true enough. But it didn't mean anyone from the community behind her house had stolen Ruby. They might have thought she was lost and taken her in with the best intentions. I'd also found in the past that gypsies were often extremely helpful, and I was keen not to jump to conclusions. I had learned not to direct all my resources to one area and to keep an open mind.

I explained to Valerie that Jacob and I would begin conducting door-to-door enquiries in the street that Ruby had escaped into and expand the search area from there. As she was a Lurcher, with long legs, we had to consider the possibility that she had walked or run some distance. We needed to put up posters in several key places. I turned to Valerie for her local knowledge: 'Which places around here would most people visit at least once a week?'

She scratched her head. 'Umm, the garage, I suppose.'

That was a good starting point. Although Ruby might not necessarily be hiding near it, everyone would see her face at some point that week when they went to fill up their tank.

I asked Jacob if he could leave bundles of leaflets at the garage, the shops and the schools, the bus station and bus stops while I kicked off with the door-to-door enquiries. The bus stops were particularly effective because people stand and read the posters while they wait for the bus – a captive audience, so to speak.

Jacob scooted off in the Astra while I worked my way along the road. The front door was wide open in one of the first houses I approached. I peered into the hallway and called out to see if anyone was inside.

An elderly gentleman appeared, shuffling from the kitchen to the front door. 'You're a bit late today with the delivery,' he said, mistaking me for the postman in my luminous jacket.

I quickly corrected him, revealing my pet detective status. All I needed was a badge to flash. 'Have you heard anything about this dog here?' I showed him a picture of Ruby.

He leaned against his door with his elbow, holding the poster in his other hand. He studied it closely, then looked up at me. I was expecting him to say no.

'I saw her in my garden on Sunday afternoon,' he said, handing it back.

Jackpot on my first knock.

'Which way did she go?'

'I called her over but she didn't respond. She ran off that way,' he said, pointing to an estate nearby.

'Was anyone with her?'

'No, she was by herself. She had a multicoloured collar on.'

That matched up. I was pleased he had confirmed Ruby had escaped rather than been stolen from the garden.

I couldn't wait to tell Jacob the good news. 'Tom to Jacob. Receiving. Over. We've got a positive ID of Ruby!'

He had just finished dropping off the leaflets so he said he would meet me at eleven hundred hours. We were going to tackle the estate together.

Jacob parked the pet-mobile in the main road running through the gypsy community. We could see the curtains twitching as we opened the boot and loaded our pockets. The residents might have been wondering if we were the police. That was a mistake many people had made in the past.

North Street wasn't a particularly steep hill but we had to dig our heels in as we were laden with equipment. We were armed with dog leads, dog food in our trouser pockets, two-way radios clipped to our belts, a microchip scanner (in my inside jacket pocket), posters, leaflets and clipboards.

We were a bit overloaded, but we managed.

I was slightly apprehensive about knocking on doors because the area was a bit rough and rundown. But I was relieved to find that after a few enquiries everyone was extremely obliging, helpful and cooperative.

The community was really friendly but some of the gardens needed a bit of work. As I approached the next property I noticed a rusting child's bicycle, an upturned toy pram and some black bin bags slung into a corner, not to mention ankle-high grass scattered with dog mess.

Just as I reached out to knock, the door opened wide. I was greeted by a man in his mid-twenties, wearing jeans and socks, but nothing on his top half. He had several tattoos, one of a Staffy's face on his upper arm.

'Are you Animal Search UK?' the man said, as he stepped towards me with his hand outstretched. 'That was quick. Well impressive!' He turned and shouted into the house to his partner: 'You ready, love? Search team's here. Have you got Ozzie's photo for them?'

I couldn't quite comprehend what was going on.

'Shall we come with ya?' asked the man. 'I can show you Ozzie's normal walking route and where he likes to go.'

The penny dropped.

This fella had lost his dog, Ozzie. At a guess Ozzie was a Staffy, and he had registered with us. What a coincidence! 'I'm in the area looking for a dog called Ruby – we've been hired by a lady around the corner.' I cleared up the confusion. 'Has your dog gone missing today, then?'

'Two hours ago. When I registered with Animal Search, I read about your team and saw the photos of you guys,' he said, then told us he was called Gaz.

What were the odds on that? We turn up in the middle of Surrey to conduct a dog search and within ninety minutes of our arrival a neighbour loses their dog and finds us online, registers, then thinks we're the search team that's been automatically deployed. 'It's a coincidence, I'm afraid,' I said regretfully. Gaz looked crestfallen.

I hated the idea of Ozzie being lost while we searched for Ruby. I asked Gaz for his surname, so Zoë could send us across all the case-file details. Jacob and I could then have pictures of Ozzie on our phone while we searched for Ruby. I reassured Gaz that we'd do our best and said goodbye.

Wouldn't it be incredible if we found Ozzie and Ruby on the same day? I was more determined than ever with my enquiries. As I approached the next front door, my walkie-talkie came to life.

'Tom, it's Jacob. I've got something.'

I hooked my radio back into my belt, then sprinted back down the drive and a hundred yards up the road. Jacob was standing outside a council house, a three-bedroom semi-detached red-brick.

He was with a tall guy, who was wearing tracksuit bottoms and beaten-up old trainers.

'What have you got, Jacob?' I said, as I approached.

Jacob's face was lit up like a Christmas tree. He'd clearly uncovered a clue to our case. 'This gentleman has a picture of Ruby on his phone,' he said excitedly.

I wasn't expecting that kind of lead. 'Let's have a look,' I said.

The guy, who was called Steve, showed me a friend's Facebook page. *Anyone know who this dog belongs to?* Below the posting was a picture of our missing Ruby. She was staring up at the camera with those beautiful eyes. I wanted to reach into the screen and rescue her there and then.

'That's her!' I yelped. I could see the multicoloured collar in the photo. 'Who's Seth, then?' I asked. He had made the

Facebook posting. All we needed to do was find him and we'd have Ruby back. I thought it was going to be a piece of cake. Case solved.

I couldn't have been more wrong.

Steve knew roughly where Seth lived – on another estate nearby, past the park and over the main road. But he didn't have an address or a telephone number for him. 'My girlfriend might have his number, though.' Steve turned his back to us, cupped his hands around his mouth and yelled for Lexi.

She appeared from upstairs. She seemed a bit shocked to see Steve with Jacob and me in our high-visibility gear on her driveway.

'These guys are pet detectives.' He chortled.

'What? Ace Ventura?' Lexi raised her eyebrows in surprise.

'Sort of,' was the short answer. I then launched into the case file. Luckily, Lexi did have a number for Seth and Steve gave him a call from her phone.

Jacob and I waited with bated breath.

But it rang and rang and no one picked up.

I asked Steve if he could send Seth a message on Facebook instead. It would sound better coming from him rather than me, a total stranger. I didn't want to scare Seth off. I wasn't going to leave it at that, though: we could be waiting hours, days, for him to get back to us. I needed to make contact with him ASAP.

'Come on, Jacob.' I told him it was time to get back in the pet-mobile. Steve and Lexi said they would be in touch as soon as they heard anything. Meanwhile we would cross to the other estate and see if anyone knew where Seth lived.

Seth came with a warning, though. Steve's last words were: 'Be careful, he's a shady character!'

I didn't have my policeman's hat on now. I was a pet detective and bringing Ruby home was my priority, not arresting criminals. Even if Seth was mixed up in illegal activity, it hadn't stopped him attempting to find Ruby's owner.

It was a close-knit community so we knocked on just a few doors before we worked out where Seth lived. My heart was racing as we drove up the road. *We're on to a winner here. This is going to be the Golden Door.*

For the first time since my uniforms had been delivered, I was about to conduct a door-to-door enquiry without them. In the force I'd learned that sometimes it was better to approach certain individuals in civvies so as not to scare them off. If Seth was indeed involved in dodgy things, he might not want to answer the door if he thought we were coppers.

Jacob parked the car in a layby a bit further down the street. We threw our luminous jackets into the back. It won't surprise you to know I had two jumpers to hand – I'm prepared for every eventuality.

As I counted down the houses, the tension was almost palpable. We were so close to getting Ruby back.

Seth's place was a ground-floor flat. It was another with an overgrown garden and an unruly hedge. The knee-high grass was littered with beer cans and a faded red tricycle, and cigarette butts filled a yellow plant pot by the door. Plastic bottles lay everywhere. The front door looked like it had seen better days. The glass pane had been smashed in and replaced with a sheet of cardboard, held in place with gaffer tape.

Jacob stood behind me as I knocked.

No answer.

I knocked again. More forcefully this time. But there was still no answer.

My heart sank. This wasn't going to be as straightforward as I had first hoped.

A neighbour a few doors down must have heard or seen us and came out into his front garden. Clearly everyone seemed to know everyone else's business around these parts. 'He's not in – he's hardly ever there,' the middle-aged man shouted. He was smartly dressed in chinos and a white shirt.

'What's that you said, sir?' Jacob and I approached the friendly neighbour.

'He comes and goes at all times of day and night. Real oddball.'

That was not what I wanted to hear. I felt a knot tighten in my stomach.

'Does he have a dog?'

'Well, he did the other day, but I haven't seen him for a couple of days.' The bloke described the dog as looking similar to a greyhound, just like Ruby. He said Seth had attached a piece of string to her collar to use as a lead.

My main concern at this point was that Ruby might have changed hands, which meant she could be anywhere right now.

There was nothing else for it. We were going to have to carry out surveillance of Seth's property.

'Cheese sandwich?' Jacob asked, as we sat watching the house from the pet-mobile.

'Thanks, mate.' I unwrapped the tin foil. Jacob's girlfriend had carefully prepared lunch for us that morning. He washed his down with a can of his favourite energy drink while I sipped orange squash.

I'd been on stakeouts before, but never for a dog.

We watched cars come and go, kids running up and down the

street, mums pushing prams, dog-walkers coming to and from the park, but no Ruby.

Three hours passed with no sign of Seth or the Lurcher. It was seven p.m. and I needed to make a call about what we did next. We couldn't waste any more valuable search time waiting outside the house. We had to continue our investigation while also coming up with a way of finding out whether Seth had returned home.

I drew on an old police method. A simple but effective technique.

Tucked away in one of my many trouser pockets was a small but essential piece of equipment. I dug deep and pulled out a reel of Sellotape. I tore off a strip the size of my thumb with my teeth, got down on my hands and knees and carefully placed the piece of sticky tape over the join where the door met the frame.

Jacob looked bewildered.

'If the seal is broken we'll know he's been back,' I said. If the neighbour was right, and Seth was coming and going, at least we'd know he was still in the area and hadn't taken off somewhere with Ruby. Even though he'd put the post on Facebook, Ruby had been missing for four days, and Seth should have handed her over to the vet or the dog warden.

I wanted to think the best of this chap but I knew dogs like Ruby were worth money and he might have sold her on. It was a possibility I had to consider.

I was unsure whether he was genuine or not.

I was uncertain whether we would find Ruby.

Both Jacob and I felt exhausted and defeated as we made our way back to Valerie's. As we snaked our way through the estates I flicked my indicator on. There was one more thing we needed to do before calling it a day. As I parked outside Steve and Lexi's place for an update, who should stroll up but Gaz and a very energetic, happy-looking Ozzie, straining at his lead to have a stroke and a pat from me and Jacob.

'Hello, mate.' I reached down and was greeted with a big wet nose in the palm of my hand. Ozzie jumped up at my legs, resting his white paws on my thigh. He was brown and white with one black sock.

'He turned up outside a mate's house,' said Gaz. 'He hadn't gone far, thank goodness.'

Ozzie's ears pricked – he must have known we were talking about him. He looked like the mischievous type that liked to go for a wander. He was panting gently as his eyes ping-ponged between us, looking for attention.

I was overjoyed that one dog had returned safely home that day.

'Have you found the dog you're looking for?' he asked.

'Ruby,' I reminded him. I insisted on calling pets by their names. 'Sadly not.' I was feeling a little despondent, although the reunion of Gaz and Ozzie was an encouraging sign. I pulled myself together. It might take some serious detective work, but we were going to find Ruby.

CHAPTER TWENTY-FIVE
RUBY TRAP

After a good night's sleep at our B-and-B and a full English breakfast, Jacob and I were ready to take on the world. We were in the pet-mobile, en route to see whether Seth had come home last night. I took a detour via the garage to check whether we needed to replenish the supply of leaflets we'd left on the counter.

As Jacob and I walked across the forecourt armed with a bundle, the cleaner, who was sweeping up next to one of the pumps, turned to us and said, 'Well done, lads, excellent result.'

I'd experienced something similar with Gaz a day earlier. 'Sorry, what do you mean?'

'You found that dog, didn't you? Is she at home now?' he said, leaning the broom handle against the pump.

This was very confusing. 'Er, no. What makes you think we did?'

The cleaner revealed that a woman had come into the garage early that morning saying the pet detectives had found the dog and that he should chuck away the leaflets.

My eyes flashed at Jacob. All alarm bells were ringing. Who

was the woman, and why was she telling the garage to get rid of our leaflets? Did she have Ruby and wanted to get us and everyone else off the scent?

'I'd never seen her before in here. She was driving a black Mercedes convertible,' he rattled on.

I quickly scanned from left to right, high and low. 'Does that camera work?' I pointed to the roof.

The cleaner said they used it a lot to catch people who drove off without paying for their petrol.

If I could get the vehicle registration number (VRN) of the woman who had wanted to get rid of our leaflets, we might find Ruby. As we chatted, it transpired that the cleaner, whose name was John, also used to be a policeman. He said he was intrigued by my Ace Ventura job and would happily let me look through the CCTV footage if it helped our case.

Brilliant, I thought. Perhaps the local bobbies would run the VRN through the Police National Computer (PNC) to find out who she was, then keep an eye open for the car. She might innocently have got the wrong end of the stick, thinking we had found Ruby, or she might know Seth and was trying to stop us finding him and the dog.

'The gaffer will be happy to show you the recordings,' the cleaner said. His boss was manning the tills.

We all squeezed into the tiny office, which was filled with boxes of crisps, sweets and drinks cans. We huddled around a miniature square TV monitor. It had a digital video recorder, which the boss rewound to seven a.m., the time at which the cleaner thought he'd seen the woman turn up in the black convertible.

As we stopped and started the footage, fast-forwarding over the bits we didn't need, I had a flashback. I used to spend hours looking through CCTV footage for shoplifters when I was a police officer. It was like coming home.

My eyes were on stalks, searching for a black convertible. 'There it is!' I shouted, as I saw the vehicle park in one of the spaces outside the entrance.

John, Mr Singh the garage owner, Jacob and I were all glued to the monitor. My heart was racing as I watched the woman walk into the garage and enter into a conversation with John. She pointed to the leaflets and a few moments later we watched John remove them from the counter and put them in the bin behind him. She then left with a packet of biscuits.

'Pause it!' I said.

The picture froze on the woman's face. She was about thirty-five, her dark hair tied back in a ponytail, and was wearing an all-black outfit. She was wearing jeans, a roll-neck jumper and high heels. She looked very presentable, although that didn't mean much: I'd learned never to judge a book by its cover. 'As she leaves with her biscuits, which camera would show the vehicle she gets into?' I needed the car's number.

With a few taps of the keyboard, we were now all staring at the garage from another angle. A white wave rippled across the screen as John fast-forwarded the footage until we caught up to the place we'd left off – the woman walking over to her convertible. She passed the biscuits to a young girl sitting inside it – she must have been around eight.

'Pause it! Can you zoom in?' I asked.

'I'll try,' John said, tapping at the keyboard. The screen enlarged, zooming in on the number plate.

'Damn it!' We could only make out the first letter and numbers. That wasn't going to be much use, unfortunately. Unless someone had been murdered, I knew from experience the police would not waste time trawling through the records if they had only the first three digits of a vehicle registration number. Especially if they knew it was for a dog, not a person.

I was forced to drop that line of investigation and pursue the leads we had already. I thanked the garage people for their help and time, then Jacob and I jumped back into the pet-mobile.

First stop was Seth's place. I kept the engine running as Jacob checked whether the sticky tape was still intact. He turned and shook his head, which I knew meant Seth hadn't come home.

Jacob ran back to the car and we sped off in the direction of Steve and Lexi's place. They were our only hope now. I could hear a second hand ticking in my head, a constant reminder that time was running out. I imagined how Ruby must be feeling – frightened, pining for her mum. Being a rescue dog, she would be particularly sensitive and vulnerable. I hoped whatever she was going through didn't evoke horrible memories from her past.

To cut a long story short, we spent the next half-hour with Steve and Lexi repeatedly trying Seth's phone number. Every time it went to voicemail my stomach clenched. 'Come on, pick up,' Steve muttered under his breath.

Finally, we got lucky.

'Hiya, mate, you don't know me but you know my girlfriend, Lexi. I'm helping someone find the dog you put on Facebook.' Steve introduced himself.

Jacob and I were quiet as mice as we listened intently to one half of the conversation.

'You haven't got her, you say?'

Jacob and I locked eyes. It was the news I had feared most.

'Well, where is she?'

I waved at Steve to pass the phone over to me. It was time I had a word with Seth.

I went in strong and officious. 'Good morning, Seth. My name is Tom Watkins. I work for Animal Search UK, a pet detective agency that helps people find their missing pets. I gather you found the dog we're looking for on Sunday. Is that right?'

'Yeah. I've given her to Derrick,' he replied.

Steve's face crumpled. He signalled to me that Derrick was bad news.

'When was this?' I asked Seth, with even more urgency.

'The day after I found her.'

'Where's Derrick now, then?'

Seth sounded articulate and friendly but started to become cagey when I tried to get Derrick's details. He wouldn't give me his phone number.

I wondered if it was because he thought he or Derrick might get into trouble. I tried to reassure him I wasn't a copper. 'I know you made attempts to find Ruby's owner, but we need to speak to your mate as her owner is missing her badly. Have you got his number?' I pushed for it again.

There was a long pause at the other end of the line. I could hear a rustling noise. I was hopeful Seth was going to come up with the goods.

Sadly, I was mistaken. Seth said he would text Derrick's number to Steve's phone shortly. It was another waiting game.

I called Valerie and filled her in on the latest. She didn't waste any time driving to meet us. Five minutes later, Jacob, Steve, Lexi, Valerie and I crowded around Steve's phone, anxiously waiting for it to beep with Derrick's number.

Valerie was playing with the sleeve of her jumper in an attempt to calm her nerves.

Ten minutes passed. Nothing. Thirty minutes went by and still nothing. I had a terrible feeling Seth had done a bunk.

But then *beep beep*. Steve's screen lit up. It felt like winning in a casino. Finally, we had the number of the person who had Ruby – or so we thought. There were still a lot of unknowns, such as who the woman in the garage was. I had a feeling she might have been a red herring.

I rang Derrick and, bingo, he answered first time.

'Is that Derrick?'

'Who's asking?' he replied gruffly.

I played down the search as I didn't want to scare him off. I told him I was helping a friend look for their missing dog and that I knew he had recently acquired one.

'Yeah, I have been given a dog, but she's not with me.'

Here we go again!

'Where is she?'

'She's at a mate's flat,' he said.

'No worries. I'll go there and collect her. What's his address?' I cut to the chase.

'I don't want to give his address out.'

It was turning into a wild-goose chase.

'Where are you now?'

'I'm in town.' Derrick explained that he had left Ruby with a friend while he did a few bits and bobs.

'When are you going to be back at your mate's flat?' I asked.

'Don't know. Might be a bit later.'

I got tough with him. I told him that the dog's family were going out of their mind with worry. It was at times like this that I had to use my powers of negotiation rather than lose my temper. 'We can pay you a small reward,' I said, trying to whet his appetite a bit, 'and cover the cost of any food she's eaten.'

Valerie was nodding furiously, desperate to agree to terms just to have Ruby home. We were all feeling desperate at this point. Even Steve and Lexi were rooting for us. The search had brought the divide in the community together.

Derrick wasn't budging, though. He said he would call me later, when he had a better idea of his movements.

It was a waiting game all over again. We had to trust that Derrick would come good.

During the course of the conversation I'd quietly drifted off down the drive so I wasn't in earshot of Valerie. I didn't know how I was going to break the news to her. I looked across at her and she gave me a hopeful thumbs-up. I shook my head slowly. Her face dropped and her hands flopped at her sides. She opened her mouth to say something, but nothing came out. In the silence, I walked over to her and gently laid my hand on her arm. 'We're nearly there. We know who's got her,' I reassured her.

Valerie lifted her gaze.

'We'll get her back, I promise.'

Valerie let out a hint of a smile. It was nice to see she trusted me. And I wasn't going to let her down. I'd find Derrick, come what may.

While we waited, we went to Valerie's for a cup of tea. We chatted about how many hands Ruby had passed through, and Valerie worried that Ruby must be scared and confused. She asked how Derrick had sounded on the phone – genuine or worried?

The truth was that Derrick had sounded as if he had grown attached to Ruby. There had been something in the way he had described taking her for walks and feeding her. I was concerned he wouldn't want to part with her easily.

I didn't want to make Valerie more upset and anxious than she already was so I kept my fears to myself. Instead we looked through a photo album of Ruby. Valerie took great delight in describing the story behind each picture. It somehow seemed to bring Ruby closer to home, which was what Valerie needed.

Two hours passed, then finally Derrick rang me back. Valerie was perched nervously on the end of the sofa, rubbing her hands together as if she was washing them. My heart was racing.

Derrick agreed to meet us at his house in North Road.

Yeeees! I clenched my fist in celebration.

'But I'm not going to be there until tomorrow,' he continued.

Oh, for goodness' sake! I rolled my eyes in exasperation.

We reluctantly agreed to go along with Derrick's plans. We all felt utterly exhausted and desperate to put an end to the business, but Derrick was holding all the cards so we had no choice but to go along with what he wanted. He was also after forty pounds to cover the cost of Ruby's food. He didn't ask about the reward, though.

Derrick now had Valerie's phone number and he would ring her the next day with a time to meet. It was the end of our two-day search but I reassured Valerie that I was at the other end of the phone whenever she needed me. I insisted she take her twenty-five-year-old son with her to Derrick's place. You can't be too careful when meeting strangers.

We had said our goodbyes and were into our journey back to Hereford when my phone sprang to life. Valerie was speaking so quickly that at first I couldn't decipher what she was saying.

'He wants to what? Meet you now? . . . Jacob, turn the car around,' I instructed.

We had officially finished our work on the case but I wasn't going to leave Valerie at her time of need and secretly wanted to meet the man who had kept us so busy over the last few days.

'Right, boss.'

We zipped back along the motorway as fast as we legally could.

I told Valerie we would meet her down the road from Derrick's place, as I didn't want it to look like the cavalry had arrived and scare him off. If Derrick and his friends were of dubious character, then he might mistake us for the police. We were so close to getting Ruby back that I couldn't afford any more hiccups.

It was seventeen hundred hours when we pulled into North Street. The road curved round in a semi-circle. There were about a hundred and fifty council houses, divided into flats. The address we had was 12A, which was on the first floor.

Valerie and her son Paul were waiting in her red estate car in front of us. As I left the search vehicle I took off my orange jacket and tie, leaving me in my white shirt and black trousers. I looked more like a door-to-door salesman than a pet detective, which was what I was going for.

Valerie wound down her window and handed me eighty pounds – the reward and dog-food money – to give to Derrick. 'Good luck. Bring our Ruby home!'

'Don't you worry! I'll not be leaving here without her,' I promised.

I had a radio in my pocket in case I needed back-up – i.e. Jacob. If I had any problems, I would secretly press the transmit button: he would be able to hear everything that was going on and rush to my rescue, all guns blazing.

I could feel everyone's eyes watching me, rooting for me, as I made my way up the yellow-paved pathway to the front door. I took a deep breath. This was it. There was now only a door between us and Ruby.

I gave the door a good knock and took a step back. There was a long pause and then I heard footsteps coming downstairs – two heavy feet followed by four lighter paws.

The door opened a little way and a guy with a shaved head

and a tattoo of a lizard creeping up to his right ear stuck his head out. Once he could see I wasn't the police, he pulled the door wide open, and there, attached to a lead in his right hand, was Ruby.

She was trembling on her long legs, her little fawn ears were pinned back, and her wispy whippet-like tail was curled between her legs. The poor thing looked shell-shocked.

I wanted to snatch her out of his hands there and then, but I had to follow procedure. To be fair to Derrick, he seemed a nice enough guy.

'Here she is. Sorry for any problems,' he said, handing me the lead.

Ruby was so frightened that I dropped to one knee to meet her at eye level. I held out a hand and she shimmied back fearfully. 'It's okay, mate,' I whispered. I rummaged around in my trouser pocket – I was sure I had a Digestive biscuit in there somewhere. Ruby watched me intently. 'Here you are,' I said, holding out the treat.

Ruby cocked her head, as if to say, 'What's this?' She then stepped gingerly towards me on those dainty paws. She sniffed the biscuit, gave it a bit of a lick, and when she felt confident enough she took it out of my hand. She chomped it down as though her life depended on it.

'I have been feeding her!' Derrick said, observing Ruby's ravenous appetite. 'Here's the food we bought her.' He handed me a bag of dog biscuits.

I took the lead from his hand and slowly rose to my knees, so as not to scare Ruby with any sudden movements. 'Here's eighty pounds for the food and your trouble, sir.' I handed over the four twenty-pound notes. 'I'll be off now.'

It was at that moment, when Derrick gave Ruby a pat goodbye on her head and a ruffle of her belly, that I could see he had grown attached to her. I understood that such moments were hard for everyone involved.

With a gentle tug on the lead, Ruby followed me out of the door and into the hot May sunshine. I hadn't realized I'd been holding my breath those last few moments and exhaled with a sigh of relief.

I felt like I was in a Hollywood film, as Ruby and I slowly and steadily walked side by side along the pavement, back to her family. Valerie and her son were waiting for us. I could already see the tears of joy in her eyes. And as soon as Ruby saw her mum, her tail went from hanging between her legs to high in the air, wagging excitedly.

Ruby was straining on her lead, desperate to be let go. I unclipped it and she flew along the pavement at rocket speed. Valerie had her arms outstretched, ready to welcome her dog back. 'Ruby!' she cried.

The wiry Lurcher yelped for joy as she launched her front paws onto Valerie's thighs. She was standing as tall as she could on her hind legs to get a cuddle. Valerie was crying with happiness.

'Isn't that a magical moment?' I turned to Jacob. It was what made all our hard work worthwhile. We'd cracked the case and it felt brilliant. Jacob and I high-fived there and then.

I'm sure you can guess what happened next. Yes, we drove back to Valerie's for a cuppa before hitting the road. I also wanted to see Ruby settle in at home.

We stood back to let Ruby go in first. As soon as she had stepped through the front door she trotted into the living room where she proceeded to sniff the chairs, the sofa and the carpet – familiarizing herself once more with her territory. We followed her into the kitchen, where her water and food bowls stood side by side. She took a few noisy laps of water, then trotted back into the living room, this time heading straight for her bed.

Ruby pawed at her bedding, turning circles in her basket as she made herself comfortable, then flopped down and let out a little whimper of satisfaction. She looked over at us, her eyebrows bobbing up and down as she watched what we were doing from the comfort of her bed. She gave a noisy sigh of contentment.

I'd sleep well that night, knowing Ruby was home safe and sound.

CHAPTER TWENTY-SIX
DOGGELGÄNGER

'So *you* must be the dog thief?'

By all reports, Colin was a dead ringer for the alleged dog-napper. With his thinning brown hair, white shirt, brown corduroy trousers and silver hatchback car, he matched the description to a T. 'I suppose you could call me that.' He grinned sheepishly.

I was filming a *Crimewatch*-style reconstruction of a dog-napping.

A moment later another car pulled up.

Here's our dog lookalike, I thought, walking over to greet our next volunteers.

The lady in the passenger seat wound down her window and the little Border Terrier stood on her hind legs and stuck her head out to greet me. I held the back of my hand towards her nose and she gave my fingers a lick.

'This is Millie, and she's ready to be stolen,' Jane, the owner, joked.

'Woof,' Millie barked in agreement. She was a willing participant.

It was my directorial debut and I had only one shot at getting it right. In exactly thirty minutes' time we would be streaming a re-enactment of the suspicious disappearance of Toby the terrier on the internet for the entire world to see. I wanted to encourage people to come forward with information and to make Toby such hot property that someone would come clean or dump him.

Three-year-old Toby had vanished exactly a week ago. His owner, Kaylee, was beside herself. So much so that she was willing to pay a thousand-pound reward to have him home. Toby had slipped out of the front door when she had gone to fetch something from the car at around three o'clock on Sunday afternoon. As soon as she'd noticed the brown and black Border Terrier had vanished, she immediately began door-to-door enquiries in her local area of Maybury, near Woking in Surrey. Kaylee, who was a vet, had met a teenage boy who said he had caught Toby.

The lad had been asking at a few houses whether anyone knew whom the dog belonged to when he was approached by a man driving a silver hatchback. Pulling up alongside the boy, he had volunteered to drive Toby to the vet to scan him for a microchip. The boy had handed him the terrier in good faith. The man had passed Toby to another young lad sitting in the passenger seat and they had driven off. Toby had not been seen since.

Kaylee was convinced Toby had been dog-napped – he was microchipped and a week had passed since he had vanished: she couldn't think of any other reason why no one had been in touch.

She had asked me to come up with an idea to raise Toby's profile. I couldn't think of a better way to generate press attention than a live reconstruction. Well, there was another way, but that came later.

Now Kaylee greeted the lookalikes and me on the street outside her home. Millie, who had been found through an ad on Facebook, was restlessly tugging on her lead, itching for some attention. Kaylee was drawn like a magnet towards her. She dropped to one knee and gently cupped both hands around the little terrier's face. Millie stopped fidgeting and gazed into Kaylee's eyes. It was as if they were making an unspoken agreement. Millie knew she was there for a good reason and that she had to put in an Oscar-worthy performance to bring Toby home.

It was easy to see why Toby was so missed. Kaylee had nicknamed him her 'first born' because he was so much a part of her family. He was especially close to Kaylee's six-month-old daughter, Pippa, and Peggy, their three-legged crossbreed rescue dog. Toby guarded the baby and, since she had been born, had never been far from her side. When he heard her crying he would run to Kaylee and her husband to check that they were coming. He had been a companion for Peggy and they had always slept together curled up in a ball. Now Peggy wasn't eating and refused to go out.

The pressure was on to bring Toby home.

We were filming the re-enactment in a few stages. The first bit was of Millie legging it from the house and being picked up by the boy. Within minutes I was hit with my first directorial crisis. Millie's owner, Jane, didn't want to let her dog off the lead in case she, too, legged it. However, the whole point of the short film was to show how Toby disappeared.

I came up with a solution. I would get a bunch of volunteers – neighbours and friends of Kaylee – to line the pavement so they would be ready to grab Millie if she did take off. I would have to make sure no one's legs were caught on film, though!

Jane seemed reassured by my plan and I told everyone to go and say hello to Millie so she would be familiar with their scents. You didn't have to ask twice: Millie was so adorable she was getting strokes and cuddles from every direction. She was lapping up the attention, her tail going like a propeller as she sniffed everyone's hands and shoes.

I glanced at my watch – we had five minutes. Stolen dog? *Check*. Youth wearing hoodie? He was a son of one of the neighbours. *Check*. Colin the dog-napper? He was around the corner of the cul-de-sac, waiting for his cue. *Check*.

'Okay, everyone, get into position,' I directed.

There was a flurry of commotion as everyone took their places. Jane's friend was holding Millie in Kaylee's hallway, out of sight of the camera. I could hear her little paws scratching on the wood, like a racehorse waiting for the starting gun.

'And . . . action!' I sliced my hand through the air.

Alex, the cameraman I had hired for the day, zoomed in on Millie. Jane's friend let go of the little dog and she bolted out of the door, up the driveway and onto the pavement, where her mum was calling her.

Like a true star, Millie put in the perfect performance. Alex gave me the thumbs-up.

'Cut!' I shouted. We'd managed to capture the scene in just one take.

Everyone scurried around again as they prepared for the next bit.

Millie was having the time of her life getting so much attention. She thought it was one big game. She was jumping up at our teenager lookalike Darren's legs, ready to be picked up.

'And . . . action!' I shouted again.

Darren knelt down and scooped Millie into his arms. Millie positioned herself so she rested her head on his shoulder, looking back at us longingly.

'Did you get that?' I asked Alex excitedly, about the cracking shot.

'Got it.'

We only had one more scene to film – Colin driving around the corner and taking Millie out of Darren's hands. I'd given him a walkie-talkie so he would know when to step on the gas.

'Colin, are you receiving? Over.'

'Hiya,' Colin chirped. I hadn't had time to get him up to speed on radio protocol.

'Are you ready to steal the dog, mate?'

'Ready as I'll ever be.'

I'd marked on the road where he needed to stop just in case there was any confusion.

'Okay, go – I mean, action!' I roared.

We heard the revving of an engine. Seconds later Colin and his silver hatchback emerged from around the corner.

He screeched to a halt next to where Darren was standing on the pavement holding Millie, a.k.a. Toby, wound down the window and asked Darren if he could take the dog off his hands.

Millie was paddling her paws in the air as Darren gently handed her to him through the car window. Colin passed her on to his son, who was sitting in the passenger seat. They drove off into the distance – well, a few yards up the road.

'Did you get it?' I turned to Alex.

He gave me the thumbs-up.

'And that's a wrap!' I circled my finger in the air. Not too shabby for my first time at directing. I gave myself a pat on the back.

As Colin's car reversed to where we were all standing, Jane's head popped up. She'd been lying across the back seat the whole time, hiding from the cameras while saying some reassuring words to Millie to keep her calm.

Jane opened the door and Millie bounded onto the pavement, as if she had springs for legs. We gave her a little round of applause and she strutted up and down, loving every second of being in the spotlight, like an A-lister on the red carpet. Kaylee gave Millie a dog treat to say thank you for helping her, which she demolished in two seconds flat. She licked her nose and looked up to see if there was more where that had come from.

'Sorry, matey. We've got to get on and find Toby now,' I said, and headed back to Kaylee's house for a debriefing.

I'd hoped the re-enactment would get press attention, but I wasn't at all prepared for the media frenzy that ensued. It captured the nation's hearts. The video went viral, attracting thousands of views, not to mention the half-dozen celebrities who got on board. Tennis player Andy Murray, singer Will Young and TV presenter Lorraine Kelly, plus Border Terrier owners, who included Dermot O'Leary and the comedians Keith Lemon and David Walliams, retweeted the @FindTobyTerrier profile. I had journalists calling me left, right and centre.

I was certain it would lead to someone coming forward. But Kaylee wanted to cover even more ground. She had made extensive door-to-door enquiries of her own in the local area and felt confident there wasn't any need for me to do so.

'Can you think of anything else we can do to let people around this area know?' Kaylee asked me.

Six years ago Sandi Thom, Zoë and her mum had laughed at me for coming up with the idea I was about to propose. I was still convinced it was a winner, though. And if anything was going to get Toby home, this idea would.

'How do you feel about the idea of flying a banner from the back of a plane across Surrey?' I suggested.

Kaylee's eyes widened. And then her face lit up. 'Yes, let's do it!' She didn't have to be asked twice. She jumped at my quirky suggestion.

I picked up the phone and started ringing around for stunt plane pilots.

CHAPTER TWENTY-SEVEN
HOT DOG

Not surprisingly, there weren't many pilots in the local area who had the skills and the equipment to fly a banner from the back of their plane. As I explained who I was, I had flashbacks to my conversation with the Dyno Rod guy who had searched for Ollie the cat down a drain, thanks to a premonition from psychic Sarita.

'Hi, my name is Tom Watkins. I'm a pet detective and I'm looking for someone to fly a banner over Woking to find a missing dog.'

There was a long pause at the other end of the line. 'Yer what?' came the reply, finally. 'Is this a joke?'

'No, I'm not joking, this is serious. I need a banner for a missing dog,' I said flatly.

After a bit more explaining, and a lot of chortling at his end, the pilot, who was called Simon, came up with a quote of £650 for an hour.

I gasped. 'Gosh, that's expensive.'

Simon explained that I had to take into account the fuel, and that there was only a small number of airports at which he could attach the banner and take off. The closest one to Woking was Dunsfold, in Surrey, where they filmed the TV series *Top Gear*.

I asked why that was and Simon explained the mechanics of banner flying. I was surprised to hear that it wasn't just a case of attaching a bit of material to the end of the plane and taking off. Simon would have to fly into Dunsfold, swoop down and hook on the banner while he was in motion. It sounded like a stunt you'd expect from the Red Arrows.

'Crumbs!' I was lost for words. It sounded elaborate, but just the sort of stunt we needed to draw attention to Toby's disappearance. 'How does tomorrow sound?' I asked. Saturday would be the ideal day of the week to fly over a busy town, as everyone would be off work and shopping. With a stroke of luck Simon had just had a cancellation and could fit us in. In less than twelve hours, Animal Search UK would be taking to the air.

Jenni was used to my wacky ideas by now, but for the first time she was left speechless. She stared at me dumbly. Eventually she found her voice. 'So, how's this going to work?' she asked.

I explained that the banner would have #FINDTOBY@ AnimalSearchUK written across it to direct people to the Twitter and Facebook campaign pages.

'So, let me get this right, people will look up in the sky and see our search?'

'Yes, Jen.' I grinned.

'Well, I hope you catch it on camera.'

I was going to go one better than that: I planned to photograph and film the big moment so we could generate even more press attention for Toby. I called on cameraman Alex's skills again.

Alex was ready and waiting outside his house with a packed lunch in one hand and his tripod in the other when I pulled up at the crack of dawn the following morning. It was a 130-mile journey to Dunsfold airfield and I needed to avoid getting snarled up in traffic at all costs. We had just one chance to capture the footage. As we tore down the motorway I wondered where we were going to set up the camera to get the best shot of Simon flying over. Alongside the runway?

The entrance to Dunsfold airfield was blocked by a large red and white barrier, which was manned by two security guards. They looked like ASUK troops in their white shirts and black trousers.

I decided to approach the situation in an upbeat manner. I wound down my window and greeted them with a smile. 'Morning!'

'Morning,' the guards grunted back.

'We're hoping to film a plane picking up a banner from here at one p.m.,' I told them.

Simon had designed the banner the night before.

They stared at me blankly.

'We would like to film that small sequence. Could you please lift the barrier so we can set up?'

They might have been guard dogs, the way their lips curled up. The response from the security guard in charge was a point-blank 'No can do, mate.'

This wasn't going well. I glanced at my watch. Time was

ticking past. We got out of the car and approached the guards. 'What's the problem? We're in uniform. We have ID cards. We're driving a marked car . . .'

The boss crossed his arms. 'Don't care who you're here to film.' He shrugged. 'The rules are no one films on *our* land.' The producers of the popular show didn't want anyone to record *Top Gear* test-driving prototype cars and leak the footage onto the internet before the show aired on TV.

'Is there anyone you can ring who can authorize our entry?'

'Not on a Saturday. I'm the boss. That's it.'

Alex, the cameraman, cleared his throat. 'Tom, time.' He tapped his wrist.

It was getting on for twelve o'clock. Simon would be in the air now, heading our way. I could either stand there arguing or we could rush off to find another place to film before we missed the fly-past altogether. 'Thanks for nothing, pal!' I snapped, and stalked away.

We jumped back into the car and I crunched the gears of the pet-mobile into reverse. Just as we were leaving a reporter from the *Daily Mail* was arriving. It was Paul, who'd been to the reconstruction the day before. I'd tipped him off about the story. I wound down my window again and said, 'You won't have any luck with them, mate.'

Luckily, Paul knew of a pub half a mile down the road where we could film. It was handy having a journalist with local knowledge on our team. We drove in convoy along the country roads until we saw the signboard for the Red Lion.

'Oh, thank goodness,' I muttered, as we turned into the car park. I'd begun to think we were going to miss the fly-past.

My phone was singing in my pocket. It was Simon calling from his mobile. He was laying the banner on the runway ready for his stunt and would be taking off in three minutes. 'I'll be flying east from the airfield,' he said.

Which way is east? I panicked.

I asked the guys.

'I'm pretty sure it's this way,' Paul said, pointing.

'No, it's that way,' said Alex, waving in the opposite direction.

Three minutes passed, and there was no sound or sight of a plane and a banner in the sky. All three of us were craning our necks, our heads bouncing back and forth, like a tennis ball at Wimbledon, trying to work out which direction Simon would be coming from.

Ten minutes passed, and still nothing.

Surely he's taken off by now.

Alex rang Simon to see what his coordinates were.

All I heard was 'What? Ten minutes ago? We didn't see you!'

It was clear we'd missed the plane!

'This is not good, chaps!' I exclaimed.

We had one chance now to capture the footage – on his return to the airfield. Toby the terrier's future rested on us not messing this up.

The Red Lion clearly did not offer the best seats in the house. We needed to get closer to Dunsfold and work out which way was west.

The clock was ticking again. We had less than an hour to find a better vantage point.

I proposed that we go right up to the perimeter of the airfield, sprint into the open when Simon flew over, then race back into the bushes for cover before the guards caught us.

We drove around, hunting for a place where we could park close to Dunsfold. I found a grassy verge, where there were only a couple of fields between the runway and us. I removed my luminous jacket. We had fifteen minutes to wait until the plane arrived.

'Come on, chaps!' I hurried them along.

As we traipsed over the fence and across the field, dodging cowpats, Alex was struggling to keep up. He was a big guy, weighed down with his camera, while we were carrying a heavy tripod, camera case, binoculars and walkie-talkies. 'Come on, mate!' I shouted back at him.

'I'm coming as fast as I can,' he huffed. Then he yelled – he'd lost his footing and plunged into a cowpat. He was now looking seriously hacked off. The whole thing had become a bit of a circus.

'Nearly there!' I tried to keep up morale as I spotted the bushes up ahead.

We were panting and sweating bullets by the time we reached the perimeter. 'Quick, get down!' I pressed Alex's shoulder as a Jeep with blacked-out windows cruised past. Alex skidded in the mud and landed on his bum.

All three of us were now crouched behind one bush. With an arm, a leg and a camera tripod jutting out from the sides we were hardly invisible. I pulled out my binoculars to check if the coast was clear.

I could see something happening on the airstrip, with cars racing around. They were clearly filming an episode of *Top Gear*. If we ran out of the bushes to the track to get our shot, an angry security guard might well chase us off in a four-by-four.

I wondered what the best plan of attack should be. As I was contemplating our next move, Simon rang. 'I'm four minutes away, coming in from the east!' he said.

Once again we didn't have the foggiest which way was east. It was just going to be a case of looking up into the sky and hoping for the best.

'Sssh, can you hear that?' I asked.

It was hard to hear above the sound of cars revving and tyres screeching, but there was the distinctive hum of a Cessna plane engine.

'Over there!' Alex exclaimed.

We all looked to the right and, sure enough, there was the little plane with a massive banner trailing behind it, flapping in the wind. Seeing the Animal Search UK logo in the sky was one of my proudest moments. 'You getting this?' I checked to see if Alex was recording. Meanwhile I was snapping away on my camera, capturing every second.

'If this doesn't help find Toby, I don't know what will,' I said, imagining the reaction in Woking as the banner had flown over the town.

I rang Simon and explained where we were hiding and asked if he could fly past us just to help us get the perfect shot. Good as gold, he turned the Cessna in the sky, dropped a bit lower and flew right past us. We emerged from the bushes. We were in the enemy's sights but there was no way I was going to miss that moment.

Click. Click. Click.

We snapped away.

The black Jeep was headed back in our direction.

'Quick, let's get out of here before they nab us.'

We grabbed all of our equipment and ran through the trees, bounded over a fence, across a field of cows, over another fence, and back to where we'd parked. We dumped our stuff in the boot and tore off in what we now knew was an easterly direction. Five minutes down the road, Alex and I were still trying to catch our breath.

'Do you think we lost them?' Alex peered out of the back window.

'I think we're safe, mate,' I said, still panting from all that exercise and adrenalin.

While we had been running around Dunsfold airfield, Kaylee had been driving to the multi-storey car park in Woking to catch a glimpse of Toby's banner. I wondered what she had made of the fly-past. I didn't have to wait long to find out. My phone came to life with a text message: *It looked brilliant. He went over four times! Are you guys ready to upload the footage?*

We were more than ready. We were on our way back to Hereford so Alex could work his magic and put the video on Facebook and Twitter.

Within hours of the pictures and footage going live, we had hundreds of likes and shares on social media. Jenni and the kids gathered around the computer screen in the shed and we all watched with amazement as the campaign snowballed before our eyes.

Sam was particularly excited by the pictures of the plane and asked if he could go up in one.

'Don't even think about it!' Jenni wagged a finger at me.

She knew exactly what I was thinking. I was already dreaming big about a new pet-mobile – in the form of a Cessna aeroplane.

As the days passed, the 'Find Toby' campaign gathered even more pace, the Facebook page attracting thousands of new followers. The story had captivated the nation. Members of the public and celebrities were sharing the information, while Kaylee handed out ten thousand leaflets to residents in the local area.

But despite our massive efforts, there was still no sign of the loyal Border Terrier. After another week had passed I was still staring at the phone, willing the hotline to ring. I refused to put Toby's picture on our unsolved-cases map.

'Do you think Toby is ever coming back?' Polly asked, as we walked through the local park. We were on a family day out in the sunshine, but Polly is intuitive and can tell when my mind is elsewhere. She also loves animals, just like her dad, and the disappearance of Toby was plaguing her as much as it was me.

'Don't worry, love, we'll find him,' I promised.

You may be thinking this was an over-confident thing to say when all the evidence suggested otherwise, but I was convinced that whoever had dog-napped Toby would be panicking about what to do with him. They could hardly sell him – I doubted there was anyone in the country who wouldn't have recognized his cute little face.

It was a waiting game, although I didn't have to hang on for too long.

Early on Sunday morning, my mobile bleeped with a message. I was half asleep as I reached to grab it from the bedside cabinet. Since I set up Animal Search UK, my phone hasn't strayed more than three feet from my side.

It was Kaylee, and she had four magical words for me: *We have got him!*

I was now wide awake and sitting bolt upright in bed.

'What is it, love?' Jenni croaked, from her pillow.

'Toby's back!'

'You're joking?' She was also now wide awake and desperate to find out more. 'How? Where?'

'Hang on, love, just finding out now.'

I thought I wasn't speaking to Kaylee at first, she sounded so different. Her serious, formal voice had morphed into a bubbly chatter.

'Is this Kaylee?' I double-checked.

'Tom, we've got him!' she told me again. The unbelievable news was taking as long to sink in for her as it was for me.

'How on earth did you find him?'

'He was dumped in Kent!'

I'd been right. Our campaign had made Toby too hot to handle.

Kaylee explained that Toby was spotted wandering the streets of Ashford in Kent, some eighty miles from his home, and was taken to a local vet by a concerned dog-walker. His fur was caked with mud, but he was otherwise safe.

What was even more startling was that Toby had been trotting alongside another dog that had also been reported stolen two weeks ago. Apparently the other dog was licking Toby's fur. They had clearly formed a friendship while locked up by their captor. It must have been incredibly disorienting for them to be dumped in a strange town, miles from anything they knew, after they had already suffered two weeks away from their owners. Thank goodness they'd had each other.

'And thank goodness Toby was microchipped!' I exclaimed. If he hadn't been, he might never have found his way home.

Kaylee said Toby's new friend had also been reunited with its owner, thanks to that magical bit of technology. She relived the moment she had taken the phone call.

'A woman from the vet's rang me and said, "I think I've got some good news for you,"' she began. 'I took a breath, and then the woman said, "We've found your dog. A client was walking hers and brought him in." At first, I found it hard to believe. I was shopping at the time and I just shed tears of happiness. But I pulled myself together and drove to that vet immediately. I rang Les [her husband] at work on the way there. When I broke the news, the first thing he said was that our family is complete again.'

I could tell Kaylee was on the verge of crying as she told her story. 'How's the little chap doing now?' I asked.

Kaylee told me the vet was still looking after him. Toby had been a bit peaky when he was picked up so they wanted to keep him under observation for a little longer.

'Good idea,' I said. I couldn't imagine what the terrier had been through in the last fourteen days. I just hoped his captor had been kind to him.

Looking back over what had happened, I concluded the man in the silver car was most likely a dishonest person who had passed Toby into the hands of a dog-theft ring. Sadly, dog-thieving is big business and is becoming increasingly common. The dog-nappers sell the stolen animals to unsuspecting families or, worse still, to people who use them for fighting. Toby might have been spared a fate worse than death.

I suspected Toby's captors had seen the publicity surrounding him and thought he wasn't worth the trouble.

'I'll send you a picture of Toby when we pick him up this afternoon,' Kaylee promised.

I was in the office with Zoë and the team when the message came through at three p.m. We all crowded around my small screen as I opened the file. A smile spread across our faces, like a Mexican wave, as we enjoyed the sight of Toby, safely back in the arms of Kaylee. She was sitting on the sofa with one arm wrapped around him, the other holding her baby. Toby seemed overjoyed to be back with his family.

I wished I could have been there in person for the happy reunion.

'Well done, team!' I said, closing the manila file on Toby and slipping it into the appropriate box.

It was another mystery solved. Another case closed. I swung my feet up onto the desk, leaned back in my chair and let out a deep sigh of relief.

EPILOGUE

Animal Search UK is going from strength to strength. My pet detective agency continues to be the UKs largest missing pet organization.

I have just launched a new website with state-of-the-art technology. Anyone who registers their missing pet will be sent alerts of possible sightings made by members of the public. ASUK now has more than seventy-seven thousand Pet Patrol volunteers searching the country for missing pets. These are kind members of the public who receive alerts about lost pets in their area. I finally have the pet police force I've always dreamed of.

Seven days a week, 363 days a year, I continue to dedicate my skills to reuniting pets and their owners.

Sadly, my devotion to finding animals has taken its toll: Jenni and I are no longer together, but we are the best of friends and I wouldn't be where I am today if it hadn't been for her unwavering support. She still likes to hear about my capers, as do the kids, although Polly is getting to the age where having a conspicuous dad isn't cool. She gave me a ticking off the other day when I picked her up from school in the pet-mobile. 'Daaaaad, I'm trying to blend in!' she said. Although even she has to admit the new thermal-imaging cameras I've splashed out on are amazing. They may have cost thousands of pounds to buy but they will help us find missing pets in the dark.

And they were going to come in handy for my latest call-out . . .

It was seven p.m. and I was in the shed, sipping a cup of cocoa, when the hotline started ringing.

'Hello, Animal Search UK, how can I help?'

'Hi there – I need some urgent assistance!' a man said.

I could hear from his tone that he was panic-stricken. 'We're here to help. What seems to be the problem?'

'My llama's escaped!'

'Sorry, sir, can you say that again?' I wasn't sure if I'd heard him right.

'My llama has broken out of his field and we don't know where he's gone.'

I pulled my feet off the desk and reached for my luminous jacket. 'You've come to the right place, sir,' I said, preparing myself for our next big case.